Autumn
OF THE
Moguls

Also by Michael Wolff

Burn Rate

Where We Stand (with Peter Rutten and
   Chip Bayers)

White Kids

Autumn OF THE Moguls

My Misadventures with the Titans, Poseurs, and Money Guys Who Mastered and Messed Up Big Media

Michael Wolff

HarperBusiness
An Imprint of HarperCollins*Publishers*

HarperCollins books may be purchased for educational, business, or sales promotional use. For information, please write: Special Markets Department, HarperCollins Publishers Inc., 10 East 53rd Street, New York, NY 10022.

FIRST EDITION

Designed by Nicola Ferguson

Printed on acid-free paper

Library of Congress Cataloging-in-Publication Data has been filed for.

ISBN 0-06-662113-5

02 03 04 05 06 DIX/RRD 10 9 8 7 6 5 4 3 2 1

for Alison

Bloodless Lunch in Media-Land

The maitre d' at Michael's must have a sense of humor. The other day, he placed USA Interactive chief **Barry Diller** back-to-back at an adjacent table to *New York* magazine's often far-fetched media columnist **Michael Wolff.** (Among other howlers, Wolff once predicted that the *Post* was on the brink of closing and that Michael Bloomberg had no chance of becoming mayor.) Diller, a winner throughout his career, recalled earlier this month at the annual meeting of Steve Rattner's media-investing Quandrangle Group how Wolff had called him a loser in another wrong-headed column. Wolff also whined that Diller had once threatened to kill him. "I should have killed him when I had the chance," Diller reportedly quipped to the high-powered investors. So all attention was on Diller and Wolff during lunch to see if any words, or thrown drinks, would be exchanged. Sadly, for fight fans at least, the two didn't seem to make eye contact.

—*The* New York Post's *"Page Six"*

Notes and Acknowledgments

In the summer of 1998, I began writing a column called "This Media Life" for *New York* magazine, from which much of this book is derived.

More than any other magazine, *New York,* through its 35-year history, has made the media business and the people in it a subject of social, political, and gossipy interest. The word *mogul* itself—applied not just to Hollywood showmen but to a new media business class—was a *New York* magazine appellation.

It certainly seemed fitting to use the pages of the magazine that had charted and celebrated the rise of the media age to chronicle its decline and fall.

My idea about the way to do this was not as a media critic—that dour schoolmarm figure—but from my view as participant. It was, after all, my business and livelihood and aspirations that were also coming apart. While the great moguls of the age are certainly responsible for the world they have wrought, I too have been along for the ride. What's more, in part because *New York* magazine has such proximity to the people I have been writing about, the more I wrote about the business and the people in it (however unflatteringly), the more I got drawn into it. People in the media love nothing so much as the media. Hence, every enemy I made in writing about people in the media produced a hundred friends in the media. Such is the weird condition of being part of the media about the media.

Indeed, I have often found myself in an unexpectedly intimate relationship with my subjects, admiring them for the very faults and personal ridiculousness that have resulted in the mess herein described. In that sense, the column and this book are less a traditional business view than a kind of *Nanny Diaries* of the media world. I have, I confess, taken advantage of the intimacies that have been extended and have helped myself to the conversation of other people who have had intimate exposure. The media, of course, is not a business you want to be in if you value discretion and loyalty.

So let me dispense from the start with any claim to objectivity. This is a book of fishbowl observation and proximity. I'm one of the fish.

This is the life we lead. Welcome to it. It won't be around too much longer.

This book would surely not have been possible without the support, counsel, friendship, amazing tolerance, and nearly intravenous flow of ideas that I've gotten, more than I would ever have imagined possible, from my colleagues at *New York:* Caroline Miller (who has defended me against many an irate mogul), John Homans, Sarah Jewler, Joanna Coles, Marion Maneker, most recently Serena Torrey, and, most of all, Simon Dumenco. It was his idea that I write the column, and he has been its faithful steward. Likewise, he tackled this book when it seemed like it would never go down. There is no writer who has ever had a better partner.

HarperCollins has been an encouraging and patient publisher. David Hirshey, Stephen Hanselman, and Nick Trautwein have seen this book through from mud slide to tended garden. Adrian Zackheim, late of HarperCollins, has been a good friend and advisor.

Andrew Wylie, my agent, is, well, Andrew Wylie.

My children, Elizabeth, Susanna, and Steven, have been among my sternest taskmasters ("Are you working on the book, Dad?").

And my wife, Alison Anthoine, is still my wife, for which I am most deeply grateful.

—Michael Wolff

Manhattan

michael@autumnofthemoguls.com

Contents

CONTENTS

PROLOGUE

A flashback, already

On the tenth day of the new millennium, Bruce Judson, a former Time Inc.-er, left a long message on my machine. Judson, who had formerly been an assistant to various high-ranking Time Inc. ministers, was making a joke, which I only half listened to, about some meeting we had been at together.

Judson and I—with *Time* managing editor and future CNN chairman Walter Isaacson—had sat on a committee at Time Warner that had decided to recommend that the company *not* buy AOL in 1994. *But why was Judson talking about this now?* I wondered as I got into the shower.

It was only in very slow motion that Judson's message started to seem coherent in a more or less breathtaking way.

Indeed, it is almost impossible to convey now, from several years' remove (even knowing the ultimate outcome), the unlikeliness, the utter disconnect, the *lunacy* of the entire far-fetched scenario: that AOL would buy Time Warner, that Time Warner would *let itself be bought.*

Nothing, perhaps, in business history, had ever been this . . . far-fetched.

Jumping from the shower, dripping wet, grabbing for a towel, I flipped on CNN.

A moment later, I got a call from Caroline Miller, the editor in chief of *New York* magazine, where I wrote a weekly column about the media business. She seemed both aghast and excited at the same time.

"What do you want to do?" Caroline asked, balancing the mundane and the momentous.

In fact, holding my towel, I was not at all sure what to do. I felt small and inconsequential.

"I don't know," I said. "I guess I better get over there."

As I might run out to cover a fire, I threw on some clothes and caught a cab over to the news conference where they were getting ready to announce the merger.

What was the proper affect here? Were we supposed to regard this as just a business story? Market reach, share price, boardroom stuff, instead of alignments, power shifts, and virtual geopolitical moves? The auditorium was filling up with business, media, and technology reporters, which for a second seemed surprising—why were they here? Where were the reporters from the national desk? The foreign desk, even? (Is this just my bias, not thinking of business reporters as real reporters? And technology reporters as an even lower order?) *We're going to miss the meaning of this story*, I started to think, *because the right desk doesn't exist*. Perhaps there should be a corporate-state desk. In that light, the AOL–Time Warner merger might be up there at some Munich Pact–Suez Canal–League of Nations level, or an entirely new kind of corporate-historical concept.

Something else: Reporters at other kinds of events—political events, disasters, crime scenes—are always nosing about, kibitzing, asking each other what they've got, but at this event, everyone just sat down and waited to be told what was what.

For a black-helicopter moment, a power move so amazingly tectonic that history would be written from here, this joint press conference was pretty bland.

The long lenses and porta-video packs were down in front of the auditorium when Time Warner CEO Jerry Levin, looking professorial and rumpled in what would be much-analyzed chinos and open shirt, came onto the stage, followed by AOL chairman Steve Case, in J.C. Penney-ish gray suit, then CNN's Ted Turner, then the new co-COOs Bob Pittman (from AOL) and Dick Parsons (from Time Warner), and then Mike Kelly, AOL's CFO. Everybody but Case sat down on the *Dating Game*–like chairs. Case opened, forcefully. But did this mean that he was the big cheese or just that he was introducing Levin? Levin indeed turned out to be the real presenter. He gave the details, such as they were, of the deal, and the philosophy, such as it was, and sent the clearest signals, to the extent that any were clear, about what was actually happening here.

It was not a businesslike presentation at all—none of the overload of information that is customary at merger announcements, the charts and bullet-pointed handouts—but, befitting a moment of at least as much political as commercial significance, a wholly symbolic tableau, although all the symbols were carefully veiled.

To do justice to the many conflicting and various unuttered messages that were being sent here, it was, I thought, probably best to look at this the way we used to look at the lineups and hierarchies and seating positions on May Day in Red Square. But the press, much of which was now owned by the merged company and therefore suddenly (as long as I am in this metaphor) something like the Soviet press, took the most literal of views.

In this view, all mergers are good mergers. Or, if not, they are superseded by even larger mergers. Mergers, in other words, are inevitable—and therefore, in some sense, unchallengeable.

Indeed, just a few months before, in what was then the biggest media merger, CBS had combined with Viacom. (The CBS and Viacom merger and now the AOL and Time Warner merger received more column inches of coverage than any other mergers before them—not least of all, of course, because they were about the media itself.)

Win-win was the most popular instant analysis. I wonder if we were this brain-dead just because we were so caught off guard, or because we or our colleagues had, instantly, made so much money off the deal (nearly 2,000 Time employees made, at the moment of the merger, $1 million or more, estimated the *New York Post*) that it was hard to think through the euphoria or jealousy, or because, as business reporters, the whole point is just to analyze with respect to up-and-down and not with an eye toward character, or consequence, or forest-for-the-trees.

It was not just the biggest deal that had been done by any company ever—the capstone of twenty years of more and more outsized business mergers—but it was a statement of philosophy too. This is how the world will be; this is the future. Indeed, all big deals had always portended more big deals—you were just upping the size of the big-deal measure.

As I sat in the auditorium, I was pretty sure nobody was thinking about how we had reached this point.

It took an odd person to be able to remember all the deals that had led us here.

Indeed, part of why we were here was that Time Inc. was a terrible deal maker.

All but faded from corporate memory was the name Temple-Inland, a paper mill that Time Inc. had bought in the seventies—though, arguably, the paper mill had bought Time Inc. Forest products became a third of the Time Inc. business, and the Temple family, from Diboll, Texas, among Time's largest shareholders. This hilarious combination was undone not too many years later in a deal that led Arthur Temple, who, in effect, was given his company back, to remark (apocryphally or not) that he felt like a whore—he sold what he was selling but got to keep it too.

But then you had Warner's Steve Ross, who had converted his father-in-law's chain of funeral parlors into a controlling interest in a parking garage enterprise, which in turn he had traded into a talent agency and then acquired the fabled, but mostly moribund, Warner name—and, virtually overnight, reconstituted an entertainment empire.

And yet, being a good deal maker did not necessarily mean you did successful deals. Because a great many of the deals that Steve Ross did were lousy. There was, for Ross and Warner, most memorably, and in a weird foreshadowing of what happens when old guys get enamored with technology, the Atari deal. In 1976, Ross acquired the go-go technology enterprise, and, in short order, it brought Warner to the edge of bankruptcy.

Indeed, most deals, we learn from the fine print of the history of mergers and acquisitions, turn out to be lousy deals.

But there are good lousy-deal makers and there are bad lousy-deal makers.

The Time Inc. guys were historically bad lousy-deal makers.

The good and the bad in this context most often emerges from what is called company culture.

The Time culture (which does not exist anymore at Time) was

aloof and clubby. Working at Time was a higher calling than other professions. It was avocational more than vocational—you worked there because you were better than the people who were not working there.

If you looked a certain way, had a certain sort of Ivy League, good-sport-jacket, furrowed-brow assurance, the elevator crowds would really part for you at the Time Life Building. The secretaries and salespeople and whoever else worked there expressed an almost physical deference to the true Time man. And you always knew who he was, as clearly as you would a priest among the functionaries at the Vatican.

Much of this culture—this aloofness from the real world—came from *Time* founder Henry Luce himself: the son of missionaries, inheritor of Wasp rectitude and old-money Republicanism, he valued assorted snobberies more than mere money.

Hence, Luce's corporate offspring, or the offspring of his corporate offspring, were, or feared themselves to be, corporate weaklings.

They were, for instance, afraid of Steve Ross. And, out of that fear, admired him.

Because he did deals.

But it wasn't only gonifism on the rise, the triumph of the vulgar Hollywood Jews over the buttoned-down Wasps. It was not just a philosophical or temperamental tide, but a technical one as well.

You had to understand deals not just as the process of putting companies together to make bigger companies, but as a process of using money in a way that increased your ability to use more money.

Leverage was the thing.

Media was a financing game. Media was like real estate.

One asset was meant to mortgage another.

The more you mortgaged, the more you could mortgage.

The more deals you did, the more deals you could do.

It had been said before: If you borrow a little, the bank owns you; borrow a lot and you own the bank.

This required a head for numbers and hubris too—somebody with a big ego who could count. (Although there were many failed instances of men who tried to step up merely on the basis of hubris.)

Such men became the instruments for the creation of vast companies that were—sometimes to a fully realized degree, other times frustratingly falling short of their radical idea—not really companies at all, not collegial enterprises, not thematic expressions, not coherent functions, but extreme reflections of themselves *and of their ability to do deals.*

Simply, moguls led media companies. If you didn't have a good mogul, you didn't have a good media company.

The entire Darwinian process of the media business was not about the winnowing out and promotion of good media, or good companies, but the natural selection of good moguls.

And the whole game was the rise and fall of these sui generis, savantlike beings—around them, you might argue, the business itself became something of an afterthought.

And so, in the nineties, there was the Time and Warner merger. Then there was the deal under which—to hold down the massive debt incurred from the Time and Warner deal—a piece of Time Warner's entertainment and cable companies was sold to John Malone, another of the media business' great lousy-deal makers. Then CNN was acquired (ruining that company). And along the way there were hundreds of other transactions, bigger and smaller. Then, on January 10, 2000, Time Warner announced it was merging with AOL. (Days before the announcement, I was flipping channels and paused for a moment on a CNN show that had on its panel Jerry Levin, Isaacson, media and culture commentator Kurt Andersen—also a former *Timer*—and the *New Yorker*'s mogul-fanzine writer Ken Auletta, talking about the future of the media. Suddenly, in the discussion, Levin, who probably knew he was soon to announce the largest merger in history, started to talk about governments' fading and some new sort of corporate city-states' rising and how the world would be mediated in some vaguely sci-fi-ish New Agey *Rollerball* digital way.)

The *Time* Ivy Leaguers (grown weary and depressed through the nineties), the Warner Hollywood heavies (many of them *alter cockers* now), and the ever-more-furious Ted Turner were married to some suburban database hucksters from Dulles, Virginia.

There was certainly no sense in the auditorium that this was the last merger. That this deal might define a level of overreach and prompt a turnaround.

After all, deals had always gone wrong, and we all still had jobs.

But, in fact, no deal had ever gone wrong like the AOL–Time Warner deal was in short order going to go wrong. This would be the worst deal ever made, defining not just a level of bad deal making, or of inimical corporate cultures, but of the profound lack of science in any deal. Not just a tissue rejection, but a whole set of doctors who had no idea what they were doing. Forevermore, in every media deal, this would have to be an operative question: Do they know what they are doing? Do they know what they are talking about? What planet are they on? And what do they smoke there?

Nobody knew it yet, but we had commenced a new phase, a whole new era, of resistance and revision.

January 10, 2000, was the beginning of the end.

Book
ONE

Spring and Summer 2002

1 THE COMEDY

The media business is collapsing. The structure is caving in, like a monarchy, or colonial rule, or communism.

The handful of companies that control the consciousness of our time are trembling and heaving, about to fall victim to internal weakness and external obsolescence.

If by the spring of 2002, this seemed obvious to many logically minded people, what logic did not account for were the moves and countermoves, as well as the pure denial, that delayed the inevitable end. Logic was up against the kind of powerful men, progressive business theories, public relations resources, and mountains of financial analysis—not to mention lots of charm and brutishness—that make most reporters and columnists end up believing that the moguls and their henchmen who run these businesses really do know what they're doing and that the next big deal is the big deal that will bring about a perfectly realized, synergistic business condition.

Now, it is not just spin and spreadsheets that obfuscate the real predicament of these colossuses, but the media culture itself. The media, like all social and political systems, works on its own behalf. The social reality—to be a player in the media is to be among the most powerful people of the age—belies a contrary business reality, that the business barely supports itself.

We are in a novel of manners—the pretense is the thing.

Therefore, to tell the story of the media, you have to tell the story of the rituals and conceits and behavioral norms and notions of propriety that hold it up.

Instead of a purposeful business story, it should be something more like a drawing room comedy—not a story about corporate success and failure as much as one about individual need and weakness and, of course, opportunism.

How to reduce such vast companies and so many divergent players to a small stage? How to bring such outsized men with their praetorian retinues into the same room?

The task was to find these people in their element, to move among them seamlessly. To be of them—but not employed by them (or, even worse, sucked up to by them—because their charm is not ordinary charm).

How to find the functional equivalent of a weekend at an English country house with a representative set of mogul kingpins as the guests?

Indeed, if business is the center of the modern world, which most certainly it is, then we have to find the dramatic context in which to reveal its true character.

Let us wait for such an opportunity.

2
MY
TABLE

In the spring of 2002—in the year of the autumn in question—I received an official, even ceremonious, invitation to have lunch with two journalists I knew from the Internet years (already sounding like some druggy past, or a best-forgotten unpopular war). They had a proposal to discuss. *We want to bounce something off of you,* one of them said in an email.

And so we met at Michael's. To have lunch at Michael's seemed specifically part of their point here.

You step into the door on West 55th Street, in a building once owned by the Rockefellers, and get a greeting from Michael himself (when he's in from the Coast—Michael's has a sister restaurant in Santa Monica), in brilliantined hair (recently he's been sporting a new floppy cut), or from one of the oddly nurturing ("You look great today") front-desk people. Then, from the top of the few steps leading down to the spacious dining room with good art and many flowers, you see everybody else in the media business who wants to be seen.

I have a table. It's table No. 5, which is a very good table very near the front of the room. Its sight lines go directly to the entryway, and its back is secured by the east wall (in view of table No. 1 in the bay with Caroline Kennedy playing with her hair or Mick Jagger drumming his fingers or Bill Clinton monologizing his luncheon companions). Among the things I have never expected or wanted to achieve is a table of my own (like Winchell at the Stork Club). Still, this takes nothing away from the satisfaction of having gained a contested piece of turf. (There is a menacing back room at Michael's where faceless people are led every day, never to emerge.)

Before Michael's was Michael's, it was the Italian Pavilion, which in a former heyday of media life had a serious following among advertising and network types. My father was in the agency business and once took me to lunch here and pointed out Bill Paley, the chairman of CBS and the most powerful and elegant man then alive.

I think this is part of the Michael's attraction: It recalls the other, more salubrious, three-martini era (occasionally, someone will even have a martini at Michael's), when media was the easiest game in town, when the world was made up of a passive audience and eager advertisers, when the money flowed like gin—as opposed to now, with media being a tortured, hardscrabble affair. A bleak, unpromising, Darwinian struggle.

I sometimes think this is part of the running joke. When you're making a lunch date and say to someone, "Michael's?"—they're in on it. The joke is that all these media bigs show up for lunch and pretend everything is just fine and still supporting these incredibly expensive meals, while waiting for the person at the next table to break down in tears (at any given moment, everyone knows who will likely be crying next).

In other establishments like this—the Four Seasons, for instance—there's a certain sort of pretense. People in a gated community pretend that they live the lives of people outside the gated community, or pretend the gated area is normal life.

But Michael's isn't like that. Everybody is open about being on the inside. It's like a prison yard.

We've crossed the existential Rubicon from social and economic anxiety to an oddly pleasurable self-loathing.

If there once was a media Eden, we are its wastrel and prodigal children with bad work ethics who messed it up and were cast out of the garden. In another sense, we are just unfortunate children, who, through no fault of our own, inherited overplanted fields and poisoned air and changing weather conditions. Whatever.

I have another metaphor, which is Vichy. This makes Michael's a kind of Rick's Café Americain.

Pushing this metaphor, the media business, through this last twenty years, has become occupied territory.

The media business used to be run by insiders. People who grew up in those businesses, and people, who by virtue of a certain New York-ism were of a family. But then outsiders, not-of-our-class outsiders, took over.

In a twenty-year period, virtually every media company and every sector of the media industry—book, newspapers, magazines, radio, television, movies, music—came to be controlled by people from outside the clan.

The mogul invasion began—not just your usual business types, but a whole new class of rougher, ruder, preternaturally cunning businesspeople.

A sense of insider resentment or snobbishness or rebelliousness would occasionally express itself. But the stronger sensation was clearly a desire to adapt. Resistance in this situation, where economic ownership passes from one regime to another, is, strangely, almost unknown. Ownership is granted a kind of moral standing. There is no model for saying we will not submit to capital. (When Rupert Murdoch bought *New York* magazine in 1977, the staff walked out—but that really may be the last time there was clear resistance, and, of course, it was pointless.) It isn't like, for instance, France. Even though these are cultural industries, you can't talk about cultural patrimony—or a cultural exception. Although there have been federal rules that regulate exactly this, that notion—that there is something here that transcends the marketplace—that this is a special and fragile area, seemed feeble and pantywaist. For a while book people said it, but then nobody said it anymore.

The world is as it is. The idea of having no place in it became the scariest thing. (We all knew people, too, who came to have no place in it—from people at the *Village Voice,* to correspondents in a network's foreign bureaus, to old *New Yorker* writers—who fell outside a sense of economic with-it-ness. Indeed, there are long mastheads of the missing.)

Therefore, we became collaborators: the quisling media.

Collaboration is, of course, a complicated emotional predicament, in which you often come to root against yourself—root for our own ruin. That's the Michael's patois. Who is going down. Who is fucking up. Whose ridiculousness will finally be exposed.

It is this self-consciousness and self-loathing that forms not only the subtext of Michael's conversation (this is a highly verbal and analytic bunch) but the subtext of the media's view of the media itself.

We are all here every day working to chip away at whatever is left holding up this insupportable business.

Which is why lunch is so satisfying.

3
LUNCH

Now, my lunch companions that spring afternoon were both accomplished men—ambitious, high-end achievers who had become significant figures of the great boom.

They had transformed themselves from striving hacks into men of wealth and affairs. They were not just journalists, but had become players in the media business, working the levers of association and finance and business theory.

So of course when they unexpectedly faltered in their transformation—when the reinvention seemed to be reduced to mere overreaching—a certain degree of pathos and Sammy Glicksterism quickly attached to them.

This was, I suspect, part of the reason I was on their lunch list. I, too, had overreached—my Internet business had risen and fallen—but had, surprising nobody more than me, come back from the edge.

The media business—at least if you knew how to work the media business—turned out to be regenerative. The notoriety that attached to you going down could become, with a little craft, the added notoriety that was needed to take you back up.

John Heilemann, a journeyman magazine writer who had gotten himself a million-dollar advance for his first book, and John Battelle, who a few years after graduating from journalism school had become the CEO of a multimillion-dollar publishing company, were now just two unemployed guys in the middle of a nagging recession in more or less urgent need of a paycheck.

At the same time, they were, I didn't doubt, planning their rehabilitation and resurgence.

Lunch with me, I was not displeased to sense, was part of their plan.

Heilemann was the more forceful of the two, although, interestingly, the more dependent—he needed Battelle to be the business guy, the feet-on-the-floor guy. Heilemann was the showman.

He was major-sport-athlete size—although he obviously wasn't an athlete—with a stud and two hoops in his left ear. He seemed like something of a sight gag: Too big to be smart, too big to *need* to be smart. Like a blond bombshell in kludgy glasses.

He'd already had, by the age of 30, an impressive journalism career, first at the *Economist,* then at the *New Yorker,* and then at *Wired* magazine, writing about media, politics, and technology—but all the time seeming way too large for those jobs. Those were for intelligent scriveners, whereas Heilemann was taking his measure not against other writers, but against the big men he was writing about.

In 1997, as the decibel level of the great boom had unmistakably begun to build, Heilemann wrote a profile of John Doerr, the greatest of the Silicon Valley venture capitalists, for the *New Yorker.* It was one of the first formal introductions of Doerr and of the Valley financial phenomenon ("the greatest legal creation of wealth in history," in Doerr's famous, and regrettable, phrase) to the East Coast audience. On the basis of the Doerr profile, Heilemann had gotten his million-dollar advance to write the story of Silicon Valley. Heilemann promptly moved to San Francisco and almost immediately became a prince of the Valley himself, a celebrity second only to the highest levels of Valley celebrities themselves—indeed, he courted and was in turn courted by those same celebrities, famously, ostentatiously, consorting with Doerr and cohorts up and down the Valley.

Once, during the boom, at a party in San Francisco—and during this time everything was a party in San Francisco—Heilemann was telling a small group of people, confidentially, that he had just met with Jim Clarke, the co-founder of Netscape, who had confided something startling to him. Should he take Clarke at his word? Heilemann was wondering aloud. I, who had already failed as an Internet entrepreneur, said obviously not. Heilemann, from his great height, said, with what I remember as quite impressive scorn, that he was certainly inclined to give a man who had founded *two* billion-dollar companies the benefit of the doubt.

I'd been reduced to a sour-grapes sort, and Heilemann elevated to part of the new, muscular, elite corps of technology intellects— and for several years we didn't like each other very much.

But then the boom ended (without Heilemann having finished his book—indeed, Heilemann's lack of writing had become legendary too) and since then there had been no reason for us not to get along. It was possible that some of the same kind of credit that Heilemann awarded Clarke for founding two billion-dollar companies now accrued to me for getting out (even if by failure) of the technology business before the bust.

If Heilemann was too large and imposing to be a mere journalist, his cohort Battelle—Heilemann and Battelle were often billed as a Stan and Ollie or Lewis and Martin combo in Silicon Valley—

was too handsome. He was distracted, it sometimes seemed, in the particular way of a too-handsome person—concentrating on people looking at him, rather than concentrating on other people.

Partly because of his distraction, and his failure to ever make eye contact, I had no real insight into whether he was secretly thoughtful or genuinely obtuse. His pure momentum, the imperviousness of the way he moved ever forward, might mean there was another dimension here—or not.

If there was anyone who had been close to achieving a version of professional perfection, even in an era when so many people had been close to achieving that, it was Battelle.

He had lost his no-hitter on the last at-bat.

He'd come out of journalism school at Berkeley in the early nineties to become the number two on the launch of *Wired* magazine. After a period of wild success, when *Wired* was thought to be worth many hundreds of millions of dollars and Battelle himself worth various millions, he had then started the *Industry Standard,* a business magazine about the Internet, promoting himself from mere editorial type to CEO and publisher. I cannot recall anyone initially thinking the magazine had any promise. (I briefly wrote a column for the magazine, while at the same time thinking it had no promise—and figuring that, as soon as I could, I had better find something else.) But the *Standard* promptly became the most successful magazine of all time in the quickest amount of time, before it, too, crashed—with Battelle being arguably responsible for both its great success and inevitable failure.

Heilemann and Battelle were badly beaten up—but standing. Their wounds contributed to a certain dashingness (a lasting stiffness in the leg, and hint of a limp).

At any rate, here they were, both of them fully aware that

everyone else was aware of their hubris and fall, formally calling on me, someone they had reason to believe might be taking some pleasure in their circumstances.

Heilemann began the specific business presentation.

Heilemann is an inarticulate monologist. He can't stop talking, can't find a clear way to an end point. He is always restating. There's a constant quest for synonyms, for adjectives, for new ways to emphasize. It's a form of buildup, of preface, of drumroll:

He and Battelle were going to hold a conference.

They had together staged some of the most grandiose gatherings of the technology boom, and now . . . drums . . . they were back, planning the biggest, the best, the mother of all media conferences. The greatest meeting of media moguls and bigshots ever!

It was nearly Barnum-esque in the telling.

Now, I have been to so many conferences—as many as twelve a year for as much as fifteen years—and there have been so many more that I have managed to avoid going to (while conferences were built on the idea of exclusivity, their sheer numbers made it really hard to make the exclusivity argument anymore—although, of course, conference organizers did), that I was not, at that moment with Heilemann and Battelle, thinking the conference, *this* conference, might be the perfect setting for my weekend of media moguls.

Instead, I was thinking, *Not another fucking conference.*

Of course, I knew what was in it for Battelle and Heilemann.

The money could be very good. In the boom years, you could do four or five or six hundred people at a conference like this, for three or four or five thousand dollars a head, with your talent, your presenters, your headliners even, getting nothing whatsoever—which was, I knew, the deal they were going to cut with me (the economic principle was that participants benefited from the same association that everyone else benefited from, that a good conference supplied new and valuable connections to everyone who went). Indeed, if you got a conference going, got on people's schedules, a once-or-twice-a-year sort of thing, you had a sure multimillion-dollar annuity.

What's more, there was an opening in the market niche. For twelve years, the TED conference (technology, entertainment, design), held in Monterey, California, had been a vital date on the media-technology-communications complex calendar. It was the big one, regularly attracting nearly a thousand people, at $4,000 a head, with sponsors covering many of the underlying costs—and a staff, functionally, of one. Richard Saul Wurman, a Sydney Greenstreet figure, ran the conference and every year collected the $4 million or so; the educated guess was that his profit margin might have been as high as 75 or 80 percent. But now he had sold the conference—and whether or not the new owners could do it as well was far from clear. If you could take that place, you could build yourself a powerful base of operations in the media world.

This is where Battelle stepped in. He explained the money part.

It occurred to me that that's what Battelle did now. That this was perhaps all that interested him: the deal. He knew, better than most—as well as any banker, or mogul—that you lived and died on the basis of the deal. The deal was the force.

The deal was this: Quadrangle, a New York–based investment fund specializing in the media industry, was backing the conference, to be called Foursquare, which would be a partnership among Heilemann and Battelle and Quadrangle. And while, ideally, this was to be a moneymaking enterprise, Quadrangle would absorb any deficit. (Of course, I knew that if Quadrangle was accepting the losses, it was a far from equal partnership, if it was a partnership at all.) What's more, Quadrangle was contributing its influence to attract the desirable level of speakers and participants.

This made sense. If no one at all paid to attend, if everyone became an invited guest, this was still an acceptable marketing cost for Quadrangle. Everyone they'd ever want to do business with would be a captive audience for three days. The Quadrangle guys would be able to strut their stuff.

But lest this appear to be just a marketing ploy, bankers sucking up to prospective clients, Battelle argued the opposite point:

"This isn't just schmooze. There'll be schmooze, but this is an editorially driven conference. We want to tell a story. What we want is for journalists to be interviewing and questioning the seniormost executives in the industry. So this isn't just guys, like in most conferences, giving sales pitches and the usual patter, this is people with information being questioned by people who know how to get information."

This is the pitch, I realized, they had sold the Quadrangle people. It was a serious affair—a serious affair with money.

"So what do you think," Heilemann asked, "is going to happen? Go wide. What are the trends? What's the—"

"I think everything is going to collapse."

"Everything? Beyond AOL Time Warner?"

"Certainly Disney and Vivendi are totally fucked."

"Messier," said Battelle, naming the Vivendi chairman, "is on board to speak at the conference."

"Really?" Messier was surely doomed, yet I was impressed that they had gotten him. I had been wanting to meet him. He was even more interesting, I thought, a greater "get" because he was out there in free fall.

"And Viacom is obviously an armed camp and can't last after Sumner—" Sumner Redstone, Viacom's 79-year-old chairman and controlling shareholder, was in a standoff with his handpicked successor, Mel Karmazin. "The same thing for News Corp.—it's not a company that makes any sense whatsoever without Murdoch."

This hypothesis—predicting the inevitable collapse of the five megamedia-opolises which dominated the industry—was as workable a theme as any.

It was 1914 in Europe.

"What about Bertelsmann?"

"Totally fucked."

It was some measure of both the peculiar nature and commonplace self-loathing of the media business that you could hold an industry conference and be relatively nonchalant about proposing that the industry was going to implode. On the other hand, it was part of the conceit here that this was a kind of true congress, at which representatives would converge and we would discuss the future of media nations.

"Can we interest you? Who would you like to do? If you did a one-on-one, an interview on stage, who would you like to do?"

It was a time to grab a big enchilada. It was certainly no time to be modest. There weren't that many enchiladas.

It was Diller or Murdoch.

Because more mystery attended them, more cult of personality, more secret of success, more mogul history, the interviews with Murdoch and Diller would be the big draws of the conference. What's more, if you could do it right, cannily and subtly, and have them reveal themselves—that would be a score.

Their existence, it seemed to me, had never been adequately explained. Murdoch certainly had held more power longer than anyone else—from his arrival in the U.S. in 1976 to now, he had just kept growing, just kept becoming more and more significant. As for Diller, he may just have defied more conventions of power than anyone else. And it often struck me he was doing this with a certain humor or irony, which might be the ultimate defiance of the power convention.

"If I could face either Diller or Murdoch I would certainly be interested—definitely count me in."

4
THE POWERS
THAT BE

Possibly, I've thought, I'm something like an old-time Washington columnist—Drew Pearson, James Reston, even Walter Lippmann—in this new kind of ultimate power scene.

They dealt with matters of state and with the egos and idiosyncrasies of statesmen. I deal with the consolidation of the global media's power and with the strange and compelling men who control much of the world's information supply. Lippmann's interest in Bernard Baruch might be, with a little critical interpretation, not all that different from my interest in Barry Diller.

After all, the media *has* replaced politics. The media is the root of consensus; it's the organizational motor of society, now that media demographics define us; it's the place you go if you have a cause, or a gripe, or desire for reform. It's a great patronage machine too; loyalists and courtiers and suck-ups are rewarded with immensely valuable publicity. The media, surely, is a more influential force in our lives and in the world's changing beliefs than politics or government ever was. Certainly, more people participate in the media than ever participated in democratic politics or government. Media is the currency of our time—the less access you have, the poorer and less successful you are. Likewise, the highest order of power and prestige is to be in the media yourself, or to control people's access to it; people may say they hate the media, but just let their mothers see them on television. Hence, moguls became the political barons of the age. And we, the mogul underlings, became the officials and ward heelers and apparatchiks and bureaucrats of the new communications-technology complex that runs the nation.

Media has become not just the political system but the biggest industry too (a convergence which, like fascism before it, has been most comically demonstrated in Italy, where the head of state is also the head of the country's media monopoly).

It is almost impossible to find a business that does not see itself as in some part a media business. In a transformation of vast and meretricious proportions, everybody plunged into the media game. Recognition, connection, meaning, transcendence, was something sought by even the dullest men.

Westinghouse became CBS; France's biggest water company got reborn as a media megalopolis; GM enjoyed a period as the nation's major television satellite company; Microsoft again and again lost billions trying to develop media savvy. And GE's flagship business moved from lightbulbs to NBC.

You even had media companies creating other media companies to promote their core media company. The more media you owned, the more you could promote the media you owned. (Disastrously, Disney and Miramax created *Talk* magazine, for a time rationalizing their investment as a marketing instrument for the companies' movies and executives.) Indeed, the modern notion of brand is really about access to media rather than the older notion of brand, which was about habit and dependability.

Every American knows the secret of success: more media. The

more media, the more recognition, the more value, the more power, the more influence—the greater claim on, well, the media.

I don't believe any greater power has ever existed.

So I began to think it could be for me just like it was for Lippmann in Washington during the thirties and forties, observing the transformation of the U.S. into the world's great consolidated megapower.

Of course, I was no Lippmann. And I wasn't the only one in the media business who had a clearly nagging sense of disappointment, of being less than the circumstances ought to have made us.

As big as the media got, as central as it had become to everyone's dreams, almost nobody took it very seriously. In fact, the bigger it got, the less seriously it was taken—even though one of the reasons it got big was precisely so that it would be taken seriously.

Jerry Levin created the AOL Time Warner monolith not least because he wanted to be a great man, a creator of worlds. But, as was apparent to all but the people closest to it, Time Inc., a company which used to be reasonably well thought of, became sillier and sillier as it grew larger and larger in its successive incarnations.

No matter how big media companies became, they just could not transform themselves into stately, or even manly, enterprises.

Politics and government, even though they are explicitly about power, have, or at least used to have, a carefully developed rationale for the need for power—they are, in a sense, about that rationale.

The media isn't so remote—isn't so Waspy. In the media business, everybody's motivations are clear. Every aspect of the enterprise—from the back office side to the talent side to the news side—is about achieving notoriety. The media is, in fact, in the business of being noticed by the media.

The more insecure and narcissistic you are, the better equipped you are to rise in the hierarchy. And because there is no limit to insecurity and narcissism, the hierarchies are always being remade.

Let's say it: The media business at its most exalted level attracts emotionally needy, attention-demanding, nerdy guys. And worse, unlike a former generation of media people, who reveled in their personal excesses, the present generation is uptight about its desperate desires.

But, in fact, they're here because they're dissatisfied with being just business guys. They aren't, or don't feel they are, temperamentally suited to just counting stuff. In fact, the media suits who are always derided as just being bean counters, don't, in fact, count beans so well. They have quixotically higher ambitions for themselves.

But they're not good-looking or funny enough or imaginative enough to be the talent either. They're stuck in the middle ground: They're not the talent, but they can't stand to be so far from the talent that there is no chance for the spotlight to ever hit them.

So they puff up their businessman mission.

Media business talk is among the most serious business talk there is. It's all about being a serious person—a visionary businessman.

No sane person (at least no sane person not on a mogul's payroll) who has ever sat down with one or another of the halfwit overlords of the feudal media states and listened to the rationalizations for the twenty-year rise of the media cartel system has ever had any idea what these people are talking about. The patter—about content and distribution and scale and outlets and platforms—is clearly designed to mask wild personal needs.

I can't do justice to the true asynchronous pitch of halfwit-overlord talk. But I think I can say what they are actually trying to say—which, even if they could say it properly, would still be ridiculous. Also, I think I can analyze why they have so much trouble saying it clearly.

At the root of the blather are some basic case-study-type business principles. Great industries are built on the concept of commoditization. You take something expensive and by making lots of the same thing you make it cheaper, and, through a larger distribution system, you make it more widely available. Cars, for instance—like the Model T.

Now, part of the premise here is that the thing you're selling, because of the more efficient standardized process you're using to create it, becomes more and more like the thing everyone else is selling, a mass-produced, unspecialized product. And therefore, you as the business guy—the person who knows how to do things more efficiently than the next guy—become all the more valuable to the process.

The media, like all other advanced industries, was going to begin trafficking in commodities. Content was going to become *commodified*. Therefore, gaining the business advantage was going to be about how the organization could most efficiently create the product and bring it to market. It was going to be about *management.*

Plus, it was going to be about *value.* Or value *added.* When you commodify something you devalue it, but if you manage to convince people (using, of course, the media) that your cheap-shit commodity is the better cheap-shit commodity, then you've won their hearts and minds. In a world where everything is the same because everything has been commodified, the only way to distinguish what you sell from what everyone else sells is to create certain neural stimulators that make buyers *think* it's different. This is called *brand.*

There's a precious irony here. The value of the media used to be that it could create that illusion of difference, that value distinction, for a whole range of products—from soap to cars to nail polish. But now media people were saying, *Why don't we use the power of the media to create the illusion of difference for mass-produced media! Why should we give somebody else the advantage that we own? Damn!* Accordingly, as the media commoditized and devalued itself, and then turned around and overhyped itself, this made it increasingly difficult to create illusion and distinction for the products and producers (the soap and cars and nail polish) that were paying the bills.

Naturally and logically, the consolidation that happened to all other great-industries-which-shaped-history would happen to media too. (Anybody who went to business school, or, for that matter, has ever read a business magazine, will tell you that there were once hundreds of automobile manufacturers, which became three.) Of course you would go from a large number of disorganized, independent, mom-and-pop media companies to a few professionally organized supercompanies. You would *con*solidate. (This really is among the sexiest business words—it is, after all, in the process of consolidation, the making of deals and trading of assets and the cost of recombination, that the vast and immensely profitable financial services industry makes most of its money.) You would combine many businesses doing the same things inefficiently to realize one business doing the same thing efficiently, hence creating a more-widely-available-less-expensive product that would be adopted by billions of people everywhere, changing human behavior and the course of history!

Making you, the person who did the organizing, a historically significant person.

One obvious problem here, however, is that the media business is nothing like a business. No mutuality. No common function. No similar objectives.

It's a made-up concept, *media.* In all the huffing and puffing

---

about the media, we forgot that *media* doesn't mean anything. The entire industry is a fluke of semiotics.

In the fifties or so, ad agencies gave *media* its first use as a singular construction. "What's the media?" "What media are we using?" Meaning the literal paper or film or tape or billboard.

From there, it became a salesman's word. *I sell media.*

My dad ran an ad agency during the fifties and sixties in Paterson, New Jersey. One of the guys who used to hang out there was a young radio salesman named Mel Karmazin, who, when he grew up, would buy radio companies, then television, and eventually joust for power at the Viacom cartel. At any rate, in those days, Mel, as a callow youth, was called a media sales guy. He was selling space, and the space was called media. Media was the thing that the advertisers bought. It was the space *between* what you listened to the radio to hear or turned on the television to see.

There was too, during this time, the growth of *media* as an arcane academic word. Media was about the abstract function of communication. Mass media. It was sociological. Large numbers of people were getting the same information in the same way—this must mean something; this must be having a *societal effect.* There was too this other element of academic self-consciousness, of the media being the mediated thing. This was McLuhan. The media was the go-between, the intermediary. This was, obviously, a point of philosophy rather than business. There was much talk about the media as a distortion field. There was real reality, and then media reality.

Then there was a thing called multimedia—a sixties thing related to drugs, mostly. The Joshua Light Show at the Fillmore East was multimedia. (In some sense, the concept of multimedia would have its finest expression as PowerPoint.)

And then, suddenly, emerging in the 1970s, you had something called media companies. This was just inflation. A useful bastardiza-

---

tion of an already obtuse word. It was a Wall Street thing. We're more important than we were yesterday because we're no longer a broadcast (notice how old-fashioned that word sounds) company, we're a fucking media company.

But at no point in the development of the word and of the concept of media was there an assumption that the television business and the magazine business and the radio business and the billboard business and the music business and the movie business were the *same* business—that they should be run by the same person, that they required the same talents, or would, even, logically have the same investors or the same stars or the same audience.

Indeed, for a while, there was even a kind of formal resistance to the word—and to the notion. One day, shortly after I went to work as a copyboy at the *New York Times* in the early seventies, a memo appeared on the copydesk bulletin board, advising reporters and editors that, in fact, there was no such thing as the media per se. There were newspapers and magazines and television and radio and movies, and to group them under one very vague umbrella was, at best, a lazy usage.

It's as ridiculous as if someone had come along and invented the "transportation" business and, within the same company and under the same management, because they were all somehow related to the same word, put car companies and train companies and ship companies and airlines together.

You get the exact opposite impression of the media business from *The Powers That Be,* David Halberstam's epic 1979 book about the media industry. Instead of assholes run amok, in Halberstam's version the media is a rational, smart, competent, inspired enterprise: the pivotal force in the rise of the civil-rights movement, the opposition to the war in Vietnam, and the investigation of Watergate and the end of Richard Nixon.

Halberstam's media people not only have vast social and political clout, but they have businesses that throw off great amounts of cash and which have increased in value as significantly as any businesses ever have.

It's a golden age chronicle: The media from 1925 to the late seventies (just as Murdoch is coming to America).

For a few years our kids went to school together. Halberstam was a lugubrious presence at the school, trotted out for benefits and lectures.

On the one occasion we had lunch together, I found myself thinking of him as a missing link. He's a certain, stuffed-shirt, media establishment type—which really doesn't exist anymore, except in some kind of martyred form.

He believes in the worthiness and primacy of civic institutions—the nineties idea that politics may have been replaced by the market, and politicians by entrepreneurs, is sacrilegious for him. He believes in owners—proprietors—over managers and opportunistic entrepreneurs.

He believes in lots of prose (anathema in modern media) and discursiveness. He's all long form—ceremonious even.

Pop culture dismays him. Celebrities don't interest him.

He certainly does not accept the new financial-media-technology power structure—the American Establishment as it is, for instance, annually described by *Vanity Fair.* ("Do these people really influence society?" he asked, and answered, at lunch. "No, not at all. This is just a scorecard of who made the most money.") He has a different idea of power, who should have it, how they should use it, and who might challenge them on its use. The quick and the glib are not at the center of his power grid.

At a dinner shortly after Barry Diller formed USA Networks (his disparate collage of television stations and cable channels) in 1998, Halberstam stood up and, in his deep voice—with such an undifferentiated bass range that it's often hard to understand him— asked Diller what USA Networks planned to do in the area of public affairs.

That must have quieted the crowd: You can hear the rustle of embarrassment.

The creation of media power is, in Halberstam's telling, the creation of civic power. The Paleys and Meyers and Luces aren't press barons (marginal, corrupt, eccentric figures). These are true American enterprise figures, as large in his telling as the Rockefellers and Henry Ford and the Kennedys. (Indeed, the Kennedys would not have been the Kennedys without the aid of many of the people in Halberstam's book.)

Before the advent of these people and their organizations, the media was vaudevillian. Here, midcentury, the media, with its ever-expanding reach, becomes both a vastly powerful voice and amazingly lucrative business.

This is, however, the *news* media.

There is no entertainment in Halberstam's media view. Movies, rock and roll, prime-time, celebrities, as late as 1979, when Halberstam's book is published, have no place in a serious discussion of the media landscape. Even Paley's great sitcom-and-variety-show empire is overshadowed by the position and power he acquires through his news division. The focus in the book is the American commonweal, rather than the media commonweal, political culture rather than pop culture.

Serious men engaged in serious matters.

It would never have occurred to Halberstam or anyone else he profiles and mythologizes in his book that the media industry would, over the next generation, become the nation's largest industry because, in part, it would provide escape from this boring civic world. (*People* magazine, launched in 1974 by Henry Luce's company—after Luce died—and which becomes the most successful magazine of all time, surely helps invent the new, alternative, celebritified, noncivic power structure.)

And yet while Halberstam misses the soon to be inescapable and elemental point about the media business, he nails another fundamental point: The media has suddenly become a really great business. He gets the hunger for media. People are eating this stuff up. It's totally hot.

You can't read *The Powers That Be* and not start to think, That's where it's happening.

It's like the West: free land.

The romance of Halberstam's world is not only in its cleverness and toughness and even nobility, but also that it's so easy. Anybody could do this. Anybody could be this kind of success.

It's the first structural analysis—who knew this person and who knew that person and how the web of connections and being in the right place at the right time intersected with the nation's changing education levels, its advancing aspirations and the laws of supply and demand—of a media career. And it's the first time that the media business is considered as not just the story of newspapers or magazines or television, but in the aggregate, cross-platform sense which makes it all so much, well, bigger.

Everybody I know of a certain generation in the media business read *The Powers That Be* and took it ever so seriously. Many of us, I'll wager, came into the media business, rather than, say, government or academia, because of *The Powers That Be.*

5
THE
PARTNER

Heilemann and Battelle had gone into partnership with one of the really deft and canny hotdogs of the post-Halberstam media age.

He was the senior figure at the Quadrangle investment firm. Before that, he was one among a handful of bankers at the center of the mergers and acquisitions that had remade the media industry.

But before that, he was a journalist too—which made everything about him all the more surprising and confusing.

Let me defer to Steven Wolff, my then eight-year-old son, just arriving home from a play date—his first at his new friend Izzy's house.

Where I work in our apartment is close enough to the front door to hear my son's comings and goings. By the end of the day there's a reluctance and crankiness and heaviness—the backpack thumping, shoes dropping, coat dragging. The nanny cajoling . . . *Just one more step . . . Just hang your coat up. . . . Just . . .* Only the most dogged parent would inquire, at this moment, about the day or the play date or the state of the second grade. The kid needs a cocktail before he's going to be civil. And indeed, Steven almost always heads to the other end of our apartment—to avoid disturbing a father theoretically at work, or, more threatening, a father who might want a sociable chat.

But something different was going on in the foyer. It was an audible change in the energy level—there was a frantic excitement, everything quicker, louder: the backpack not thumping, but being flung; shoes being kicked. The nanny's voice rising, control being lost. The chatter level going off the scale, "Izzy this . . . Izzy that . . ."

I almost went out.

But I know Manhattan play date etiquette. It's not all right to recruit your children as spies.

What's more, children—and Steven has two older sisters who have had countless play dates before him—are not very reliable reporters. They don't readily perceive real estate or class differences (although this changes with adolescence when they become canny appraisers and breathy gossip columnists). This may be because an eight-year-old, as yet, lacks envy's power of observation, and it may be too because the differences between upper-*middle*-class real estate and upper-class real estate is not, in Manhattan, all that great. Most truly grand apartments in Manhattan are four or five thousand square feet, an American professional's right anywhere else. An overdecorated billionaire's apartment on the Upper East Side is a doctor's home in Scarsdale or Shaker Heights. In Manhattan, millions are in the nuances.

And so, as difficult as it is, and as disappointing as it is, I have learned not to ask too much of my children about other people's lots in life.

The nanny was sharply calling Steven now. There was a clattering, and I heard an impermissible flying leap between the arms of two chairs, and then my son was flinging open the French doors which I look out of, over the laptop screen, as I work.

His eyes were large. His face lit. His shirt askew. It seemed like a vast sugar high, but more profound. Revelatory. It was one of those moments as a parent that you anticipate and dread—when some piece of information, some experience gained on a play date (i.e., the street) takes your child from you. I held my breath for his epiphany.

"IZZY," he said, momentously, his voice soaring and eerily distorting, his eyes becoming ever more saucerlike, "IS RICH!"

I inquired closely and guiltily.

In the telling, Izzy occupied a Harry Potter apartment. Some fantastic and fabulous interior world.

Great halls and monumental public rooms.

A complete Toys "Я" Us inventory.

Marble.

Columns.

Statuary.

A bathroom as big as a whole normal apartment!

The most delicious cookies ever served anywhere.

Izzy's father had gone to work at the *New York Times* just around the time when I did (for me it was the Watergate–Yom Kippur War–overthrow-of-Salvador Allende fall of 1973).

Manual typewriters—rows and rows of them on the third floor. Dirty linoleum floors. Rotary dial phones.

It was a preyuppie age. A prebusiness age. Another world, really.

I wonder if everyone in their careers finds themselves at some point thinking they are fundamentally from another era—and that they will be found out one embarrassing day.

Actually, I most wonder if there are people who have never experienced such a temporal break. Are there people whose lives and careers have a logical continuity?

There are, after all, still people—as though in some parallel world—in the *New York Times* newsroom. And while the floors are cleaner, and the office equipment up-to-date, they are still doing the same job that we used to do. I know many of these people, but I do not know if they know that, in a manner of speaking, the industrial revolution began and they stayed on the farm.

But perhaps they do know this, because among the two most irritating words to a generation of *Times*men are "Steve Rattner"—that is, Izzy's father.

During the seven or eight years he was at the *Times,* Rattner did better than almost anybody else. He was really golden. New York, London, Washington: These were assignments that already put him in a sphere to make him one of the most powerful journalists in the world. His career path was the path of a Reston or Rosenthal or Frankel.

Now, no one, in that age, even far-lesser achievers, gave up the *Times.* It was like giving up the Church. You couldn't replicate the career, you couldn't improve upon it, you couldn't substitute for it. Achievement at the *Times,* just being *at* the *Times,* was sui generis achievement.

Merely reaching the *Times,* like the priesthood or Harvard, was an accomplishment, and then, as a separate or additional process, you moved up inside the institution.

The exceptions were people who fell out because of weakness or eccentricity. Or you could in some risky, prodigal endeavor leave the *Times* to *write.* This was in some sense like leaving the priesthood for a contemplative order. Or like leaving the priesthood, in South America, to pursue revolutionary activities. But you didn't and wouldn't just leave the *Times* for some canny career reason.

Just as, one day, Steve Rattner did, upping and going into *investment banking.*

Everything argued against this. There was a line in the sand, deep and meaningful, between the business side and our side.

If you were one kind of person you couldn't be the other kind of person.

These were inimical interests.

Male. Female.

And to discuss people who did business was hardly even to discuss people who did *investment banking.*

When Izzy's father decided to leave the *Times* and become an investment banker, it was hardly clear—certainly hardly clear to virtually all the reporters at the *New York Times*—what investment banking even was. Or, at least, if it was anything grander than being a stockbroker.

In 1982, investment banking was still a dumb-dumb business. In the long shadow of the sixties, and the darkness of the no-growth seventies, Wall Street was a redoubt of C-students, and sons of former Wall Streeters (who were C-students).

So when Izzy's father made this leap, crossed this chasm, he was seeing something that few other people saw—not just a series of opportunities, but, I think, a new identity.

There is a way that Rattner is described during his early years at the *Times* which is telling. First, he is always described. He is singled out. He is perceived as being different. Now this could mean that among highly ambitious people, which lots of people at the *Times* are (lots too, interestingly, are not ambitious at all—they are, in all aspects, lifers), he is just more ambitious. Or it could mean that his ambition is of a different order. *Times*ian ambition is very much of a corporate kind. It is Organization Man stuff. It is to rise up within the *Times* but always with the implicit understanding that without the *Times* you would be nothing. It's a very precise individual-to-institution calculation. You are its product—almost never the other way around.

But there was something different when people talked about Steve Rattner. A further wariness. An additional respect. An uptick of interest. And often, an undercurrent of envy and dislike.

For his part, Rattner, a short, slight, fair young man, seemed cooler, more remote, more *aware* than others.

He began his *Times* career as James Reston's assistant—which is something like beginning a legal career as a Supreme Court clerk. Chosen. This was, then, the most honored job for a young man in journalism.

From Reston's office he went to the Metro desk and then, in the OPEC-obsessed seventies, to writing about energy and shuttling back and forth to the Middle East, and then, at 24, to the Washington Bureau.

As it happened, his Washington rotation intersected with that of the publisher's son, Arthur Sulzberger Jr.

This circumstance of having the heir working in Washington, as a journalist among other journalists, is played, of course, as a normal one. But everyone knows it's weird and loaded.

Now, nobody is at the *New York Times* by happenstance (whereas most people find themselves working in professions and at companies they couldn't ever have anticipated—it's pure randomness). Everybody who is at the *Times* has aimed for it, considered it for years, fetishized it in greater and lesser ways.

The Sulzberger family is a complicated part of this fetish. It is one of America's longest-lasting, and last remaining, instances of primogeniture.

In any conventional career strategy at the *Times,* there really isn't much advantage in having a relationship with the family. It presents more complications than benefits. The line of demarcation is too clear. It's not just a hierarchical distinction, but a class line. And the family occupies a class of one—you can't get into it. It would be like someone trying to rise up in Labor Party politics by befriending the Prince of Wales.

But Steve Rattner does befriend young Arthur (always called *young* Arthur). Indeed, young Arthur is befriended by an assortment of people in the Washington Bureau in the early eighties. That is young Arthur's job at this point in time: to experience the *Times* as its reporters experience it—and to experience *Times* reporters.

But it's situational. While he befriends these people now, he will unbefriend them as the situation changes. He will say later, in his surprising blunt-speak way, that he can't be friends with *Times* reporters. That it doesn't work. That it complicates things.

But the person he will stay friends with, best friends (they will later live in the same building in New York and, every morning, go to the gym together) is Izzy's father—no longer at the *Times,* but now an investment banker, a media money guy, whose clients include the Sulzbergers.

I remember when I heard this: Steve Rattner had left the *Times* to go to Wall Street.

It was unclear what this meant, and yet it was clear to me that it was large—disturbing. If no one had ever done this, but someone, someone like Steve Rattner, was doing it now, what did it mean?

But I wasn't that far from understanding.

When I had arrived at the *Times*, I'd known, within something like minutes, that it was all wrong.

It was Gothic. Dickensian. It did not look like the modern world. It lacked any feeling of affluence. It was dirty and gray and unfriendly. The men had tics and limps and hairpieces.

You could romanticize this—this was a newsroom, after all. And that's what lots of affluent, suburban college boys must have done.

But I couldn't shake the sense that this was a time warp, which, if you didn't run fast, would catch you.

I sensed the grip of the place. The plantation quality. Still, I did not think that the career itself, the economic proposition, was flawed: to be a journalist. A writer in the culturally important person sense. A writer in the pre-rock-star sense. A writer in the sense of there being a recognized profession.

I left the *Times*, as Steve Rattner was moving up in the ranks, to enter what might fairly be called the late renaissance of the magazine business. These were terrible economic years, but in fact, there were plenty of alternatives to the *Times* in New York. It was (it borders on the bizarre to remember) a time of thriving, independent, Zeitgeisty magazines.

New York magazine, started in 1968, was a vast success. *Rolling Stone* moved to New York from San Francisco in 1977. *New Times,* a biweekly alternative newsmagazine, where I went to work, was started by former Time Inc.-ers. Mort Zuckerman bought the *Atlantic* with great fanfare. *Harper's* was not that far removed from the era of Willie Morris (the great editor of *his* generation). Even Condé Nast, then just a rag-trade publisher, wanted in on the game, and launched a revival of *Vanity Fair. Manhattan, inc.,* and *Spy* would shortly come onto the scene.

And yet, if you had a truly special sensitivity you might have recognized that there were roiling waters. You could have read these magazines themselves—so many of them doomed—and learned everything you had to know: The rise of Hollywood and the value of celebrities and the rise of a business culture full of its own Zeitgeisty cowboy personalities, which, every day, was setting a new baseline of what represented real and attainable wealth, was changing everything.

I was trying to make my writerly way when I heard that Steve Rattner was leaving the *Times* to go into investment banking.

How did he know, I have spent a lot of time wondering since then, that everything was about to change?

In hindsight, the business explanation is clear: One result of the late-seventies fiscal crisis in New York was that the financial industry and the power of finance, public and private, expanded vastly. Then too, there was the Reagan era of deregulation, an end to inflation, massive deficit spending, and the bulge of baby boomers in their prime earning years.

But this still does not explain the scale of the transformation, neither the economic nor the cultural transformation: Virtually *everything* became a reflection of how it was financed.

6
MY
THEORY

Corporate America, heretofore, was a white-bread, repressed, deeply uncool place to be—but then, all of a sudden, corporate man became a sexy thing.

My own favorite theory for what caused business to become such a compelling sport and transforming experience was the advent of the spreadsheet. This came in '82 or '83, shortly after the introduction and widespread adoption of the IBM PC: first VisiCalc, then Lotus 1-2-3, and then, of course, Excel. If you could work a spreadsheet, money suddenly became a highly fluid concept—the buck never stopped anywhere (oddly, during the eighties, *bottom line* became a metaphor for something absolute and irreducible when, in fact, the bottom line was becoming ever more elusive).

Financial strategy became like a war game. If you played it one way, you risked the end of the world, but if you changed a variable, you were safe and secure. Business reality became wonderfully plastic (running numbers has about the same relationship to actual business as sex fantasies do to sex—indeed, running numbers gets to be a sort of fetish).

Financial engineering (the term of art for the business that grew up around working a spreadsheet) becomes as complex as any activity becomes when you increase the variables exponentially. "Can he keep track of the moving pieces?" was what got asked about prospective managers of high-flying companies. The question was not, "Can he work hard and focus on the many details of the business?" Rather it was, "Can he appreciate that business has become a Rube Goldberg system of effects and countereffects, of balancing one representation against its counterrepresentation (what the Street is told versus what the media is told versus what the employees are told), of keeping not two sets of books but as many sets as can be imagined (the spreadsheet accommodates all fantasies)?"

In short order, business became way too complex for mere businessmen—the pallid, gray dad types of the past. Business suddenly demanded a different caliber of brainpower and temperament.

Everybody was catching the spirit. There was a revolutionary quality to what was going on—the old order was being swept away (indeed, almost everybody from the prior business generation was exiled).

Every day it was happening: Absolute nobodies, with only heart and imagination—and strange new ideas about how to analyze and manipulate numbers—took over heretofore unassailable, invulnerable, and oppressively dreary great American corporations. It was a class overthrow: outsiders against insiders, smarties against dopes, risk takers against old farts.

Business, which used to be a specialized, opaque, conservative activity—something like the military—became the national pastime. If you weren't taking over companies, you were getting into the stock market, watching the miracle of those mutuals and 401(k)'s going up and up. If you weren't an entrepreneur working spreadsheets to start your own dreamy enterprise, you were an option holder in someone else's dream.

Everybody was in business. Everything became business—technology, entertainment, news, even academia. And if it was already business, it could always be made more businessy—Enron was a Texas oil company that transformed itself into a global financial enterprise. Financing something, or refinancing something—the moment when reality always suffered its greatest adjustments—became the nation's central economic activity.

The culture at large may have been dumbed down, but business culture was smart, competitive, obsessive, relentless in its pursuit of the next best idea. Business became the ultimate abstraction. A new, near-philosophical language was invented to deal with the many-hued nature of reality and nonreality that the world of business was defining (it was as utopian as the language of revolution). Business became the focus of how people related to one another, of how communities were created, of how human progress was made. Business, as a system of logic that would allow you to accomplish any goal, at potential great benefit to everyone (and with a little extra to the person running the spreadsheet), was the metaphor of the age: The rich would get richer, and so would everybody else.

And the rich would get richer to a degree that had no precedent in history.

If he had not left the *New York Times,* Rattner would have earned, in twenty years, assuming a stellar career, an aggregate of $3 million to $5 million dollars (he would have been making about $50,000 in 1982 and something more than $300,000 in 2002). In twenty years as an investment banker (he was already making $1 million a year two years into his new job) with a stellar career he would have earned $300 million to $500 million.

The point is not just the hundredfold difference. It is that in the former scenario, he and his family would have lived a middle-class life in Manhattan or the suburbs, with minimal net worth to show for it, while in the latter he would have both supported his family in maximum style, while his net worth appreciated vastly, supplying his family with almost unlimited wealth for generations to come.

In other words, the difference here is not just between a reporter who makes less than a banker and lives a different sort of lifestyle (say between the Upper West Side and Larchmont—as it might have been in the fifties, sixties, and seventies), but between a reporter without assets and one of the richest men in the world, between a functionary in the information business and one of its key leaders.

Even if Steve Rattner had become the executive editor of the *New York Times*—that could hardly compare with the personal influence and freedom he had achieved.

He had gone to Lehman Bros. then to Morgan Stanley, and then to Lazard Frères, where he was the number two.

Lazard, for a long time, remained a rarefied Wall Street place. It was not so much a player as the firm that played the players. It sold pure knowingness, synthesis, metathinking. It made its money not through the amassing of so many less-dignified commissions, or through the creation and retailing of financial instruments, but through the discipline and mystique of the mandarin.

These were the behind-the-curtain players.

In some sense, Rattner finds the true value here of the *New York Times*. The $50,000-a-year job he had in 1982 is converted into a $20- or $30- or $40-million-a-year job.

This is almost a pure business-model point. You can retail your expertise the way a newspaper does, or you can do it the way an exclusive investment banking firm does. The point is about packaging and distribution.

There's a personal point too, of course. Few *New York Times* reporters, even the best business-desk people, could show up downtown and be seen to have great value to anyone. They are sloppy, and literal, and indiscreet—all flat affect.

The value, however, is in the package—in talking the talk and walking the walk.

Rattner is, too, by temperament, a social climber. This is a rarer attribute than you might think in this celebrity age; most people, in and out of business, have a natural and ingrained reticence. They're shy. Insecure. Afraid. Ashamed.

Social climbing requires complex emotional breadth and stamina—and often a novelist's, or courtesan's, understanding of individual value and distinction and of the myriad underlying relationships in any given room, or professional or social circumstance.

You have to be both arrogant and obsequious.

You have to be able to both know your place and to be able to cleverly advance it.

You have to be shameless.

Indeed, the premium on social climbing and starfucking, and people who have the shamelessness to engage in it, is so great that it has meant that a great number of vulgar, tawdry, unrefined people have been accepted into and elevated up the social and business ranks.

Rattner had the great advantage then of being an active and willing social climber but not being sleazy. He was very smooth.

He has a certain degree of Wasp aestheticism—or Wasp envy. Formality. Reserve. Efficiency. Soft-spokenness. (He was a kind of perfect museum board member.)

As it happens, none of these are particular virtues of media moguls. But Rattner's qualities turned out to be good banker qualities, especially for the Lazard kind of banker. He seemed like a wise man and a careful man, and a man who kept confidences and secrets.

There were suddenly, however, much easier ways to make much more money than the way Lazard was making it—and Lazard was making a lot of money.

For the three or four or five years of the big boom (depending when you got with the boom), what you wanted to be doing was owning pieces of these vastly inflating enterprises. You didn't want to be just in the advisory and fee-generating business—which Lazard was in. You wanted to be buying into, at a ground floor price, some of the most outrageous wealth-creation schemes (i.e., stock speculations) that have ever been created.

You wanted to be a promoter rather than an advisor.

Now, there were reasons that you wouldn't want to be this. To be an advisor was not only fiscally more prudent, but it was not sleazy. Indeed, that is what you were selling: I'm not sleazy.

But the sheer breathtaking, beyond-imagination amounts of money that could easily be made destablized these trade-offs and underlying value propositions. There was no kind of respectability that could compete with the respectability that came from billions. And the more people who made these billions, the less respectable you seemed without you yourself having billions.

So Lazard, in the last years of the boom, clinging to respectability looked dowdy, out-of-it, failing.

Now, Rattner was fabulously rich anyway. He didn't need Lazard anymore. Rather, he seemed to have already designed his segue. He had risen through the ranks of Clinton administration favorites, contributing money, raising money, playing personal host to the homeless first family. He had even now successfully transferred this affinity to Gore and his prospective administration.

He was about to be that historically important figure, the Wall Street guy who goes to Washington.

The upside here was really fabulous. He had made hundreds of millions, and now he was going to have historical stature added to the résumé (and be able to someday go back and make, potentially, hundreds of millions more). He was going to be Bob Rubin, or even Clark Clifford.

But it didn't turn out that way. The Democrats died.

Hence, Quadrangle.

You create a vehicle for economic self-expression.

It's less your business than your business avatar. It's going to represent your business, economic, organizational, and technological philosophy.

Because you have made money before, money is now going to come to you, reside under your command like the armies of lesser lords. The money is your instrument.

A fund.

To have a fund.

Pete Peterson, the former treasury secretary, started a fund called Blackstone Group, which, in addition to making him vastly more wealthy, made him more central, engaged, called upon, than he was as treasury secretary. Before Peterson, another treasury secretary, William Simon, created Wesray, and arguably created the model for the personal fund. Henry Kravis, at KKR, with his fund became the seminal businessman of the eighties. John Doerr at Kleiner, Perkins made his venture capital fund the virtual arbiter of the nineties.

Leverage, venture, hedge—it doesn't make any difference what kind of fund. In each instance, you have abstract concerns.

It's influence. That's what you have; that's what you're after.

Rattner's construct, very vague in its outline, would involve the media industry.

He raised $1.8 billion. And, what with the money you would be able to borrow against that cold cash, Rattner would have $10 billion or more to invest.

No doubt, as he considered his construct in early 2000, he was thinking about old media and new media and the convergence of platforms and distribution systems and the technology to facilitate all this.

But then the market crashed.

Now, in an ideal world, you invest your money in a rising market (ideally, you raise money in a rising market too). In the second best world, you are fortunate enough not to have invested your money in a market which the bottom is falling out of (and too, to have raised at least a good part of what you want to raise before the bottom fell out).

Indeed, as the first year of the millennium wore on, and as the millennial downturn got worse in 2001, it was more and more clear that Rattner was one of the luckiest guys around. He'd gotten lots of money together before the bust was clearly on, but hadn't yet given it to anyone. This meant not only that he was not losing any money, but that he would have all the money in his war chest ready to deploy when the market bottomed out.

When he bought, he would be buying cheap. It was an impossible-to-fuck-up strategy. The job was just to wait. The art, too.

You had to fight the impatience of having nothing really to do.

You continued to raise money—slowly, in a down market— and you had a lot of meetings in which you listened to proposals soliciting you to invest in companies that you were not going to invest in because, if you merely waited a little longer, your dollar would buy more than it would buy when you first heard the proposal.

How to be a deal maker—a deal *macher*—without doing any deals? That was the question.

How to *be out there* is the way it would have been put. *We have to be out there, Steve,* someone would have said.

Brand. Profile. Marketing push. Buzz.

A conference.

The finest marketing strategy is to associate yourself with people who do not need a marketing strategy.

Starfucking.

Allen & Company, a far-from-mainstream investment house, which had developed a media specialty precisely because it was not a blue-chip firm, had, some years ago, begun gathering moguls together at the Sun Valley estate of Herbert Allen. Not only was this good for Allen & Company business, but it helped create the illusion that Allen & Company, and Herbert Allen himself, were at the center of it all. A magnetic force.

And if, a central motivation of everyone in the media business is to be at the center of it all, well, then, if you controlled the center, if you were the force that brought people to the center, then you *were* the center.

So a Quadrangle conference.

Rattner and his partners discussed this idea with *Fortune.* The concept was, first of all, to do this with people who knew how to do it—and *Fortune,* like every business magazine, organized several conferences a year. And also, to have *Fortune,* among the eminent names in the business arena, associated with Quadrangle, still hardly a name at all, couldn't hurt.

But *Fortune,* with less to gain by sharing top billing, said no.

It was at this point that Heilemann and Battelle entered the picture. And while they were far from *Fortune* status, they had done it before. At the *Industry Standard* they'd produced conferences—which they'd had Rattner speak at (this is how they knew each other, from conferences).

What's more, if they weren't *Fortune,* they knew journalists. (While you might think that Rattner would know journalists from his *Times* career, this was a little like the Chairman of the Joint Chiefs knowing field soldiers—he would, but would not address them except through proper channels.) That's exactly the pitch that Heilemann and Battelle sold Rattner on. This wasn't just going to be a promotional thing; this was going to be a real conference. A serious business congress. Quadrangle would be at the center of a marketplace of business ideas and tough new thinking about the media.

It would be very cool.

7
THE BALLAD OF
JEAN-MARIE

As Rattner was assembling his war chest, the media business was focusing its attention on another investment banker—a former colleague of Rattner's from the Paris office of Lazard—who was the brightest and newest star of the media firmament, the first among a next generation of would-be moguls. Heilemann and Battelle, through Rattner, had already drafted him as the first big name of the autumn conference.

Now it is true that within two months of when I met Heilemann and Battelle for lunch, this star, the 45-year-old French-born-and-bred Vivendi chairman Jean-Marie Messier, would be out of a job, the punch line of every business joke. And yet the fall of their headliner was not so much evidence of Heilemann and Battelle and Rattner's foolishness, or lack of prescience, but of the weird surface existence of the media business.

The business is really quite a courtly affair, in which the most extraordinary manners and rituals are taken at substantive face value, right up until the point that disgrace intrudes. A mogul is a mogul, with all due consideration, until he is deposed. The king must be killed for him to cease being the king.

If Heilemann, Battelle, and Rattner had not been able to attract Messier to their conference—even when the smart money was already predicting his overthrow—his absence would have marked it as a pallid affair.

If his was a high-wire act, all media acts are. There isn't any mogul who has not risked absurdity and death, so absurdity and likely death should not exclude you from mogul acclaim.

This is, indeed, a crux of the matter: How is it that people vastly unworthy, by all evidence and logic, so palpably precarious, are taken so seriously?

Why don't we all break down in laughter?

How is it that our critical faculties come to be so readily suspended?

What made us such pushovers?

Certainly, from the start, the Messier proposal was an exceptionally ludicrous, even slightly surreal one: The idea was to take France's leading water utility and turn it into a global media-technology-communications company.

Why?

A substantial part of the reason, oddly, lies in the uses of metaphor.

Metaphors as much as spreadsheets are key investment banking tools. The more abstract business became, the greater business there was for investment bankers, and the greater need there was for metaphors to give some structure to the abstruse forms everybody was talking about.

In fact, it was very French: Business, as well as life, was philosophically complex. It required new tools of language and consciousness to decipher.

A water company supplied great metaphorical opportunity.

A water company was an objective correlative for the media business.

The point was the pipes. Here you had a company that moved its product—water—through a complex distribution mechanism right into people's homes.

That, in a nutshell, defined the challenge of the modern media. How do you take our content—a kind of water by any other name—and efficiently get it into people's homes? (It used to be that you wanted to get in into their heads—but the *home* offered the truer point that you really didn't have to think about, or even register, content for it to be part of your life.) And how do you get it into people's homes so efficiently that it becomes a transparent part of their daily activities? (Media ought to be on the unconscious level of water and electricity.)

Owning the pipes was the key.

Owning pipes was the millennial secret (as plastics had been the secret circa 1967 offered to Benjamin Braddock in *The Graduate*).

Literally, there were oil and natural gas companies in the U.S. emptying (and one would assume cleaning) their pipes and filling them with the fiber-optic cables that, shortly, would glut the market.

A water utility, with only a little critical interpretation, is therefore the same as a media company—indeed, let us call it a media *utility.*

This wasn't just French sophistry.

Everybody who was rising in the media business was obsessed with distribution. HOW WE GET OUR PRODUCT TO OUR CUSTOMERS.

This reflected two issues:

There was the example and threat of cable television. Nobody took cable television seriously in the seventies. It was exclusively a distribution business—"a pure distribution play"—and everybody thought the effort and cost was going to be way too great. What's more, you already had free television. So why would you choose pay television over free?

The fact that everybody turned out to be wrong here, that consumers would pay, and that owning the pipes meant you controlled what went into people's houses, was a vast shock to the media system. The paradigm, and the metaphor, changed. Instead of a media menu, with consumers selecting the radio and television and magazines and books that appealed to them, now the idea was a version of force-feeding. Could you be the doctor administering the nutrients and medication that flowed through the media IV?

At the same time, we were entering a further new paradigm in which all of the capital and technological barriers to controlling distribution began to fall, in which we were becoming a world of broadband and Napster. That made it all the more imperative, and all the more valuable, to be able to argue that you were, somehow, going to be able to control distribution and maintain control, or at least as much control as it was possible to maintain.

And then there was the second issue: the investment bankers. In addition to controlling the business language—the basic means of business expression without which you could not communicate with other businessmen—investment bankers also controlled the market. You could not sell something without bankers.

Now, if you controlled distribution, or if you could merely argue a reasonable case that you would be able to control distribution, then the bankers would certify an altogether different type of pro forma than if you were just a mere content purveyor. The difference was a difference in scale. *Scale.* After covering fixed costs, how do we grow exponentially with only incremental new expenditures?

That's *scale*. Bankers would say: "How do we scale this? I don't see any scale here. How do we show scale?"

If you controlled distribution, you had scale.

And if you had scale, then the value of your business—what someone, some investor, or some other business that might acquire you, would pay you for every dollar you earned (the "multiple")—increased geometrically. At least according to the bankers.

The fact the Messier's and Compagnie Générale des Eaux's water pipes had nothing to do with media was beside the point. He'd nailed the metaphor.

There were two other big themes in the rise of Jean-Marie Messier and the transformation of Compagnie Générale des Eaux: national pride and personal vanity.

Neither should be underestimated.

Each European country had its media barons who could play on an international stage. The Germans had Bertelsmann. The Italians had Berlusconi. The English had Murdoch (however strained this relationship might be—and, even though he was actually an Australian). Being a media power was something like being a nuclear power: It brought you to the table; you were a player in the world. Another world now existed which was made of digital networks and cross-culture brands and, largely, the English language. You didn't want your country to not have a stake in this.

So Jean-Marie came into the media-mogul game not only with the right metaphor but with lots of French capital.

And then the vanity: What was required in the transformation of Compagnie Générale des Eaux was someone who was willing to gamble very safe and stable wealth and power in a business of fathomless risk and low reward. Someone who valued the reward by a different measure than just a financial one. You had to understand the value of personal exaltation—of being a powerful individual and puffed-up popinjay on the world stage.

Now, possibly the vainest thing a human being can do is go to Hollywood. More precisely, the vainest thing a human being can do is go to Hollywood with money. A step further: The vainest thing a human being can do is to be a foreigner who goes to Hollywood with money. You are, ipso facto, conceited and deluded enough to assume that while all other foreigners who have gone to Hollywood with money have had it ignominiously taken from them, you will not.

It is possible, perhaps, that Messier was thinking something like, Lightning doesn't strike twice in the same place. Considering that his vehicle of going to Hollywood was a vehicle that, previously, had been the instrument by which another ludicrously vain pretender had been fleeced.

This was Edgar Bronfman Jr., who, in the same way that Messier was trading his stable and conservative water business, had cast aside Seagram's, his family's old-hat liquor business (with a big and lucrative interest in chemicals which Edgar sold to finance the Hollywood adventures), for the high-risk entertainment business.

The Bronfman story is an unexpected and extreme tale of paternal love. A father, Edgar Bronfman (along with his brother, Charles, the uncle, who must really be pissed off) acts as a good, if passive, steward to a great family fortune based around the Seagram's liquor company. He has a son, Edgar Bronfman Jr., with no demonstrable business talents or career focus. Rather than go to college, Edgar Jr. goes out to Hollywood, begins a long association as a friend to movie stars, and, briefly, considers a career as a songwriter (he writes "Whisper in the Dark" for Dionne Warwick) before being given unspecified duties in the family business. Then, placing filial regard above profit motive, the father allows the son, now in his mid-forties and still keenly infatuated with Hollywood, to redirect the family's historic business interests. The company liquidates its enormously profitable holdings in the chemical industry and in 1995 acquires, from the Japanese, Universal Studios, and then goes on to buy a substantial interest in the music business. After vastly overpaying for these acquisitions, Edgar Jr. engages in several years of almost nonstop mismanagement during which many of his Hollywood friends, most notably Barry Diller, take great advantage of him. The family fortune is not only compromised, but the family is suddenly the object of great ridicule—almost as hurtful as great financial losses. Father and uncle direct Edgar Jr. to sell all of the family holdings.

Edgar Jr.'s single victory in the entertainment business is managing to sell his company, at what seems like a significant premium to its worth (although at a significant loss for the Bronfman family), to Jean-Marie Messier. ("The best thing about owning an entertainment company," Edgar Bronfman Jr. memorably said, "is selling it.")

This would have been the reasonable point for everyone to break down in laughter. But no one does.

Jean-Marie Messier, heretofore unknown, is treated as a great foreign potentate—rather than a doomed and comic figure engaged in an act of hubris and narcissism so transparent as to, in any melodramatic rendering which Hollywood people ought to understand, broadly foreshadow an inevitable and desperate end.

Let me offer a conspiracy theory here. People in the entertainment and larger media business *did* know that he was doomed. But they had a clear self-interest in making Messier believe he was safe and proceeding successfully. The greater his delusion, the larger his failure, the richer other people's take.

This analysis shouldn't be shocking or extreme. There is, every-one knows, a kind of flattery that happens in Hollywood that is very much akin to fattening a pig.

Jean-Marie Messier was given the pig-fattening mogul treat-ment.

Certainly there was lavish press attention—the kind that comes not just from Jean-Marie's own people saying loving things about Jean-Marie, but from everybody talking him up, pumping him greatly.

And wouldn't this have been a smart idea?

For a period after Messier did his deal for Universal, which would bring him into frequent dealings with Barry Diller, Diller went around telling everybody who would listen how astute Messier was. He's the real thing, Barry kept saying.

At the same time, let's just assume that Barry knew Messier was the opposite of the real thing. That he was entirely a made-up cre-ation. A self-actualized creature. A . . . joke. Let's assume this not least of all because Diller has made his career on the basis of the best instincts for other people's weaknesses.

Now, surely, Diller wants to foster goodwill with the new owner of a business he's in substantial partnership with. But too, let's con-sider the advantages of getting your partner to believe he's vastly more capable and cunning and astute than he really is.

Messier receives the full *Vanity Fair* treatment—*Vanity Fair* being a kind of *Debrett's* of Hollywood power and royalty—proclaiming him the new mogul.

He is invited everywhere to speak.

He is drawn in. He even begins the process of moving to Amer-ica, of becoming an American.

I saw him speak at a *Variety* conference. Messier, who spoke a

French person's idea of good English, went on and on about his vision: convergence, the digital world, handheld devices, transactions, cell-phone movies.

What was this, if not a setup?

If you don't know who the fool is in a room full of bankers and deal makers and media bigs, it's you.

There is, further, a belief among deal doers that as a result of language and cultural barriers and compensatory arrogance (with the French, of course, being among the most compensatorily arrogant), foreigners are incapable of doing proper due diligence—that is, making a basic assessment as to the substance of what they are buying, whether the land is underwater or not. Therefore you can sell them anything—especially in the media business, where what you're buying is such an uncertain affair anyway.

This was true of the Japanese when they bought Hollywood studios, the Germans when they bought book companies, the Dutch and the French and the English (who have their own linguistic—and emotional—issues) when they bought magazines, and the French and the English when they bought ad agencies: They all bought much less than they thought they were buying. (Murdoch, as it happens, is the exception to the foreigners-always-get-brutalized-and-robbed paradigm. But then, he did what most foreigners would never do: He became an American—which, oddly, and comically, and in Murdoch's image, Jean-Marie Messier tried also, haplessly, to do.)

Foreigners may do okay when they buy factories (although the Germans don't seem to have done great buying Chrysler), but media really complicates the buy-sell equation.

The cool factor is one of the big complications. You buy media to be cool; and paying attention to details (like leases and contracts and trademarks, and, in general, who owns what, and what moneys are reliably due and what the kettle of fish should actually be worth in a reasonable world) is not cool. Indeed, foreigners to assert their own cool often cultivate a dismissive attitude about the silly American obsession with details (and low-class obsession with money).

This casualness and assumption of superiority on the part of the French allowed the Bronfman family to sell Jean-Marie Messier an illusion as much as a film studio.

"Everybody makes a lot of money when the French come to town," said the advertising man Jerry Della Femina when I called him to ask about his experience when the French bought his advertising agency. (The French company that bought his agency became, in the great sweep-up, part of Vivendi too—and then later was spun out.)

It is, though, in all fairness, not just a case of American (or, in the case of the Bronfmans, Canadian) media people taking advantage of foreign media people (indeed, the Japanese took advantage of the Bronfmans).

Hollywood people are surely crooks, and even if they were virtuous, they might not have been able to resist taking money from foreigners who are so guileless and yet so arrogant. (Sometimes foreigners who are ruined in Hollywood are crooks themselves. Let us not forget that Gian Carlo Paretti, who bought MGM, took the French bank Crédit Lyonnais, which financed the deal, for nearly all it was worth and has been on the lam pretty much ever since.) But at the same time, you have to consider the intent of the foreigners: Their desire is to out-Hollywood Hollywood.

The process of becoming a mogul is the assumption of mogul-like powers—you start to believe that you can outhondle any hondlers, that you can take advantage of anybody before they take advantage of you. It's a straight-up Hollywood syndrome: They've seen it done in the movies, so they think they can do it.

And so Euro moguls, in deep cross-cultural celluloid thrall, try to ape (or outape) American moguls.

In some sense, they achieve even more outsize egos and a greater sense of entitlement than their American mogul counterparts because in Europe there is a greater tradition of the one true strutting supremo (together with milder accounting rules and securities oversight).

Everyone's favorite Euro-media supremo is of course Berlusconi, the Italian in the guise of the very American figure of a smiling, affable salesman. He has managed to monopolize his nation's media (half of its television, its largest magazine publisher, its leading newsmagazine, a major national newspaper, and the biggest book publishers) as well as its political system.

Indeed, it is this connection between the government and the media, a deeply incestuous relationship in almost every European country, that suggests, not unreasonably, a lot of self-dealing and tends to create a culture of people saying things with the assumption that other people know they are saying something else.

"The French," in Della Femina's analysis, "are simply incapable of telling the truth."

The Europeans, of course, accuse the Americans of small-time literal-mindedness, hypocritical moralizing, and intellectual dishonesty. Life and business, the Europeans argue, are complex, shaded, many-layered.

As it happens, this live-and-let-live, you-scratch-me-I'll-scratch-you attitude results in many European countries in a national web of interlocking companies so tight that all companies become one and monopoly is truly complete (or else unnecessary). On the other hand, the Euros would argue that this is exactly what AOL Time Warner is about, so shut up.

Here's a Euro-media snapshot:

Havas, one of the early pieces of the Vivendi media empire and the largest and oldest publisher in France, collaborated with the Germans during World War II and, as punishment, was nationalized after the war. (So, along with Bertelsmann, that makes two of the most important media companies in the U.S. former Nazi accomplices.) Under the management of the French government, Havas added advertising agencies, bus-tour companies, and pay television to its portfolio.

Under chairman Pierre Dauzier, an associate of French prime minister Jacques Chirac, Havas arrived in the U.S. in the late eighties, when it took a small stake in the English advertising group WCRS, which owned the U.S. agencies Della Femina McNamee and HBM/Creamer. As the English group encountered financing difficulties, the Havas agency, Eurocom, continued to raise its stake, taking over all of the WCRS advertising and public-relations interests by the early nineties.

In 1991, under the firm encouragement of the French government, Eurocom merged with the ailing French advertising group RSCG ("Why should we?" perhaps the conversation went with government authorities. "Why? Because you are French" was perhaps the answer), which owned U.S. agencies Messner, Vetere, Berger, McNamee & Schmetterer and Tatham-Laird.

In 1995, Havas, officially privatized but with the French government still a major shareholder, exchanged part of its shares with French telecom giant Alcatel Alsthom, another partially government-owned entity, and took over its publishing operations. In 1997, utility conglomerate Générale des Eaux, also partially owned by the French government, and run by Jean-Marie Messier, the former Finance Ministry functionary who had headed the government's privatization team, acquired 30 percent of Havas. In 1998, Générale des Eaux, now renamed Vivendi, bought the 70 percent of Havas it didn't own, which included a 49 percent interest in Canal+. Then Vivendi bought Cendant's computer-game division for something close to $1 billion. It also took a 24.5 percent stake in Murdoch's BSkyB satellite operation. It allied too with Vodafone AirTouch, the world's biggest mobile-phone company, to create Vizzavi (for *vis-à-vis*), a wireless Web portal, which promised to revolutionize the world of media and communications by rerouting content to handheld devices all over the world.

This is what Messier was trying to do in America—and this was his fatal error. He thought that in America he could enter into a realm of Euro-ish we-all-understand-each-other-and-we-all-get-rich-together. That the mogul class, which he thought he was joining, was such a rich-get-richer realm.

And so he got close to Barry Diller, assuming that there was a great, even historic, alliance being formed here.

It's almost painful to recount the details of what happened. Diller had already taken the Bronfmans, when, in an effort to "play" with Barry, Edgar Jr. had sold Barry an undervalued position in the Universal television holdings. While this deal exposed the Bronfmans to great ridicule, the connection to Diller probably held great attraction for Messier. By getting Universal, he got Barry. I'll bet Messier's fantasy was to turn Diller into his consigliere, his Zen master even. And such a relationship—perhaps he even thought he was hiring Barry, that Barry would become something of a French civil servant—would put him in some front rank of mogul masters. Together, Jean-Marie and Barry would be a new axis.

In fact, suddenly, in a kind of ultimate conquest, an annexation even, Jean-Marie seemed even to buy Barry. The same television properties that Universal had sold to Barry at a steep discount, it now bought back from Barry (plus much more) at a great premium.

And, briefly, many people saw this as a Messier triumph. He was lovingly attended in *Vanity Fair*. The deal was part of his strange, public, and ultimately embarrassing metamorphosis, or supposed metamorphosis, from French bureaucrat into major world leader. There were other deals, more publicity, more speeches.

There are two points here:

You, the mogul, might naturally come to believe, because of all the machinations and alliances and dramatic as well as subtle shifts of power, that you are involved in a process of geopolitical moves, even that you are engaged in an historical process of taking over the world (God knows, Messier had the French briefly believing they meant something again in the global community).

But the other point is that with everything getting so very heady and estimable, it's very easy to forget that you're a con man too—that being a con man is what keeps you alive, that if you don't keep getting the better of someone, that probably means they're getting the better of you. It's easy to forget that your great historical significance depends on your workaday opportunism.

Deals are complex things: You get conned (sometimes you have to even let yourself be conned in order to do a deal) and then you have to con someone else. You have to keep the balance (and balance sheet) right—that is, you have to con more than you get conned.

Messier, in a way that you can almost bring yourself to admire (there is a certain innocence to it, at any rate), got swept up in his historic, world-beating, grandiose role—and kept letting himself be conned, without conning anyone.

Now Messier was stupid—and bad at his job. And yet, he became not an exception, but a kind of example of the inexorable forces that work on all moguls—the need to be bigger and bigger, to grow beyond proportion, to be transformed.

MICHAEL WOLFF

*   *   *

I live on the Upper East Side of Manhattan, on the margins of the neighborhood where the great moguls live. You've got Barry Diller and the former Mrs. Sumner Redstone (Mrs. Redstone threw out Mr. Redstone) at the Carlyle Hotel (and Mr. Redstone nearby). You've got Mort Zuckerman on Fifth Avenue. You've got Michael Bloomberg on East 79th Street. You've got Sean "P. Diddy" Combs on Park and 75th Street. You've had Edgar Bronfman Jr. in the East Sixties (he recently sold this home). Michael Eisner grew up just a few blocks away. And Rupert Murdoch always kept a place here before moving to a younger neighborhood with his newer and younger wife (I used to see Murdoch jogging around the reservoir in Central Park; I'd follow steps behind him—a small man in a too-dapper running suit—thinking how fragile he looked and how powerful he was and how easy it would be to snatch him away). And, of course, all around the East Side you've got the bankers and lawyers who do the media deals.

Then—and you know how the realtor must have sold him the property, telling him all about Barry and Sumner and Edgar and P. Diddy—we got Jean-Marie Messier, who moved into a $17.5 million Park Avenue apartment that the company paid for (even on Park Avenue, $17.5 million is a lot of dough for an apartment).

At the height of Messier's reign, I was walking on Madison Avenue in my mogul neighborhood with my son Steven, who was shopping for an ice-cream cone, when we saw a figure who prompted Steven to exclaim, "Look at that guy!"

There was, languorously moving up Madison Avenue, a small man, with a coat cast capelike over his shoulders and the most pleased-with-himself expression I have ever seen on an adult, whom I recognized, after the slightest moment of surprise, to be

Jean-Marie himself (I quite doubt anyone else recognized him). He occupied a wide swath of the sidewalk, with a strut to the left and then a strut to the right, nodding and smiling, or rather bestowing blessings, on passersby, who gave him wide and incredulous berth. He seemed to see himself as some combination of Pope and maestro—his idea, I suppose, of an American mogul. (Not something, of course, you could see yourself as, if what you are is a CEO of a water and sewer company.) I do not think he would have considered spontaneous applause to be out of order.

I would have thought that this was it. I could even make the argument that Messier is the final flowering of the mogul. That, with the arrival of Messier and Vivendi—the overnight international media conglomerate—it suddenly became clear to everyone that the jig was up. That the long joke had reached its anticlimactic punch line.

But if the media puts a vast premium on association, it also has a special talent, and keen appreciation, for disassociation.

He is not one of us. That was only his delusion—his overreach.

What's more, one mogul's failure is another's success.

The market is speaking.

And then, in a complex social realm—Edith Wharton's New York updated—there have to be morality plays. You cannot have an inner circle of the influential and powerful if people are not regularly, and dramatically, expelled from it.

8
IN THE
SAME BOAT

After Messier was fired, Thomas Middelhoff, the *über* manager's manager at Bertelsmann, bought the farm; then Bob Pittman, the COO at AOL Time Warner, got the shiv only months after AOL Time Warner CEO Jerry Levin's sacking. In the summer of 2002, three of the six largest media companies, almost in tandem, dismissed their CEOs and top managers. When any big company throws out its management, you know something pretty extreme is going on—it's akin to a coup in a mostly stable nation. But when half (to date) of the leading companies of one of the nation's leading industries all at once begin firing their leaders, it's destabilization on a continental scale.

And too, in the summer of 2002, it seemed increasingly possible that Martha Stewart, that symbol of media wholesomeness and ubiquity, was going to go to jail.

This was all, of course, against the background of Enron and WorldCom.

It seemed highly problematic for Heilemann, Battelle, and Rattner—they were going to celebrate the media business just when there wasn't one. They had called a meeting of the crown heads of Europe in 1915.

We appeared to have gotten to one of those historically precarious moments when any catastrophe that you predicted was sure to come true. Anyone could go for it: What's your most satisfying darkness-at-noon vision? Who do you want fired and humiliated? Who do you want convicted?

Indeed, what if, after thriving for twenty years, the business culture itself—the broad social power of private enterprise, the no-guilt thrill of making vast amounts of money, the inevitability of an ever-increasing net worth, the great art of the transaction—was finally over? Kaput?

Thinking just this, on a fine Manhattan summer evening, as WorldCom was collapsing and Messier was getting the boot, I found myself on the Forbes family yacht—once a very potent symbol of upper-class American capitalism, before capitalism got hijacked by the arrivistes and entrepreneurs and spreadsheet accountants.

It was one of those meet-and-greet affairs that magazines are always hosting for advertisers and other media people. *Forbes,* the capitalist tool, had once had an advantage in this kind of promotional thing because of the yacht, the *Highlander.* But in the age of G4s or even larger personal jet transport, the boat seemed quaint.

Still, if the business culture really was kaput, I was thinking, we could well go into a new era, or back into an old era, in which one could not be self-respecting (that is, a self-respecting liberal-type person) and be on the *Forbes* yacht. The *Forbes* yacht might again stand for something other than what it stood for now, which was just a promotional thing; it could, possibly, go back to being a resented symbol of wealth, class, and exclusivity.

Now, I like Tim Forbes—son of Malcolm, the over-the-top father and protomogul, and brother of Steve, who keeps running for president—who is a kind of counter media mogul. He's a self-effacing, none-too-hip, always somewhat-pained-looking anomaly of a modern media executive. Tim might be, you suspect, a lot happier having inherited a more anonymous sort of business—for instance, a water utility—but he seems dutifully to make the best of his fate. In fact, this aura of dutifulness, rather than ego gratification, may be one of the reasons that he seems popular among his staff—something unusual for most ego-charged media executives.

We sat together at one of the little tables on the yacht, eating the catered dinner and marveling at this whole breathtaking moment of corporate humiliation.

Now, we were both old and jaded enough to appreciate that in all likelihood this was just a periodic blip. Various deserving people would be pilloried and hung out to dry, and there would be a requisite shocked, *shocked,* moment of sanctimony and contrition, and then the markets would get going again. This made sense.

"It's very hard to imagine the end of this," said Tim.

The business culture was just way too ingrained in careers and aspirations and relationships to be undone by what was, relative to the vastness of the American economy, just rounding-error-level corruption. We shared a moment's amusement about the recent *Wall Street Journal* story naming this business era as the most corrupt since just before the Great Depression.

And yet that the *Journal,* of all places, could so easily be caught up in the antibusiness fever—partly, of course, trying to distance itself from the current mess—was precisely the point. It really could happen. It really could come apart. And not just the economy, but the central organizing faith of our time: that personal ambition, relentless salesmanship, financial savvy, and, well, greed were the most efficient and even liberal agents of societal advancement and harmony. All of that, almost in the blink of an eye, could go back to being not just uncool but really nasty stuff. Quite possibly, business would return to being the province of only bores and bad guys. Certainly, people everywhere were rushing for the doors (our M.B.A. president himself has seemed to be frantically searching for an exit from any identification with the business culture).

But Tim Forbes seemed much more awestruck than depressed by this possibility.

While such a turn of events, an epochal rejection of the business culture, might be a deeply dispiriting notion for his colleagues at *Fortune* and *Business Week* and the *Journal* (not least because many of these people would want to participate in the repudiation), for Tim Forbes there was the possibility that this might be very good news.

"You know, we have always been," Tim said, with a certain twinkle, "the magazine for true believers."

If you go back twenty years, it would not at all be a prosaic thing to say *I am a capitalist* or *I believe in unfettered markets* or *Government is too big.* Rather, saying something like this would have defined you as a contrarian or country club member and, quite likely, a *Forbes* reader. I remember my own grim fascination with the *Forbes* motto, "Capitalist Tool"—it seemed so brazen and taunting.

To be a *Forbes* reader was not to have any sort of liberal or youthful or ambivalent impulses whatsoever. Dick Cheney surely read *Forbes.* Certainly, there wasn't any greater cheerleader for the Reagan revolution than *Forbes.* Deregulation, laissez-faire capitalism, hands-off government, pro forma anticommunism, was *Forbes* stuff. Caspar Weinberger, Reagan's secretary of defense, even became—and in some preserved-in-amber state remains—the ceremonial chairman of the company.

Nor was there any greater voice in the eighties for the sheer *joie de vivre* of wealth. *Forbes*'s "400 Richest Americans" issue, which debuted in the early Reagan years, may rank as a seminal work of the business culture. For one thing, it vividly established a new benchmark of riches—there were really, it turned out, a whole lot of people who had achieved mythic levels of dough. Absolute-freedom money. Start-your-own-nation stuff. For another, it was a folksy instruction manual. Anybody, apparently, with a head for business and a modicum of audacity could make a few hundred million bucks.

And then there was Malcolm himself. He was a Reagan complement. While each man represented stiff and conservative and unemoting constituencies, they were both showmen. Hollywood was, ultimately, the point (Malcolm Forbes's 70th-birthday party in Morocco, with Elizabeth Taylor on his arm, was a pivotal Hollywood-business-culture moment). Both men helped foster the most profound transition of our time: making business sexy, expansive, embracing, even polymorphous.

But this left *Forbes,* especially after polymorphous Malcolm died, as an awkward cultural fit. That it neither acquired nor was acquired; that it remained in private hands; that the company was known for a yacht instead of a G4—all of this suddenly made it seem quaint and fragile. The fact that Forbes remained an independent company was not so much an accomplishment as an eccentricity—and probably a costly one. (If the business magazine *Fast Company,* an unproven title with limited revenues, sold for nearly $400 million, how much would that have made *Forbes* worth—$2 billion or $3 billion? How could the Forbes family, if they had any head for business at all, not have taken the money and run?)

So much about the magazine seemed out of sync. The brothers, with their odd primogeniture plan (Steve, by dint of first birth, got the top title and biggest share of the business). The crotchety old editor, James W. Michaels, on the job for decades, only to finally retire and be replaced by another lifelong veteran of the magazine, William Baldwin (just a somewhat younger icon of crotchetiness). And then you had the magazine's uplifting quotations and mini-sermons and ritualistic pomposity. And, of course, there was Steve Forbes's loopy quest for the presidency and efforts to restore the Republican Party to its place as the party of the pants-pulled-up-too-high set.

Like all business magazines in the nineties, *Forbes* raked it in. But as business became the big media subject, and one of the great media revenue generators, *Forbes* also got roughed up by the competition.

Forbes may have remained the magazine of true believers, but *Fortune* and *BusinessWeek* (and so many other New Economy comets) became the must-reads of the yuppies and entrepreneurs and opportunists and faddists and marketers and digital schemers and reconstructed radlibs. These magazines were not fundamentally about business but about celebrity, heat, fashion. They were the new business culture. *Forbes* was the old.

But both old and new in the summer of 2002 were in bad shape. *Fortune* and *BusinessWeek* were certainly no fun anymore. And at *Forbes*, for the first time, they'd had to lay off staff, sell from the collections (those preposterous Fabergé eggs!), even ask senior execs to take pay cuts.

So, what if? What if the market didn't soon recover? I couldn't help wondering—my anticipation was growing. What if we continue to see corruption behind every boardroom door? What if I and other chattering sorts get to be socialists again? What if the pendulum has really swung as dramatically as that?

This was exciting: the collapse of monoliths, the end of business talk, a return to a cottage media industry (oddly, not unlike the *Forbes* company itself), the rise of new (old) values to complement a falling GDP (this really will be weird), and a new, widely shared antipathy for CEOs and fat cats everywhere (Cheney and Halliburton—ha!).

And it might well be, I thought, an exciting possibility for Tim Forbes (and for Steve and their brothers, Bob and Kip).

"If the world becomes more hostile to business, it just makes our job easier," Tim said, with something like irony.

I would not say that there was, on the *Forbes* boat, exactly a mood of giddiness (or that the Forbeses have ever been giddy). But, possibly, something was in the air: a sense of renewed mission. Dennis Kneale, the Young Turk (at 44) who was brought in from the *Wall Street Journal* a few years ago as managing editor to liven things up, was energetically announcing a "Free Martha" campaign. There was a not unhappy sense of this being time to circle the wagons, of capitalism having to be defended once more from the hoi polloi.

"I do believe we do things right in this country," Tim remarked, with, for him, a fair degree of passion.

It will, of course, not be the business culture that *Forbes* is defending but, rather, business itself. The Forbeses, too, may well take some pleasure in the collapse of monoliths, the end of business talk as a popular pastime (business talk, business secrets, should be the province of businessmen), and an affirmation of their own, standalone business model.

It occurs to me that while subscribing to the *Forbes* attitude might not have made businessmen more ethical, it would certainly have been wise on everyone's part to play it, *Forbes*-style, a little more conservatively. Businessmen get into trouble not just because of accounting tricks but because they think they're something more than faceless businessmen—whereas at *Forbes*, a businessman plays it close to the vest.

Yes. The arrivistes and wannabes screwed things up, but now the natural order may be righted.

On the yacht, you'll have the true believers in capitalism (in their madras jackets), and on dry land, everyone else—hurling insults at them.

I began an email to Heilemann and Battelle on how this conference could be the first postbusiness conference. That that should be the subject here: What replaces business? What is the new energizing, organizing force?

What would all the ambitious guys do now?

9
BOB PITTMAN—
A DIGRESSION

I was sorry there'd be no Bob Pittman at the conference. He had become—at least for a moment—one of the media business' most significant entities.

This has to do with a certain cult of personality—he has a kind of suaveness which makes everybody else feel so small-time—but it also had to do with function. There was, everywhere, this sense of corporate limitations. As corporations got bigger and bigger, as indeed they all recommitted themselves to getting bigger and bigger still, there came the simultaneous understanding that bigness was paralyzing too. While you might be unassailable, you were also immovable.

Pittman was wily and foxy and came to be thought of as the person who could move the modern corporation. This wasn't just because he was a smart manager or a brilliant salesperson (and he was the latter), but because he was rumored to have the touch.

To understand, in a way other managers did not, pop culture.

Certainly, he had the bona fides.

He was attended by the magic of being from out of town. He was a heartlander—not a medialand dweller. This implied a kind of oneness with the great rolling public out there. Indeed, he had an actor's look—and what is an actor, if not a sculpted every-man?

He was almost Elvis-like. He came from the South and had come out of radio. There was no more basic American media than radio: teenagers and ad space.

Plus he had social abilities. More important even, he had media abilities. Great press surrounded him.

Social abilities, of course, were not necessarily distinct from media abilities (arguably, media abilities had become social abilities): Pittman and his wife would live for a period on Central Park West across the hall from Steve Shepard, who would become the editor of *Business Week*. Shepard would come to conclude that Pittman was an exemplary manager and grant him favorable coverage for years to come, including the crowning cover story in *Business Week* after the AOL Time Warner merger was completed.

And then, most of all, there was MTV.

Pittman either single-handedly invented the notion of a cable channel that would air (at no cost to itself) the promotional videos which had become popular for music acts, or he did not.

This has become like the scholarly wrangle that surrounds certain not-precisely-authenticated works of art. The dispute does not so much discredit Pittman as put him at the exact center, even if its details are disputed, of the most brilliant media development in postmodern memory.

After MTV was bought and Pittman exited, he founded the kind of enterprise that would become popular later: a no-company company, or a no-function company. Its product was Bob Pittman. We have Bob Pittman and you come to us with opportunities for Bob Pittman. It was a Mafia thing. People lined up outside the door of Bob Pittman's Quantum Media and were granted audiences with Pittman and, if he agreed to cooperate, then various terms were discussed wherein Bob Pittman lent you his approval.

You were then in business with Bob Pittman—or with Bob Pittman's cachet.

Pittman's model, his rabbi, his godfather, was Warner Communications' Steve Ross. Pittman was to be the next-gen Ross, an entertainment executive with charisma (that is, salesmanship) and vision (that is, a sense of the next step, the next move, the audacious opportunity).

After MTV, and his brief, independent career, Ross brought him back into Warner, where he came to run the theme parks, and where, in a more controllable world, he might have succeeded Ross. The merger of Time and Warner in 1990 complicated that (the fight between the Ivy League-ish Time side and the unreconstructed Warner side would still be a company theme until the AOL merger) but made it a bigger prize—which Pittman might still have gotten, had not Ross died, of prostate cancer, in 1992.

With Ross gone, Pittman was a homeless gun.

He became the CEO of Century 21, the national real estate firm, intending, perhaps, to show that he was a manager for all seasons— all products, all services, all functions. (This is really a manager's holy grail, to be able to manage anything at all.) But really, he had a country club air of underemployment.

Indeed, going to AOL in 1996 did not seem really any more directed than going into the residential real estate business—it was just Pittman casting about.

And yet suddenly, almost within weeks of his arrival, Pittman turned on the gas that would inflate and then explode the Internet bubble.

He took AOL from an hourly charge to a fixed-fee basis (i.e., from three-something an hour to $19.95 and all you can eat a month). This became the most significant engine of Internet growth. Instead of being on the meter, America was suddenly on an unlimited ride.

The fact that what was created here was largely an illusion—that the company had gone from a proven, profitable pay-as-you-use scheme to an unproven new vision of infinite more-customers-more-advertising-and-direct-selling scalability—was, as yet, unrecognized.

It may have been Pittman who recognized it first.

Hence, by engineering the millennial sale of Time Warner to AOL, at precisely the highest reach of the market, he was able to accomplish the most difficult but most elemental feat of modern business: He turned vast theoretical paper money into incredible real dough. (Viacom's Sumner Redstone, more streetwise than TW CEO Jerry Levin, said that when he had been approached about merging with AOL, he'd told Mr. Pittman, "I really don't trust your currency.")

Pittman and AOL's detached founder Steve Case were following that most basic (if never publicly stated) business principle: You only make money, real money, off people who are stupider than you, and the stupider they are, the more money you can make.

They knew (and Pittman, who went back to the Time and Warner wars, knew as well as anyone) that since Jerry Levin had made being smart the raison d'être of his moguldom—he was the mandarin mogul—it was even more unlikely that anyone would say to him about the AOL deal, "Don't be stupid."

It wasn't just Levin who was stupid. The entire Time Warner

board were know-nothings too. In a sense, their collective view was as simple as, technology is the future, so let's do something technological—even though they knew precious little about technology.

It was just a perfect moment of pervasive and confident know-nothingness at which Pittman and Case struck. The buyer (and in truth Time Warner was the buyer) was caught unaware.

Then, 18 months later, in a fascinating paroxysm of elemental capitalist blame (where there is profit, there is loss), as the summer of 2002 began in earnest, and as what had happened became clearer and clearer (that Pittman had really taken Time Warner to the cleaners), Bob Pittman was ripped apart by the crowd (i.e., the media).

I suppose it is a kind of ultimate character note, the ultimate cool—slick, fast, and coifed—that having done what he did to Time Warner, having become fabulously rich while great numbers of Time Warner people (including Jerry Levin) got much of their net worth wiped out, he still thought he could hang around, even become the CEO. (It didn't help matters when Pittman took to telling people that he too had lost a lot of money—that he wasn't even a billionaire anymore.) He, quite possibly, figured he'd be held in awe for pulling off the greatest bait-and-switch in business history.

Here's what happened: Within a few months of the merger, it was clear AOL couldn't make its advertising numbers and that its subscription growth had seriously slowed (within weeks of the merger announcement the Internet bubble was obviously bursting; by the time the merger closed, it was a wrecked economy); what's more, Time Warner's own broadband service, Road Runner, was becoming a significant competitor to AOL. And yet AOL's lightning rod, Bob Pittman, was taking over the combined company. Then too, the AOL guys were talking about spinning out the Time Warner cable business—Jerry Levin's baby.

This was the elemental dish: It had become the two former allies, Pittman and Levin, the two guys most associated with the AOL deal, against each other. Each of them trying to grab the company, each of them trying to shift the greater blame onto the other (actually, each of them trying to grab the company before the blame crushed them).

There was even a proxy war: It was Levin's PR guy, Ed Adler, in New York, against Pittman's PR guy, Ken Lerer, in Dulles, Virginia. The first pitched battle was over the spring 2001 Pittman cover story in *BusinessWeek,* which had a crystal-clear subtext: Levin doesn't count; Parsons doesn't count; *I am the heir apparent.* Levin fired back with a story in Time Inc.'s own *Fortune* and one in the *New Yorker* by mogul Boswell Ken Auletta about the triumph of Jerry Levin. (Then there was a second story in *Fortune*—this one including Levin on the cover as one of the most brilliant thinkers of the age.)

At the same time, there were other rumors out of the rumor-mad Time Warner camp (never many rumors out of the AOL side): Levin couldn't get the support of an ambivalent board to buy AT&T's cable system (which would have made AOL TW *the* national media monopoly); Levin was having trouble getting that same ambivalent board to extend his contract. Levin's people were pushing Levin, and Pittman's people were pushing Levin.

Here is the Talented Mr. Ripley theory about Jerry Levin: He seems harmless enough until he kills you. The weapon of choice against Bob Pittman was Levin's surprise early retirement (forced though it may have been) and the sudden inevitability of Richard

Parsons as the new CEO—Levin was out, but, with a certain sort of kamikaze style, he had scuttled Pittman too.

It is necessary here to point out that taking it out on the guy who outsmarted you does not, in turn, make you smart.

Indeed, part of the subtext, at this point in the undoing of AOL Time Warner, is that everybody (shareholders, employees, media, fellow execs) got mad at Bob Pittman, not just because he pillaged and decimated TW but because of the widely circulated suspicion that Pittman turned out not to believe in AOL. (Here's a question that was constantly asked: "When did Bob know that the company was going to go south?")

Time Warner, however it lashed out, could not make itself undumb.

The logic that advanced thinkers (or hustlers) were championing in, say, 1995 was the same logic that the highest-ranking people at AOL TW were still stoically dealing in by the summer of 2002: *The Internet is the future; platforms will converge; the winner will be the one with the most eyeballs.*

Whereas Bob Pittman, by the summer of 2002, wanted to get as far from the division and the Internet as possible. It may be that Bob Pittman didn't believe in the Internet business anymore because he was the man who destroyed it.

Here's what he had done: He convinced every Internet company that it would be a loser unless it became what he called an "anchor tenant" on AOL. That is, these companies would pay AOL fantastic sums of money, often hundreds of millions of dollars, to have first crack at the legendary mother lode of AOL eyeballs. Accordingly, every Internet company went to the public markets with, fundamentally, this one proposition: If you give us money, we can buy access to AOL eyeballs, and then we can't lose.

Of course, everybody lost (except AOL, which, on the basis of these anchor deals, managed to trick Time Warner into the ultimate anchor deal). AOL eyeballs turned out to be worth much less than AOL was selling them for—and, accordingly, the whole industry, which had been paying AOL much more than it got, went belly up. Ergo, Bob Pittman, like no one else, came to understand AOL's real value—that there was a profound discrepancy in the accounts.

I hasten to add that inventing a reality in which everyone, however briefly, comes to believe is a metaphysical rather than an accounting fraud (although sometimes it can be both).

Pittman's idea (and I suspect he had this idea as he was doing the merger with Time Warner) was to get as far away from the break in the space-time continuum known as AOL as fast as he could. His idea was that you take the Time Warner behemoth and you get it to obscure AOL. And for a year Pittman steamed around and held meetings and demanded accountability and cut perks and sought margin growth and insisted on integration. (He kept complaining that the real problem was that the Time Warner divisions wouldn't cooperate with his grand one-stop, cross-platform-print-TV-film-music-online-cable-advertising-merchandising-promotion vision; one of his schemes was to reward Burger King, a big advertiser, with walk-on roles in AOL TW television shows for Burger King servers.) But instead of the AOL division becoming lesser in relative size to the larger company, it grew larger as, in fact, it became ever weaker—causing the bureaucracy to revolt.

The sorry state of the AOL division meant that the old Time Warner, with all its fractious and testy division moguls, got to rise again. (Part of Levin's original merger dream was that AOL would be such a superdivision that all the other divisions would converge into it.) The company returned to being (apparently, had never ceased to be) an association of disparate enterprises, each with vast and often unassailable clout, whose highest imperative seemed to be to resist what management wants—to resist, in fact, being managed at all. Pittman, it turned out, was easy to dispose of. By July 2002 he was gone.

But a revolution does not mean that logic is restored.

There were two depressing but motivating beliefs in the AOL Time Warner corporate offices which continued the logic of the AOL merger. The first was that spinning off or otherwise disposing of AOL would probably mean the end of the larger company too (and everyone but the most hostile was a long way from contemplating that yet).

The second belief among the deeply depressed people at the highest levels of AOL Time Warner—not at all unwarranted—was that the whole media business was probably going up in smoke. Music had been the first thing to go; print was going fast; pictures would follow. The media business would lose control of the media. *Puff.* Napster. *The horror, the horror.* AOL was supposed to be the lifeboat—however uncomfortable it was that Pittman and his posse preferred to swim for it.

It actually strikes me that Bob Pittman may have been one of those guys who actually knew what they were doing.

Bob Pittman is a media guy—in a very old-fashioned way.

He's not a manager, or philosophiser, or mandarin, or even, really, a mogul.

He's a promoter, a huckster, a snake-oil guy.

He finds something to sell, and then does what he has to do to get people to buy it. Likewise, if people stop buying what he's selling, he sells something else. Music videos. Theme parks. Real estate. Online services. There's always something.

This is the source, perhaps, of his perpetually unruffled quality. He doesn't see any of this as life-and-death, or painful transition, or existential business drama. Rather, it's the same old hustle.

10
NOT GETTING IT

My problem, my analytic failure, is in always thinking *this is the end.* That it *must* be the end. That it has to be obvious to everyone that this is the end. That we have reached the point at which reformation must begin. That the moral of the story is clear.

By July 2002, there was the absolute logical certainty that AOL Time Warner, the largest company in the media business, among the largest companies in the world, could not survive. The collapse of Vivendi was nearly a fait accompli. Bertelsmann was in deep retreat—they would surely sell Random House, its vast over-the-top acquisition (again, that problem of foreigners and due diligence), if only there were a buyer. Disney had become one of those isolated nations—Romania of the Ceauşescu era, or North Korea—held together only because its own despot had so thoroughly isolated himself from reason and the rest of the world. Viacom was a company caught between two warring chief executives who would sooner see each other dead than save the enterprise. News Corp. was run by the ancient mariner, almost mystical in his leadership. (What happens when the mystical leader dies?) All this together with the fall of Enron, WorldCom, Global Crossing, and Adelphia, and an epochal challenge to the cult of corporate personality—a post-Maoist climate, almost.

If I had briefly thought Heilemann and Battelle had an extraordinary opportunity—a chance to seize an antibehemoth Zeitgeist—now I began to think, *Who would even come to a media conference? Who would want to?* The media was dead—everybody knew. Must know.

And yet, certainly I was the shortsighted one.

When you listen to the journalists and analysts covering the media business, you can actually think it's an orderly, self-correcting world we work in. Reporters might spend a day ripping Messier or Pittman or Middelhoff to shreds, but then, shortly, return to defending Vivendi or AOL Time Warner or Bertelsmann.

"In fact," said the *Times,* "once all the broken promises about being a new breed of company for a new millennium are discounted, AOL Time Warner does not seem to be in such bad shape, considering the economy."

Reporters resist following to the end the cold logic of breakdown and collapse—even for the fun of it. They can't seem to help thinking that invariably, rationality will emerge out of the current mess. If Martha Stewart goes to jail, the world will have been righted. It's all ultimately part of a healthy process. After this period of resignations, terminations, investigations, and reorganizations, normalcy will return.

The rules of reporting and analysis are that even if you have good reason to suspect that the end is near, that events are largely out of control, that very bad things will invariably happen to very bad companies, you're not allowed to say it. There's just no formula or model for applying any sort of chaos theory, or even gut sense, to business reporting or corporate analysis.

You couldn't say what seemed pretty obvious: that nobody knew how to run the superaggregated and radically transformed companies that came into being during the past decade. That these companies defied control, were too vast and far-flung and composed of too many recalcitrant people and inimical functions. This, together with the fact that the guys who ran these companies often clearly had no idea what they were doing.

Everybody but the most literal-minded knew this.

But to be a respectable business reporter, you have to pretend the world is a coherent, rational, by-the-numbers place. You *can't* report that everything is up for grabs, that the greatest likelihood is that we're deep into a process that will cause the reordering of most of the basic structures of the media business—that the sky is falling.

Now, each of the management coups at AOL Time Warner, Vivendi, and Bertelsmann during the summer of 2002 was reported as a function of internal travails, and that is obviously the case—each enterprise was reporting its own variation on a looming cash crisis, which, in business terms, is the mother of all crises. On the other hand, three is a trend. Three indicates a mass movement, a systems issue, a rapidly spreading condition. It is not just a function of bad management but of larger, converging forces. History is turning against you—and is probably out to get you. And there's no way to manage yourself out of the mess.

But responsible reporters can't say that.

Which is why I started to wonder if I might have special powers.

I wondered if I didn't see the natural unfolding of the business narrative just as the most self-absorbed and megalomaniac CEO might see it: as an existential drama that, by the sheer force of bravura narcissism, can be bent to one's will—or not, and then you lose control of it. That's the game. All or nothing. Play it well or blow it.

What we had surely learned was that all of these companies that have seen themselves as part of some new, freer, liberating economic condition are emotional creations—they are psychological as much as management case studies. And to understand them, to be able to analyze them, you have to have some appreciation of the unique dysfunction of their top managers—the nuances of their hyperacquisitiveness and unsettling mood elevations. But even now, business reporters can't break the habit of assuming that even the most imperial CEO is a tempered and rational being. And if he isn't, then he must be a crook—an anomaly, a terrible and unfortunate exception.

Now, you'd be hard-pressed to get anyone to accept my theory (to accept it as an analytic model, at any rate) that the larger and higher-profile the company, the bigger the nutcase who runs it.

But let me push it.

Many of my journalistic colleagues, an earnest and respectful lot, seem to be of the mind that what has happened at the various media companies that have replaced top executives is a generally healthy move from personality-oriented management to—in the figures of phlegmatic Richard Parsons at AOL TW, austere Jean-René Fourtou at Vivendi, and bland Gunter Thielen at Bertelsmann—less charismatic, more nuts-and-bolts, more rational leadership. Well, yes, possibly—perhaps everything works out nicely in the end. "AOL Time Warner's biggest problem—the one that its new management team is bound to tackle first—is its credibility with investors and customers, not the soundness of its various divisions," wrote Saul Hansell in the *Times,* giving the adults-are-back-in-charge analysis.

I, on the other hand, would theorize that what has happened at these companies is merely a reverse psychosis—the flip side of the same condition. We have just moved from the manic phase into clinical depression.

At Vivendi, the company is now run, in effect, by the French government, depressed for half a century.

At Bertelsmann, the company is now run by the guy who, until just before his surprise elevation, pressed the CDs.

And at AOL Time Warner, you have in Richard Parsons a canny imitation of the walking dead.

For argument's sake, and in the interest of developing a method by which we might accurately predict the coming apocalypse of the media business, let's assume that these men will not deliberately disassemble what has so irrationally been assembled. Let's assume, too, that the hubris that created these companies does not naturally convert to reason—rather, it converts from mania to helplessness. In my model, then, these companies are now being run by men much *less* temperamentally suited to run them than even the overblown figures they've replaced. The situation has not gotten better; it has gotten worse (and less fun too). More chaos.

The worst case, you have to figure, always gets worse.

And yet, everybody who should have been running screaming into the night or hanging their head in shame would be showing up at Heilemann's and Batelle's and Rattner's conference.

11
BARRY
BUFFETT

But then there was Diller, who surely would be one of the conference stars, and who seemed to transcend the calamity.

He was the most unlikely and most respected of American business figures. He'd surpassed mere media and become a nearly deified business phenomenon—like Warren Buffett, the CEO of Berkshire Hathaway, with its forty years of double-digit returns, the oracle of Omaha, the most beloved business figure in America. Diller, too, had an almost avuncular Midas touch. The oracle of Coldwater Canyon. He was, against most sense and reason, beloved too.

It was a remarkable transformation. I don't think anyone ever before has made the leap from Hollywood—that inversion of Main Street business ethics, that primordial Enron—to blue-chip, chamber-of-commerce, I-always-make-money-for-my-partners status.

This was his accomplishment: After forty years spent rising to the penultimate reaches of the American media business—through Leonard Goldenson's ABC, Charlie Bludhorn's Paramount, Rupert Murdoch's Fox, John Malone's QVC, and now his own independent

USA Networks (soon to have its name changed to USA Inter-active)—he neither looked like a fool, nor a Queeg, nor as though he were engaged in a vainglorious last hurrah. He looked like a genius.

He did not seem, unlike so many of his mogul colleagues, ineffectual, pathetic, empty.

He seemed scary and full of portent.

He was a threat.

But not just a threat, not just a bully.

Really, he had several themes going—it was a wacky, picaresque, modernist novel, worthy of Thomas Pynchon or William Gaddis:

There was Diller as the preternaturally knowing businessman. Diller as thug and lounge lizard. Diller as the brilliant, creative, finger-on-the-pulse guy. Diller as consummate, gray-suit Wall Street financier. Diller as gay man—as gay icon. Diller as media contrarian and outsider. And Diller as once and future corporate media chieftain.

It seemed that the people who really appreciated Diller were people who appreciated him as fundamentally . . . playful.

Whereas the people who didn't appreciate him felt he was fundamentally . . . cruel and deadly.

It's an unlikely means of business ascendancy to keep losing your job and blowing the deals you try to make. Interestingly, though, this has made Diller, in an age of excess, seem like the last prudent man—and a not unheroic one.

There was the widely reviled Paramount chairman Martin Davis who, in 1984, ousted Diller as head of Paramount Pictures. Davis then went on to make a run on Time Inc. (as it tried to buy Warner Bros.), eventually leading both Diller and Sumner Redstone to make a run at Davis's Paramount. At the eleventh hour, Diller lost his nerve for raising his bid, and lost Paramount to Redstone. But in time, this had the effect of gaining Diller the reputation of being the only media mogul never to overpay for a media company.

Then there was Diller and Murdoch. Diller is one of the few people ever to work for Murdoch—as chairman of Fox—to achieve some kind of parity with the boss. He didn't submit. Arguably, Murdoch needed Diller more than the other way around. Diller even openly ridiculed Murdoch's politics. And while he didn't get Murdoch to make him his partner—and left as a result—he probably was the only person Murdoch ever really considered making his partner.

Then there were CBS *and* NBC, both of which he tried and failed to buy.

After a much-publicized period of soul-searching in 1992, he took over the cable shopping channel QVC. The notion of home shopping as a reflection of Diller's media genius—a spin most of all propounded by Ken Auletta in a *New Yorker* profile—goes a long way toward obscuring the fact that these were Diller's wilderness years. Subordinates (not his biggest fan club) paint a comical picture: the ever-pampered Diller in a low-rent motel in West Chester, Pennsylvania, near QVC headquarters, or Diller bawling out the young woman staffer who teases him when he arrives at the new QVC office in Queens ("Welcome to Queens, Barry"), or Diller's persistent irritation about being called the cubic-zirconium king. And in the end, he was effectively forced out of the company anyway (at great profit, of course).

There was AOL, which he considered buying but then decided was too expensive, looking chumpish when it rose wildly in value—and, of course, looking prescient when it tanked. And there was Lycos, which he tried furiously to buy, and if he had (again, he refused when push came to shove to raise his bid), he would have been, today, a goat.

There was surely something startling about seeing Diller in the middle of the Internet business: Could there be anyone less nerd and more showbiz than Diller? The parties; the cars; the planes; the celebrity posse; the power breakfasts, lunches, and dinners? (Diller had cut an uninhibited path for many years.) Could there be anyone with a more old-media-centric point of view? And yet, there was something oddly in character too. After all, almost everyone in the Internet business had "transitioned" out of another business and turned themselves—more or less overnight—into new-media seers. This was true of Barry as much as of anyone: He was a founder and leading light of the I-get-it-you-don't school of management. And his was one of the great career shifts (a late-in-life one at that): From an exalted programming guy and talent coordinator to a finance, marketing, and technology wizard. He wholly remade himself—from showbiz cat to astute financier.

I'd certainly love to know how he suddenly came, mid-career, to learn the ins and outs of corporate finance, how he went from partying with Warren Beatty to designing deals so artful and complex that analysts, investors, and principals alike are flummoxed. Lots of people would want to take *that* course.

At any rate, instead of buying something for more than it was worth, he waited around and, whether because he was cowardly or because he was smart, did a series of comparatively low-risk deals (the Home Shopping Network, the USA Network cable channel, some UHF television stations, some independent movie companies, Ticketmaster, and CitySearch), a collection of media properties that either (1) are a hodgepodge that have no relationship to one another save for the fact that he can apparently afford them, or (2) are the basis of the first truly convergent media company, or (3) are just something you do to keep yourself occupied until opportunity knocks.

Or, in another metaphor, he was a spider weaving an intricate web, into which Edgar Bronfman Jr., who had just bought Universal, fell.

Diller, in the time-honored business tradition of parting a fool from his money, bought an interest in Bronfman's television properties for far less than it was worth. And then, in part because of this bad deal and the great ridicule it exposed him to, Bronfman, in order to salvage some portion of his family's fortune, was forced to sell Universal to Messier's Vivendi.

Whereupon Messier, too, immediately fell into Diller's web.

Messier, displaying all the way-out-of-control mogul traits that Diller himself has resisted displaying, bought back for Universal from Diller, for far more than they were worth, those same television properties that Diller had bought from Bronfman and Universal before. In addition, Diller, as part of this deal, seemed to be left running Universal.

And yet, obviously, this wasn't entirely what Diller had in mind. He might have banked a billion, but he wasn't ready yet for a retirement sinecure.

Obviously, he regarded Messier as something just this side of a personal embarrassment; there was that remarkable news conference when they announced their deal, with Diller waving the gathering to a close as Messier was happily answering questions. But if you paid any attention to the deal, it was clear that Diller had gotten himself into the catbird seat: Messier's deal to attract Diller into what was, in effect, part-time employment gave Diller effective control over the fate of the company—which was surely going to be worth something great to Diller.

Still, it was all in the details. It was an almost old-fashioned, your-father's-business kind of thing. That is, he did the thing really smart (or really conservative) businesspeople are supposed to do—bide their time and wait for it to come to them; wait for the opportunity to buy low and sell high—as opposed to what media moguls invariably do, which is, at vast cost and assuming great risk, go out and get what they want when they want it.

Diller watchers call this his "discipline," which is related in various ways to his toughness.

Now toughness is a not untypical mogul attribute. Moguls take a certain sort of enjoyment in not only taking advantage of someone else, but in humiliating them, too.

But Barry's toughness is either of a different order, or he is just tougher than even the toughest mogul. It isn't toughness just for sport or pleasure, but an ideological toughness. *I am better than you.* At the heart of his toughness is a profound condescension. He doesn't let one moment of anyone else's weakness pass.

"He won't let you forget it if you drop your napkin on the floor," Michael Fuchs—who, as head of HBO and of Warner Music, was himself a tough mogul—told me once.

It's the way to keep a certain distance. It may be a gay thing—the sneer of the outsider.

At any rate, Diller sucker-punched Messier every which way but loose—and eventually loose too.

And suddenly, at the relatively advanced age of 59, Diller seemed finally in position to get what he wanted: control of a media empire.

This included a major studio, some of the best cable properties in the business, and the biggest music company in the world. There was, too, a desperate seller, and in this season of media discontent, probably not a lot of other eager buyers. And, what's more, Diller already ran the company—meaning that when it came time to do the deal to buy the company he would know more about the company than the seller knew.

You do this deal, then you buy NBC, and you become, finally, who you are supposed to be—a top-of-the-heap mogulissimo.

And yet, you weren't born yesterday.

Also, a measure of proportion is that most good things finally come to you just when you don't necessarily want them so much anymore.

It's the existential moment: to be a mogul or not.

Possibly there is a certain innocence that attends to moguldom—or, anyway, enthusiasm. You have to have an enormous tolerance for a big mess, you have to be able to minimize vast problems, you have to be able to see yourself as greater than you are. To be a mogul is to be a little bit delusional.

Notably, moguls usually become moguls by taking over businesses they don't know a hell of a lot about. (What did Murdoch know about a movie studio, or Redstone about cable television, or Eisner about theme parks?) Diller, on the other hand, knew just about everything there was to know about running entertainment companies. He couldn't have any illusions.

And yet for the right price, how do you not do it? How do you resist? For the right price, isn't everything worth it?

Well, let's try to look at this through the eyes of Diller (nee Buffett)—a man who is no longer just a mogul wannabe but (just assuming) the smartest, canniest, most astute business guy there ever was. Let's cast as cold an eye as has ever been cast on a deal.

What you know, if you've breathed the Sun Valley air of other media moguls, is that no matter how good the deal is, no matter how great the opportunity, if you take control, if you get what you want, you get stuck. The bigger the media company, the more public the failure (and all big media companies, partly because they are so public and partly because they are so big, fail).

It's a tar-baby enterprise.

In the Buffett model, however, you create a remove between yourself and the businesses you own—let somebody else get stuck. You want to buy at a price that is low enough so that you can't lose, and you want to be distant enough so that you are never in danger of losing your cool; you never, ever make the mistake of thinking any one business is all that much fun, or any imputed glamour all that real. You don't ever want to risk damaging your legendariness—which is your added value.

There is, too, the John Malone model (which Diller would know very well—Malone has been his partner on various deals). It's similar to the Buffett model and just as unsentimental, but it has a slightly different spin. You don't try to take over—instead, you merely insert yourself opportunistically and annoyingly. (Your annoyingness is, in a sense, your added value.) TCI, Malone's cable business, was in the middle of everything (it was a crummy system too—which AT&T would painfully come to discover after buying it for $55 billion); you always had to deal with him. He was like the party boss or ward heeler—but he carefully avoided any pretense of wanting to be the elected official. His power was in the back room. In this, there may be similarities between Diller's USA Interactive (his system of online shopping networks) and Malone's TCI. Malone saw cable as the key infrastructure and transforming agent of eighties and nineties media, and it's possible that Diller, in a post-advertising world, sees his transaction model—the ability to sell everything from mood rings to airline tickets to downloadable movies—as the next.

Anyway, what you want is lots of leverage to help you do what you want to do; what you don't want is to be left holding the bag.

Diller, for instance, clearly left Messier holding the bag. Diller cozily fit himself into the Vivendi mess, gaining all of its benefits and suffering none of its consequences. Messier was just a passing dupe.

I have taken to observing Diller from afar. I have often seen him striding in blue pinstripes between Allen & Company, his investment bankers, and Wachtell, Lipton, his takeover lawyers, a few blocks apart, or setting out in the morning from his New York base at the Carlyle Hotel, jacket over his shoulder, walking alone through Central Park. Once, under the awning of the Carlyle, we might have even stopped to chat, except that I was with my children, who were crying and hitting one another. I wonder if I haven't seen something kindly come into his face. It could be that he appreciates the arc of the story—how a gay man, reckless in his honesty, without much education, beginning with no capital of his own, becomes one of America's most successful and admired businessmen. Or it could be that the possible twinkle in his eye comes from an understanding that he has beaten the mogul cycle. Been there, done that, without getting caught.

On the other hand, maybe you never get over dreaming about being a mogul—and, if given the opportunity, you just have to buy the whole deal. There actually would be some comfort here in finding out that Barry is really, in the end, just a sentimental fool.

I was looking forward to seeing him at the conference. The walk, the suits, the Mona Lisa smile—he made you feel that something interesting and terrifying was going to happen very soon.

12
AND THEN THERE WAS MURDOCH

Heilemann called to say I was on for the Murdoch interview—I'd sit with Murdoch on stage and we'd schmooze.

All right, it's a tetchy situation that this book is being published—and I've been paid a lot of money—by a company controlled by the pivotal figure in the collapse of the media industry: Murdoch.

The editor of this book at HarperCollins, having read that sentence, has now paused. His stomach and facial expression have tightened. All illusion of professional integrity and independence is now lost.

Or, on the other hand, the fact that Murdoch's people are paying me good money to write about the end of Murdoch and his ilk may actually reflect one of my basic points about mogul kingdoms—AOL Time Warner, Vivendi, Viacom, Disney, and News Corp. They're always being subverted. Any megamedia conglomerate is really, as anyone who has worked in one knows, a confederation of more or less noncooperative parts. It's quite possible that only in periods of acquisition, sale, or big stock losses (and ensuing fear of job loss) do the people who work for a mogul actually personalize their part in his grand scheme and do their literal follow-the-mogul duty. Otherwise mogul employees are mostly able to passive-aggressively defy, if not ignore, their mogul master.

And yet, equally, I've wondered in my paranoid moments if I might not be a pawn of Murdoch's, doing what he wants me to do, which is to make the case that he's a lot less powerful than he obviously is.

Moguls want power, but they want it with a certain order of ritual deniability.

Indeed, Murdoch, claiming that his influence is greatly exaggerated ("We're minnows," he's said), is constantly engaged in an effort to get the Feds to waive whatever media ownership rules have not yet been waived.

The ultimate goal he's been fighting for over the last few years is to combine his worldwide satellite properties with DirecTV and become television's nonterrestrial overlord. For that, he'll also have to convince the government that he's such a relative minnow that it won't represent any sort of extreme concentration of power if he monopolizes the fastest-growing television signal distribution system.

Yes, it could be good for Murdoch if I paint a vivid enough picture of mogul vulnerability: Certainly I believe that just as the media is being thoroughly consolidated, it is fracturing all over—and, therefore, Murdoch and other moguls would argue, needs to be consolidated still further.

Still, it's surely a sensitive spot I'm in. There exists for every HarperCollins author the specter of the last governor of Hong

Kong, Chris Patton, whose book Murdoch canceled because it got in the way of his plans to control China. Of course, that was China.

Now possibly, by anticipating this conflict, by hanging a hat on it, I may have slyly, albeit obviously, carved out some room to maneuver here for myself.

What's more, I've now even made it part of the shtick which could draw attention to this book and help Murdoch make more money (and me too—we're in this together).

And I can still punt, or at least feint. To wit: As large as Murdoch looms, as central as he's been, he is a vastly less ridiculous figure than his mogul brethren.

In some sense he's just an old-fashioned newspaperman; his early reputation was certainly as a mere vulgar tabloid guy, more a promoter and a gambler than the visionary he's now become. When you un-demonize Murdoch, when you separate him from his right-wing politics and predatory disposition, you can easily find yourself thinking what fun it must be to have been him. In fact, we admire (secretly admire, anyway) Murdoch because he's created an enterprise that only he would have created. News Corp. is an eccentric, nonrational, highly personal company. It's all about his interests: the Australian and English stuff, the American networks, the satellite systems, a major book company, not to mention the continued existence of the *New York Post* (how many people who can create a tabloid front page have great financial skills?). It's all about him.

And yet, what happened, what has become the underlying motivation for the past twenty years of media history, what has brought the media business now to the brink of chaos, is that everybody else decided they had to do what Murdoch was doing. Every other would-be media conglomerate has had to create itself in the Murdoch–News Corp. image. What's more, Murdoch laid out the way: Owning one company enabled you to buy another and another; tricks of corporate finance let you reach way beyond mortal ambitions—not just a network or a movie studio, but the entire communications and sensory apparatus.

Almost right away this got ridiculous. Murdoch was flying seat-of-the-pants and everybody else was thinking this was a brilliant, case-study-worthy, geopolitical business strategy.

Murdoch himself is a casual opportunist. (One of my all-time favorite moments of Murdoch opportunity: Murdoch, in 1976, owned newspapers in Australia and in the U.K. and a paper in San Antonio, Texas. He had taken a summer rental in East Hampton, near the home of Clay Felker, the founder of *New York* magazine, whom he invited to dinner, along with Felker's houseguests, writers Aaron Latham and Susan Braudy. As the courses were served with the help of the Murdoch children, Elisabeth, Lachlan, and James, Felker talked about the unique position *New York* occupied in the city's social and media world and the remarkable talent the magazine had attracted. He mentioned, too, the increasing disputatiousness of *New York*'s board of directors. Murdoch confined his conversation to observations about the price of paper, telling Braudy that he was in the U.S. to buy forests. Over the next several months, Murdoch first bought the *New York Post*—after being introduced to *Post* owner Dorothy Schiff by Felker—then, with Felker continuing to confide in him about the problems with his board, entered into negotiations with *New York*'s board members, who, over Felker's fierce protests, sold the magazine to him.)

But faster and faster, Murdoch's mere opportunism became a Big Idea, part of the business canon: You can't own just one media sector—you had to own all of them. *Just like Murdoch.*

So on the one hand, you had Murdoch doing his unlikely and high-risk thing. On the other hand, you had a lot of other people suddenly believing the Murdoch thing was a science, a kind of genius—a sort of historical inevitability.

Because of Murdoch, virtually everyone in the media believes that the media, from newspapers to magazines to television to satellites to movies to books to the Internet, are one big ball of wax: in for a penny, in for a pound. What's more, Murdoch's mogul (focused on market dominance to the exclusion of all other concerns), the mogul as consummate control freak—unlike the more flamboyant version (from Louis B. Mayer to Robert Maxwell to Ted Turner)—has become the enduring archetype: A mogul stands alone behind the curtain, working all the levers.

And yet, more and more, pathos seemed to attach to him.

He turned 71 in the spring of 2002. There was no way out of that.

Vulnerability crowded him.

I thought that getting close, sitting knee to knee, I might be able to open him up.

Book
TWO

Autumn

1
THE LIFE OF
THE PARTY

A few weeks before the Foursquare conference, I got an invitation to attend a book party at the Rattners'. Once before, picking up my son Steven, I'd been able to glimpse into the apartment—but that was just a furtive, fleeting look.

I RSVPed now with great (and pathetic) interest and alacrity.

Book parties in Manhattan may be the functional equivalent of Tupperware parties or bridal showers in other places. (This isn't the literary life anymore; publishers no longer even throw an author a party—you have to recruit friends or get your day job to throw you one, or find sponsors, like a vodka brand.) Book parties are like books: ho-hum, with a certain desperation too. If you are not tied to a book or its party by obligation, you skip it. But this was something else—beyond the apartment being a big draw, this was an invitation from someone with so much money and so many possibilities that it suggested command performance.

The party was for a book called *The Great Tax Wars* by Steven Weisman, an old friend of Rattner's and of mine. Weisman had started at the *Times* in the late sixties (he was a few years older than me and the first person in the heartless newsroom to be nice to me) and stayed, and stayed, and risen to the estimable but faceless rank of *Times* editorial writer. But the party surely had a larger point.

The imbalance was obvious. Imbalance? This was monumental disproportion.

There were book parties—I'd guess half a dozen were going on that evening around Manhattan—and then there was a party at the Rattners'. When you're trying to get someone to throw you a book party, you always try for your friend with the best apartment—but the Rattners' apartment utterly transcended such neighborliness, or *hamish*ness, and essential small-timeness. In some way, in fact, the party became about the disparity itself. Why were we here? What message was being sent?

Now, serious party-giving in Manhattan is a complicated statement. Careers are made around *serious* parties. (A dowager friend who I have known since long before her dowager days has exactingly analyzed it: In Manhattan, your career is who you go out with at night.) To be able to give a serious party, to have either the wealth or the will (or both) to give a *serious* party, puts you in a whole different circle of achievement and ambition.

You don't, at this level, just give a party to give a party. There is no celebration for its own self. There is always an agenda. Sometimes it's a simple one: just to create a diversion through which to introduce this person to that person (overwhelmingly more likely to be a business than romantic introduction). But usually it's a much more complex program: You're locating yourself in the hierarchy. Or, even more complexly, you're using a party as a kind of media (of course, most Manhattan parties are media parties) with which to target a set of people and deliver a message. The message may be about power, or wealth, or taste, or aspirations—or, sometimes, most grandly, all of the above. This message is most concretely delivered through the display of who you know and who you can compel to come to your party. This, you are saying, is where I am located in the great media network; and this is, too, a demonstration of my ability to effect or control the network.

The point of the Rattner party was, on the face of it, a kind of indulgence (the point was the publication of a book, but that, quickly, became rendered as, How nice, how extremely nice, how really *oddly* nice of the Rattners to do this). This indulgence established the mood, the conviviality, the theme if you will.

There is, in party-giving parlance, the *excuse* for the party. People will even say, "What's the excuse?" It's the nod to something other than one's own narcissism and desire to facilitate connections and relationships and set in motion future development which, because you've engaged them, will involve you. There has to be a selfless reason for the party, and that was Steve Weisman's book.

It was a work, obviously, of smartness and fortitude—an uncommercial book written over many years of after-hours labor. Writing the book was a good deed and giving a party for the book a doubly good deed.

It was a noblesse oblige thing.

And yet it was surely not just that—noblesse oblige is never just that.

There is a tone of money. The tone is both about self-expression and about a more strategic outlook. Unlike in many other eras, there is no *right* tone—but it is hard, not to mention pointless, to be rich and have no tone. Every hundred million or so makes you more resonant. (It is sometimes of great anthropological interest to come upon vastly rich people in New York who have actually acquired little tone. Bill Ziff, the publisher of hobby and computer magazines, and, arguably, the most financially successful media figure of the age—he cashed out of the media business with $4 billion or $5 billion, whereas everyone else's paper billions are much more equivocal—was atonal. He really appeared to have none of the social, philanthropic, aesthetic, or further power ambitions that would have given him tone.) The tonal range runs from the most slapstick and vulgar and unreconstructed. This would include, for instance, Harvey Weinstein, the obese and semiviolent New York movie producer. And moves on to a slicker, more efficient, no-nonsense, money-buys-everything-including-respectability affect (this might include, for instance, Sandy Weill, the financier who came to control Citigroup). And soon reaches a kind of lugubrious respectability (which is where most people worth various hundreds of millions fall). And then, often, there is an urge for more stylishness—possibly after a divorce—and a media and gossip page presence, and this is where you might get your Broadway investors and such. (The financier Ken Lipper, for instance, who parlayed his wife's fortune into a larger fortune, and then, after divorcing her, invested in movie and publishing projects, before going belly up, fits here.) And then there is the social tone—that desire to move effortlessly through otherwise resistant and difficult worlds. And this, among certain rich men, breaks out into a sort of forceful I-stand-for-something articulateness (this would include Felix Rohatyn, or George Soros who lived here in the same building with the Rattners on Fifth Avenue), and, often, as part of this articulateness there is an added patina of seriousness and culture (this is, ideally, the tonal group from which you draw museum directors) and too there is the political tone—*I am here to serve*—for certain rich men who have not quite ever gotten over their own boyhood dreams of being President.

The subtleties of Rattner's tone were not yet clear, except for the fact that he was reaching for the upper ranges.

He was cultured, cool, precise, and ready.

This party then not only associated Rattner with an earnest work, *The Great Tax Wars* (lending him a certain policy-wonkishness too), but was, also, a many-shaded invocation of Rattner's own *Times* connection. Rattner could have the benefits of the *Times* plus the few hundred million he'd made not being at the *Times*.

There was Weisman's wife, too, Elisabeth Bumiller, who was the *Times* White House reporter. (Weisman, older than his wife, had had this same job twenty years and three administrations before.)

It was then a party whose message was bookishness and wonk-ishness and *Times*ness and political-connectedness—that was the backdrop.

But most of all, the theme was publicness. *I am a giver of parties,* was the overriding statement, *to which other public people come.*

Rattner was, accordingly, a public man.

This was an add-on to the tone thing. Being public, being out there, was an additional commitment, and represented further longings, and an effort at being a media figure as well as someone who controls the media (hence, you hold a conference).

This role, or the interest in playing this role, may be what separates, in the late 20th century and the beginning of the 21st, one ambitious person from another. It's the thing that creates a special class of the ambitious, and a special order of compensation. How public do you want to be? How public are you temperamentally able to be?

Notably, Rattner did not seem to be obviously and instinctively a public guy. There was a lack of extroversion and of, well, sex appeal.

Will, however, was more important than nature.

The apartment obviously anticipated this larger role—this rein-vention.

The Rattners had lived here when he was running the media

practice at Lazard and jockeying for the top spot. But it was certainly not the apartment of a specialist at an investment bank, or a number two. It was a potentate's place.

It was a public apartment.

The elevators opened in a massive foyer which in turn opened into an even larger anteroom which opened into the main gallery running in front of Central Park. The room was a careful, muted, just-so green affair, with much elaborate and detailed plasterwork.

The original version of a recognizable painting hung at the end of the foyer.

It was all presentation. It was 19th century.

It was an attempt at salon life. There was very little furniture.

It pushed the bounds of self-consciousness and only just skirted ridiculousness.

In the room just after the room following the big foyer, I was grateful to immediately run into Jonathan Alter, *Newsweek*'s political and media correspondent.

I was always running into Alter at cocktail parties—which meant he was always at these parties. Of course, he could construe this as meaning I was always there too.

But I was fairly sure that he was the insider and I was the interloper.

I believed that there was, in some sense, a permanent cocktail party. A circle of observers of power and of the powerful who not only had a certain high level of connectedness—Alter was a much more credible Walter Lippmann than I would ever be—but who had the fortitude to keep showing up at all these parties.

This was the media establishment—or these people were the glue that held the establishment together, the grout between the tiles.

You couldn't have an establishment without people who acknowledged the structure and worked within it and provided the infrastructure to keep it standing.

Alter was not here as a mere observer to power, but as a participant. He was not here as an outsider, or agitator, or jaundiced eye.

The point was that I knew the permanent circle at these parties because I had seen the circle at these parties over so many years. So to come up with a justification of why I was not, by any measure, also a permanent part of this circle was less than intuitive.

I do not know if my interest in deconstructing this hierarchy actually put me further out or drew me further in.

I am not sure, either, that my own chronic sense of displacement would excuse me. Indeed, I could not, of course, vouch that Alter himself—in many ways, awkward and scattered—did not also feel displaced. He might also need a friend.

Now, Alter was in the very solid top rank of more or less Official Journalists. I would guess that there might be no more than fifty people of his rank (five to ten of whom would be at this party, one might assume). It was a rank achieved not so much by journalistic talent as by other aspirations. Social aspirations. Corporate aspirations. And a certain kind of media presence all your own. Alter was not just a *Newsweek* writer, but a frequent television commentator. Alter was not just a partygoer, but a host as well—I had interloped on his big-deal party on the beach at the Malibu Colony during the 2000 Democratic convention in Los Angeles.

And yet, there was something missing about Alter. Some status unattained.

Indeed, he was only dimly aware of Rattner's coming conference, and uninvited to the mogulfest.

The medium was the issue.

Time and *Newsweek* had been the middle-of-the-road opinion journals for the last few generations. If there was a consensus, it was to be found there. That was a powerful thing, to be part of that. It was an official thing. And there still was that officialness. The President, one could be sure, knew what was in *Time* and *Newsweek.* The problem is that nobody else did. While they had a combined circulation of some six or seven million, it was dead circulation. Millions of people who had no real interest and no true reaction. What's more, they had become, in some real sense, women's magazines—health, religion, lifestyle, recreation. For a serious—in fact overly serious—man, it was hard to rise above this.

Alter had tried to adjust, using television, but television also was not an ideal medium for a serious man.

Shortly after some trudging small talk (I liked Alter, but I am not sure we ever had a lot to say to each other), Alter engaged us in a little chatter with Mrs. Eliot Spitzer, wife of the New York State attorney general, who was aggressively prosecuting rogue businessmen and aggressively promoting himself.

She was a blonde, thin, attractive, uninteresting woman who Alter seemed to know well and whose intercession gave me the opportunity to jump from Alter into the main crowd.

I traded up from Alter to CNN's Walter Isaacson.

Now Walter, who was Steve Weisman's neighbor in Bronxville (Andy Lack, the head of NBC News, and David Westin, the head of ABC News, were also Bronxville neighbors and also in the room), was possibly the most important journalist of the age. Or the most emblematic. Or the most symptomatic.

So many of us in a certain media generation (Walter is 50) have a Walter thing. I know a dozen people who will spend their nursing-home years dissecting Walter's career, that unique confection of classicism and opportunism, remarkable diligence and rank ambition.

Walter is our fantasy life: a media-business action figure. A perfect combination of vast intelligence, adroit political talents, impeccable connections, publicity savvy, deep reserves of corporate sucking-up abilities, and an equal facility with both high- and middlebrow sensibilities. And on top of that, he's a good writer (his Kissinger biography—which he wrote when? at what hour of the day?—is a brilliant thing; his Ben Franklin biography is also an estimable achievement). What's more, he can go to an endless number of parties without apparent fatigue.

He has—or always seems to have—accomplished that thing that is so elusive to and so sought after by the rest of us: a perfect career. As able an organization man as he was a journalist, he just never made a mistake. Never got caught out. Or at least never failed to recover beautifully when he had to recover.

A decade ago, Time Warner's Jerry Levin, searching for someone to help him with his inexpert technological hankerings, vaulted the also inexpert Walter out of the ranks of *Time*'s many senior editors and brought him to the hallowed thirty-fourth floor and a big office suite and into the new role of editor of new media. Walter led the effort to create Pathfinder—history's first razzle-dazzle Website—and, not insignificantly, was most responsible for the Internet's becoming, with *Time*'s imprimatur, an advertising-driven medium. Then, just before Pathfinder flopped, Walter was whisked back to *Time,* where he was made managing editor and where, arguably, he saved the idea of the newsmagazine—by exchanging worldly hard news for domesticated soft news (a famous Walter cover headline: "TOO MUCH HOMEWORK!"). Right before the great nineties ad boom expired, Walter was promoted to Time Inc. editorial director—one step from the Henry Grunwald Time Inc. editor-in-chief job that, nobody doubted, he was born to have.

At which point the AOL deal happened. Walter aligned himself squarely with Levin and with AOL's Pittman (when Levin and

Pittman were still in alignment). Early on, he tried to become the editorial director of the combined new-media–old-media operation. When that didn't work out, he took the possibly even grander job of CNN chairman.

Walter is a yuppie Platonic ideal. (Walter, in fact, may be what we men of a certain middle-aged media generation talk about instead of talking about girls.)

It is certainly of no small significance to the Walter myth that he accomplished what he accomplished at Time Inc., and then Time Warner, and then AOL Time Warner—that he stayed within this fold right up until now. For one thing, these are arguably the most vicious and fraught companies that have ever existed—so to have risen through them for nearly 25 years almost without setback is the feat of a remarkable career athlete; there aren't a handful of others who have done it. For another, these companies, Time Inc. and its successors, represent, in their transformations and grandiosity and shamelessness, all of our media lives. AOL Time Warner is, for better or worse, *our* company (as New York is our city). And Walter, for many of us, has been the manifestation of the most extreme demands, the most difficult contortions, of this company and this life.

Walter became not so much journalist as mediaist.

Not everyone who shares the Walter obsession feels a sense of admiration. Indeed, how you regard Walter—as perfect example or bad example—in some sense defines your bias in our media generation: Do you accept the career itself as the art—and therefore see Walter as representing a sort of *Pilgrim's Progress* figure? Or do you see careerists, of which Walter would be the highest expression, not so much Machiavelli as Eddie Haskell, as the real agents of the whole mess we're in? (These anticareerists refer to Walter as "Wally," in an effort to deprive him of his very Walterness.)

At any rate, he looked terrible.

He was sallow, with dark-rimmed eyes.

As logical as the CNN job was—or, as necessary as it was to pushing his career ever onward (he would not have wanted forever to be a subaltern running *Time* magazine)—it was, certainly, an exhausting, thankless job.

I'm sure he understood that the reason he got the job was that everybody else knew there was almost no chance of success. That the job fell to him because the geniuses at AOL Time Warner had gotten rid of everyone at CNN who had theretofore made it a success.

That left Walter reporting to WB auteur Jamie Kellner (surely not Walter's idea of a genius), working in Atlanta (even though there is no more Manhattan creature than New Orleans–born Walter), competing with Fox News (as unseemly a competition as he has ever been in), and hiring Connie Chung (who Walter can't have thought was anything other than ridiculous).

Still. If you understand, as Walter does, that the world—our world—has changed irrevocably, that journalism is a sidelined occupation, and that, if you want to be a contender you have to break through to the other side of the diversified media-and-entertainment business, you do what Walter did.

But he looked terrible.

I was always too aware of Walter as media subject, rather than as media participant. The room was filled with politicians—former governor Mario Cuomo, former mayor Ed Koch, former UN ambassador Richard Holbrooke—but to me Walter was the politician in the room.

Like a politician, he thanked me for something I had recently written about him and his wife chimed in too. She also seemed sincerely grateful.

What I'd written, however, had been not a compliment, but a dig. I knew this to be a sign of an advanced media man, to be able to throw off personal sensitivity and to embrace all notice as good notice. (This was not just self-centered blindness, but a necessary survival tactic—you have to be armored against slings and arrows; what's more, you don't ever want to show public hurt.)

"I always love writing about Walter," I said, stupidly, to his wife. "I love Walter," I added, wildly, hoping as soon as I said it that it had been lost or at least muted in the party noise.

"You're speaking at the conference?" I hurriedly said to Walter.

"I guess I am," Walter said, "but about what I'm not sure. I'm not sure if I have anything to tell anyone."

This was modesty in the form of gloom—or gloom in the form of modesty.

"You're doing Rupert—will you go after him?" Walter asked.

It was odd and confusing to hear Walter implicitly cast Murdoch as the enemy. Walter was CNN and Rupert was Fox and they were competitors, but the idea that Walter and Rupert were somehow not in the same business—that there was a moral gulf—seemed old-fashioned. I thought, perhaps, I had misheard Walter. Or that it didn't mean anything, that Walter was just trying to say what he thought I wanted to hear, and I was listening to hear what Walter was not really saying.

In the end, I always found it awkward to be with Walter.

I couldn't rise to colleaguehood with him.

He was too much for me like a much-vaunted girl in high school: hair, breasts, legs.

It was all too much, too intense, too fraught, and, oddly, at the same time, in fact, too uninteresting. Walter was more interesting from afar than up close.

Then Steve Shepard, the editor of *BusinessWeek,* interrupted, pointedly.

"You're entirely wrong," he said, grabbing my arm. "I've been thinking about what you said." He peered into my blank face: "About the J-school." The Columbia School of Journalism, which, theoretically, fed the ranks of the media business, had suddenly become the subject of earnest debate—what was its purpose?—and I had recently expressed an opinion on the matter (although, at that moment, I had to struggle to remember just exactly what my opinion was).

Here were two glaring style contrasts:

There was Walter who was smooth and withholding (he waited for you to come to him), and Steve Shepard, an old-fashioned buttonholer.

Where Walter was engaged in a high level of media politics, Steve had an issue. Where Walter occupied a highly abstracted world, Steve was a literalist.

I grasped at the prospect of literal discussion hungrily—even about, of all things, journalism school.

Steve, tall and bald with a big nose and self-effacing grimaces, was nearly a generation older than Walter. He had grown up in the newsmagazines, at *Newsweek* for the first half of his career; stymied there, he had taken a brief and ill-fated turn during the last gasp of the *Saturday Review* (a publication as forgotten as a publication can be) and then taken a consolation post at the resolutely second-tier *BusinessWeek,* which covered the slow pace, minor digressions, and faceless cast of industrial America.

At the time, there was *nothing* more second-tier than business journalism.

But in a radical upheaval, during Steve's almost twenty years at

Business Week, the fundamental interests of journalism effectively re-versed themselves. The broad, worldly, political interests of the newsmagazines—the journalism practiced by Alter, and by Isaac-son earlier in his career—became specialty interests, and business journalism became protean, dramatic, addictive even, and certainly the in-the-money subject. Shepard's *Business Week* may have been, for a good part of the nineties, the most profitable magazine in the country. (Shepard himself resisted becoming the kind of media star *Business Week*'s great success might have allowed him to be.)

Alas.

With the collapse of the NASDAQ and the technology business, *Business Week* was now an ailing vessel. Shepard had become one of the names often mentioned as the next dean of the Columbia School of Journalism—a respectable retirement.

Which is what he was challenging me about now:

The journalism school, and the search for a new dean, had sud-denly, bitterly crystallized the sub-rosa debate about journalism itself—and why anyone would want to engage in it, much less spend tens of thousands of dollars in graduate-school tuition to get the chance.

It was weird, certainly, to be plunging into this discussion in Steve Rattner's house, because if anyone, Rattner represented the ultimate transcendence over or escape from this profession of ours.

And it was doubly weird to be pulled away from Walter Isaacson to have this discussion. What I had written about the journalism school had begun by noting that one of the issues in the self-criticism of the school was precisely an eagerness to be the kind of school, as a faculty member had told me, "where the next genera-tions of Walter Isaacsons" would go. (Walter himself, after Harvard, had gone to Oxford as a Rhodes Scholar.)

That, it seemed to me, was the identity crisis (not just for the journalism school but for all of us):

Did you take Walter, and even in some sense Steve Rattner, as the ultimate and highest evolution of the journalist, or did you accept journalism as a function and skill-set apart from the journalist himself being celebrated and powerful (and cool)?

Shepard was making the literal argument: Journalism was important; the Columbia School of Journalism offered something of importance. (I believe he had some other, subtler points, which I've forgotten, but in essence, he was pushing the right-stuff argument.)

I was touched by the old-fashionedness of Shepard's notion: that it was important to train journalists.

He entirely eschewed the larger absurdist and existential points:

Important schools exist, not least of all, to produce important people. And although the J-school is incontrovertibly the best in its field, hardly anyone who goes there rises to the top of his or her profession.

Columbia J-school—which is not-too-ironically called the Harvard of journalism schools—represents the world of noncoms, while Walter and friends are West Point.

The failure to groom movers and shakers may be partly due to the nature of the training itself: The basics of journalism, of fact-finding and of interviewing (and occasionally writing), are substantially lower on the food chain than the industry-shaping issues of distribution and supply and demographics and technology and the creation of hit formats. But it is also due to the outlook of the school. The J-school sees itself as different from the officer class of the media world, even opposed to officers (or at least assumes that the world runs at best in spite of them). While the Walters of the business are rising in their consolidated corporate media regimes, making whatever Faustian infotainment bargains they need to make, *somebody* has to be finding and preparing the news (and protecting old-fashioned news values).

And that's the rub: Do you want to be training people for lower rather than higher economic activity?

There is even a feeling out in the larger, more cynical journalism world that having gone to journalism school, having had that specific training, is a liability, that the first $45,000 of an employer's investment in you is spent having you unlearn what your parents paid $45,000 (or what you yourself borrowed) to have the journalism school teach you. Journalism students, especially Columbia J-school students, may well learn their skills too well. They come to the real world with a certain level of literalness and inflexibility and even stridency that is out of place in an increasingly, to say the least, plastic and accommodating media business. Indeed, at just the point in time when all other professional schools are being urged to put a greater emphasis on professional values and ethics and canons of behavior, the Columbia J-school is in some sense being faulted for putting way too much emphasis on such things as it prepares its students for what is more and more a quisling enterprise.

And then there's the issue of newspapers. No matter how much electronic equipment has been installed, or how many courses are devoted to long-form magazine writing (in itself odd, because there are few long-form magazines), or how eager everybody briefly was to be a dot-com cub reporter, this is still a newspaper school. And newspapers, as everybody kinda knows, are not long for this world.

Complicating the situation and the value proposition, many of the purists in the J-school consider themselves, in effect, the media working class, and—complicating campus allegiances—claim a higher sort of left-wing credential for themselves. They continue to do the honest work. Media is the corruption, and theirs is the truer calling. They recognize, proudly, even militantly, that to have an interest in news is to be regarded as a dinosaur. "If you're chasing police stories, you're in career eclipse; if you're covering lifestyle, you're ascendant," says a J-school graduate I know who is in eclipse. They are labor-movement people.

Shepard seemed to be stubbornly resistant to the ironies here.

He was a journalist. He had risen practicing journalism. And he was about to go into retirement proud of his life's experience and accomplishments.

To me the point had to do with, as everything else in the media business had to do with, return on investment. Universities, as much as anyone, loved a big return, and understood, too, if you didn't keep up with the accepted level of returns, you would be, naturally, superseded and finally put out of business.

But if the university can create a larger career model, larger economic horizons—not journalists but media managers—it might, for one thing, be able to sell more school (which is of course the central thing). A school for moguls is, in some hopeful mission statement, undoubtedly what someone had in mind—a school that produces the people who run the massively consolidated media combines. (Universities are often a little behind in realizing what's happening in the actual world—it may not yet be aware that the media world is collapsing.)

Since it may be that only God can create a mogul, the fallback is to make a school for mediaists—that is, for the future Isaacsons and Rattners. A new class of students who can see beyond the limitations of journalism and to the complex supply, production, distribution, and technological demands of information.

Sure.

While I was pleased to be having the conversation with Shepard—he too, it seemed, preferred going back and forth with me to having to observe the decorum and social blah blah—it would have been more revealing to have had this conversation with Walter (who had peeled away).

In short order, Rattner's wife, Maureen White, conspicuously cleared her throat. In an interesting power-sharing arrangement, she was apparently to give the evening's peroration.

She was, in many ways, much more imposing than her husband. A former Wall Streeter herself, she now sat on boards (she was on the board of the school our children went to) and convened tables at luncheons for various political figures and causes. She had something more like a Beverly Hills than Manhattan coif and whitish makeup (her lips were exceptionally shiny and pale). There was no expense spared here, no detail untended, no consideration unthought of—but nevertheless (and unlike Beverly Hills) she presented herself with a certain austerity and sexlessness.

Was she a creature of her husband's aspirations, or he of hers? was the unavoidable question (friends of theirs openly debated and analyzed this question).

She proceeded to deliver an oddly long speech—or really an elaborately prepared impromptu talk—part of the effect of which was to recast the light, if it had drifted, back on the hostess and host. She gave the sense of not just offering the space to have a party, not *just* of being the host, but of being, too, the honoring benefactor, with the author, bashfully and modestly and awkwardly, by her side. She went on at great and fulsome length. The accolade and implied honor she extended was, like the party, itself out of proportion. (Book parties tend to be filled with other people who have written books, like bar mitzvahs are filled with other 13-year-old boys who have had bar mitzvahs, so the pretense of specialness is a hard one to maintain.)

I was not the only one embarrassed here.

Still, such embarrassments are ultimately taken in stride and what is remembered is the intention. And, in many ways, that intention, to be the presenters, the benefit chairs, the larger-than-life friends, the pillars and underwriters of the journalistic community, would be remembered much longer than the book.

It was interesting, and unusual, to see the gears grind like this, openly and theatrically.

Then, turning, and suddenly filled with the sense that having gotten this far without panic or self-loathing, I should now get out, I ran into Rattner.

His coolness, or preciseness, or remoteness, was palpable. You wanted to grab and hold him.

He didn't come to you. You had to get to him.

He was one of those people who speaks in a voice purposefully too low, too modulated, compelling everyone to bend toward him.

I only vaguely, and after some delay, made out that he was talking about the conference. The words were hazy . . . *joining us. . . . I understand . . . interesting . . . ought to be. . . .*

In fact, he seemed not to be sure that I was joining him. Or, at least, he seemed to make me doubt I was joining him.

I rushed to say, to confirm, "I'm doing Murdoch!"

Had I blurted that?

"Yes," he said, simply.

"It should be really great. It's a great program. You've done an incredible job." My head was nodding like a dashboard dog.

The more I sensed his elusiveness, the more frantically I tried to make a connection.

Why did I want to?

Why do we need the approval or the affirmation or the acknowledgment of the rich? Almost everyone here at this party needed that approval and affirmation.

And if I was aware of everyone's need more than they were aware of it, which of course is what I felt, did that reflect on the further tenuousness of my relationship here?

Rattner continued to seem remote, placid, delphic, as I made my excuses.

2
AILES AND TRUMAN

I had to give a speech a few days before the conference began.

The International Center of Photography, an organization that straddles the ever-widening no-man's-land between media and art, was having some sort of goodwill or donors or potential donors breakfast, and—arranged so long ago that I was here, it seemed, much more by fate than by choice—I was the speaker.

People in the media business are always giving speeches because other people in the media business, as in politics, have given speeches before them. There is an endless desire to get in the last word, and an equal desire to have your own voice elevated by the voices that have come before you. One gasbag is inflated by another.

In this case, I had agreed to speak because at the last such meeting of the ICP Roger Ailes had spoken.

Ailes, the former Nixon and Reagan political operative (and before that, an early television whiz kid) who ran Murdoch's Fox News Channel, had, perhaps, a greater claim at this moment in time on what the media was—on its true sensibility, its clearest voice, its most basic character—than any other executive in the business.

You could argue, without too much difficulty, that Fox, with its anti-Democrat, anti-Clinton, antiyuppie, antiwonk, anti-Washington, anti–New York POV, had produced the only new, lively, thriving media of the age. Likewise, you could argue that it had, as much as the media ever has, upended U.S. politics. Indeed, if modern politics is about message, about media opportunities, about controlling the news cycle, then what's the effect, for the Republicans, of having the fastest-growing news organization in the nation on their side?

Fox and George Bush were in an interesting symbiotic relationship in which it was unclear whose body was the host.

Ailes is one of the great creepy figures of the age—and doesn't try to disguise it. He looks the way you imagine the man behind the curtain looking: That is, he doesn't care about how he looks (which is, as it happens, gray and corpulent). The ultimate operator, he's not distracted by show business. He understands it's all manipulation, so why pretend otherwise?

When he got found out giving the President ex parte advice on handling the Iraq war, he didn't for a second whinge or show remorse. (Any other network executive would have had to commit ritual self-flagellation or even suicide.) Let others pretend—he's too old and too good at his job to start making believe the world works any other way than the way it works: Network execs are always in tight with somebody.

Of course, the rap on Ailes is that he's a hopeless partisan, a true believer, a Republican agent. But that deeply misses the point. Ailes is a television guy. He's been doing television practically as long as anyone. His digressions into politics have always been more about television craft than about Republican craft. His is the singular obsession of any television guy: to stay on the air.

Fox really isn't in the service of the Republicans. Ailes can say this baldly and confidently. (The Republicans, more and more, follow the Fox line.) Fox isn't in any conventional sense ideological media. It's just that being anti-Democrat, anti-Clinton, antiyuppie, antiwonk turns out to be great television. Great ratings make for convenient ideology.

Indeed, professional political people, while surely corrupt and cynical, are also sentimentalists: They believe everybody else is as interested in politics as they are. A good television guy, who has to command the attention of the public, would never make that mistake.

Fox is not (not *really*) about politics. (CNN, with its antiseptic beltway POV, is arguably more about politics than Fox.) It certainly isn't arguing a consistent right-wing case. Rather, it's about having a chip on your shoulder; it's about us versus them, outsiders versus insiders, nonphonies versus phonies, and, in a clever piece of postmodernism, insurgent media against established media.

And, perhaps most interesting, it's about language, or expressiveness—which politics has not been about in a long time (modern politics is the opposite of expressiveness). Fox has cultivated a fast-talking garrulousness. Traditional news is rendered slowly, at a deadly, fatherly pace. Fox gunned the engine. Automatic-fire patois. Cable talk.

Fox, too, is about arguing—rather than the argument. It's a Jesuit thing. Thesis. Antithesis.

In the conventional-wisdom swamp of television, this passes for serious counterprogramming.

It's the tweak.

This is really the Fox narrative device.

The entire presentation is about tweaking Democrats and boomer culture.

The Fox message is not about proving its own virtue, or the virtue of aging Republicans (except, of course, for Ronald Reagan), or even of the Bushes, but about ridiculing the virtues of Democrats and their yuppie partisans.

Pull their strings.

Push their buttons.

Build the straw man, knock it down. Night after night.

Here's the way not to get labeled a phony: Accuse the other guy of being one.

Always attack, never defend.

And have fun doing it.

A media nation demands great media showmanship. What's more, in a media nation, it's logical to make the media the main issue. The most audacious part of the Fox story line, the point that drives liberals the craziest, is that Fox is the antidote to massive media bias—and that the Fox people resolutely stick to this story. (The wink is very important in television.)

Which brings us to what may be the central political conundrum of the era: Why do conservatives make better media than liberals? Fox is, after all, just the further incarnation of a successful generation of conservative radio provocateurs.

There aren't really even any liberal contenders except for Paul Krugman, on the *Times* op-ed page, and the peripatetic Michael Moore. And Krugman's is a victim's voice. It assumes a kind of emasculation—conservatives are doing things to him and he's helpless. As for Moore, it's comedy and pretty scary narcissism—he's satisfied being just an entertainer.

No, nobody who's seriously interested in ratings and buzz wants liberals on television or even near an op-ed page.

Part of the explanation of the conservative-media success is that in a liberal nation, conservatives have had to develop a more compelling and subversive story line. They've fully capitalized on the outsider, tough-talking, Cassandra thing. Accordingly, while the country remains more than not unenthusiastic about Republican policies, Republicans get positive ratings (go figure).

And a part of this is the dancing-dog advantage. Conservatives have been hired by the heretofore liberal media to be, precisely, conservatives—hyperconservatives, even; eager exaggerations *(wink)*. Whereas, when liberalish people are hired by liberalish media organizations, the issue is to be neutral, unliberal.

But most of all, it's an understanding-the-media point, which if you're building a media career—exactly what all the conservatives tend to be doing—you get. But which if, like many liberals, you see yourself as having a higher calling than just a media career, you may not get.

We can talk about politics as a metaphor for something else, as Fox does (and NBC's drama *The West Wing* has done—politics as a metaphor for working too hard, living in your office, being too involved with your coworkers—until it stopped doing it, and became syrupy and earnest. Likewise, there's the right-wing commentator and jihadist Ann Coulter, who *really* uses politics to talk about some S&M thing).

But what we can't do is talk about politics for its own sake. It's way too boring. It's too disconnected—it's too Al Gore. And you can't say, as almost all liberals do, "It's boring, but it's important." That would be bad writing. (It's why George Bush's patent deficiency in talking about policy has not been so great a liability.) As opposed to the Fox writing style, which is to thrust and parry and dump on Clinton and thump a liberal snob or egghead when things get dull.

So, as I arrived for my speech, I was thinking of my relationship to the absent but always present Ailes. He was the greatest, but the Antichrist too.

There was the great land of no message—of media without meaning, or interest, or sensibility, or purpose (beyond being media)—and then there was Fox, crafty, audacious, insulting, agit-propping, bold.

On some level you just had to embrace Ailes—if, on another level, you would be obliged, if you met him in a dark alley, to send him to hell.

It was a pleasant, older, interested crowd of media burghers at the ICP building on 43rd Street and Sixth Avenue, getting Danish and juice.

This was a reliably liberal group—a do-gooderish group—and, in a sense, it was mystifying why they would have been hospitable to Ailes. A similar group of conservative burghers would not be so receptive to Ailes's liberal counterpart, if such a counterpart could be found. This is probably an argument for the existence of the liberal media. Liberals think they own the media and so they were just hosting Ailes—he was in their house. The media itself, I think they felt, derived from a set of liberal virtues. To share information, to be sophisticated, to cultivate a sense of community and style. Media came from books, newspapers (the *Times,* of course), magazines, movies—it's a Jewish thing. And a New York thing. Our thing. And even to the extent that certainly everybody here had to recognize that the media was under all kinds of assault and radical transformation, we still had some kind of important ownership position.

I was being shepherded by Alan Siegel, who ran Siegelgale, one of the eminent logo-design businesses—the unconscious, or background media that creates much of the look and feel of the age (not unlike photography itself). This was an insular group here—media apparatchiks; members of the Media Party. We all lived in a neighborhood where the party honchos lived. We all went to the same media schools and media parties.

Anyway, I was told by everybody how much they enjoyed Ailes's speech—and how much they hoped I would be as provocative and entertaining as he had been. (Although, when I inquired, no one seemed to remember at all what he said.) And all of these immensely affluent New Yorkers, in important media industry jobs, looked up expectantly when I was given the floor (after an appropriately florid introduction).

I always feel, with the microphone in my hand (there was no podium, so it had a slightly Vegas aura, or that of a pitchman to a kaffeeklatsch of potential buyers of desert development homes), an overwhelming urge to deliver bad news, to present my audiences with a neatly wrapped package of doom. Good news always seems so much less interesting and funny.

The sky is falling and, because of the microphone, it is my responsibility to spare no one this message.

Most speakers, in the PowerPoint, sales-conference-corporate-meeting age, are execrable. They suffer, as almost everyone suffers, from a vast epidemic of cheerfulness and optimism, which is among the dreariest forms of self-censorship.

The point, for most speakers, is that they have a job. And everyone's real job is to protect their job.

Everybody's muzzled.

Everybody pre-processes what they say (indeed, the joy of Fox is that is seems unprocessed).

And you can extend this further: Everything businesspeople say is a lie.

Or at least a conscious departure from reality: a modification, a couching, a hedging, a smoothing, a refurbishing.

Plus many who have an opportunity to speak in public have been rehearsed by PR people. The goal of a corporate speech is the generation of some modest good feeling—it's a buttering-up job. Somebody is trying to sell you something.

This invariably makes for a very boring speaker.

Whereas I have a helpless, and undoubtedly infantile, desire to get a reaction from the audience. (Ailes must have this too.) If they throw rolls (I have had this happen once), or do the vigorous nod, or, best yet, break up laughing, I'm happy. What's more, I'm never all that prepared. So there's always a certain kind of desperation, and overreaching, and wild generalizations, and a sudden, panicky urge to go for broke.

I was thinking about Ailes as I began—and about showmanship.

Ailes, it seemed to me, was the most effective and the most dangerous media executive (not unlike his immediate boss, Murdoch himself) because he did not have the central flaw of almost every other media executive.

Every other media executive had the need to be part of the show—the need not just for attention but for approval. The modern media executive sees himself as less a manipulator, or creator, or producer, than a performer.

The modern media executive, I started to explain to my audience, is one of the weirder business creations. In essence, he throws out all the traditional business virtues. He is much closer to a politician, to a strongman, to a despot, than he is to a traditional, conservative, and accountable businessman.

"A media executive is an executive who has something wrong with him," I said. "He's a psychologically flawed, emotionally needy businessman."

This got a deep and appreciative laugh.

"The larger your insecurities are, the greater your need to be at the center of attention, to be the man in front of the curtain rather than behind the curtain, to have this endeavor, however sprawling and unfocused and complicated and senseless, be about you, the greater the chance that you'll rise up to run a major media conglomerate."

They really liked this. This was fun for them.

"What's more, you have a model of the media executive, the ultimate mogul, who is a kind of pure beast. Just a reflection, an unconscious reflection of his own needs. A primitive creature. The noble media savage. This is your Murdochs and your Redstones. And then you have your would-be savages, who, in their self-consciousness about being savages, are really nothing more than neurotics—or worse."

They really were into this. I wasn't surprised. But still, it was odd. All of these people in the room had long careers wrapped up in the media business. You might have thought they'd have some small sense of wanting to defend their businesses—that they would resist such a broad slur.

"You all work for needy, narcissistic sociopaths."

Big, hearty laugh.

I said, "This need to call attention to themselves is coupled with an absolute bias against doing anything that would be exceptional or original. So, in effect, it's the self-promotion of the bland. Of the banal. Of the invisible. The opposite of showman have become the showman."

It was not even clear to me what I was saying here—except that it was obviously true that we had elevated completely uninteresting people to positions of great mythical and heroic status—but I was getting a fabulous response.

There are not too many industries in which upper-middle management would enjoy hearing upper-upper management being casually savaged. Usually upper-middle management more clearly identifies with upper-upper. But here, in the media business, upper-upper was, as I was saying, composed of people who, if you yourself had any personal restraint and humility, you were careful not to overly identify with.

In fact, the laughs were a product of a kind of reverse identification. The larger moguls and their upper-upper echelon retainers seemed to get, and the more massive and consolidated the industry as a whole became, the more most people had to accept their fundamental small-timeness. In some sense, the media business had jumped the bounds where it was anyone's business—it was just too large, and sprawling, and ubiquitous, and amorphous, an abstraction finally, like the travel business, a category rather than an industry—therefore nobody took it personally.

In the end, everybody had had enough of the big media experience, and the ridiculousness, for the joke not to be evident. Executives in the media had become such demented self-promoters, such self-aggrandized assholes, such unreal self-creations, that you couldn't help but score with the joke. The media was like the army after the Second World War. It was at the Sergeant Bilko stage, the Catch-22 stage. It was just plainly over-the-top. At some point, after the Second World War, to merely say the word "army" was to say something funny, like "high school" became funny—a shared experience of absurdity (shared even when you didn't share it). "Media business" was close to that.

I went into a Jerry Levin riff—about his isolation and oddness. He was General Dreedle.

Now, quite likely ten percent of the people in this room had had personal dealings with Levin. But even for them, Levin had become some semifictional character. A punch line.

I pushed it further.

"In this craze of personal aggrandizement, of the creation of these bogus and corrupt empires and dictatorships, the same thing happened that happens in real dictatorships, real banana republics. Your society collapses. Your institutions become corrupt. The daily fabric of your life comes to be built on lies. Not to mention, your economy stops functioning. Everything is ruined. All is shit."

I was, for a second, Lenny Bruce.

"Movies are shit.

"Music is shit.

"Magazines are shit.

"Books are shit.

"Radio is shit."

These media professionals, average age 55, no doubt complicit in the production of shit, applauded. (Briefly, I thought, I might have struck an age divide: Would an audience of college students think it all was shit? Or was it just this group of middle-aged Manhattan Jews, most responsible for the creation of the media business, that was most alienated by it?)

In the middle of this all-is-shit rant, I saw that James Truman, the Condé Nast editorial director, was in the room.

He was, arguably, one of the nation's great tastemakers. I liked him very much and suddenly felt guilty about saying all was shit.

★   ★   ★

Nobody, perhaps, except his boss, the 75-year-old Si New-house, was more important in that most influential of media sectors: the smart magazines.

This audience at the ICP was surely a smart-magazine set.

The smart magazines—defining a powerful countermedia, and a counterculture, to mass media and mass culture (sophisticates versus Babbitts, urbanites versus bumpkins, upscale versus Wal-Mart)—thrived through most of the 20th century, creating the most influential visual and writing styles, before being consolidated by Condé Nast in the eighties and nineties.

James, who was standing in the back of the room while I spoke, with his arms crossed, and in a suit that I admired, was not the bad guy of this story. The smart-magazine business was filled with such profound incompetence that its ruination was accomplished less by any one person's ambitions and avarice than by the negligence and weakness of many men.

Still, there were notable figures in the demise of the form. Tina Brown, the former editor of *Vanity Fair* and the *New Yorker,* who, in this power vacuum, was able to accomplish legendary feats of self-promotion and to accumulate vast power for herself, is one. Indeed, she became a primary instrument through which Condé Nast managed to corner the market—not just to own much of the nation's print media, but to exert vast influence over the media that it did not own.

Condé Nast was a carriage-trade publisher fallen on hard times when it was rescued in the fifties by Sam Newhouse, father of Si and of Donald (who runs the larger and more lucrative side of the family business, its newspaper chain and cable stations) and husband of Mitzi (for whom he is said to have bought Condé Nast as a present).

Sam Newhouse promptly reinvented Condé Nast as a rag-trade publisher. Its lot was fashion magazines (not to be confused with women's magazines) at a time when fashion was something for your mother. The company was not—nor did it aspire to be—part of the journalism or cultural world.

Three things changed in the eighties: Sam Newhouse died, and the awkward and unhappy but socially envious Si Newhouse took over; fashion designers came to occupy a major role in the life of the city; and the bull market ushered in the age of status and acquisitiveness. Around his increasingly important fashion titles, Newhouse added a lineup of affluent lifestyle magazines, including *Gourmet, Architectural Digest, GQ,* and *Condé Nast Traveler.* He added journalism too: relaunching *Vanity Fair,* buying the *New Yorker,* and inflating editorial budgets. Sparing no expense, the company again remade itself, and the New York media world flocked to its doors, attracted by its parties, its courtlike atmosphere, its salaries, its perks, its curbside rows of black Town Cars. (It is odd, though, that this normally combative world was so attracted to a company that prized English manners and frowned on the garrulous, or argumentative, or even expressive; the tone of smart magazines moved from urban Jewishness to mock English gentility.)

Meanwhile, James Truman was growing up in Nottingham, England, in a middle-class family. A teenage pop-culture autodidact in the age of punk, he forswore college, took a training course in journalism, moved to London, and joined a local weekly, the *Hampstead & Highgate Express,* as a cub reporter. He was the sitcom character: the punk-rocker covering town meetings as he tried to write for London's cooler rock magazines. Soon enough he ended up in New York, where he freelanced for *The Face,* the coolest of England's rock magazines, and then got a job at Bob Guccione Jr.'s start-up, *Spin.* Within a year, he was the executive editor, and he and Guccione were inseparable friends, out on the town every night. But in short order, they quarreled over the direction of *Spin* and broke up, with Truman heading out to Los Angeles to try screenwriting.

Unsuccessful at the movies, he arrived back in New York and famously caught the attention of *Vogue* editor Anna Wintour—the story, perhaps apocryphal, has her captivated by the way he wore a checkered Armani jacket—and shortly thereafter joined her staff.

The magazine business in the late eighties and early nineties was deep in recession and identity crisis. Where the eighties had been about upscale titles, there was a recession-born belief that magazines needed to speak to a new, hipper, more jaded generation. "What's next?" became something of an obsessive question, even for the exceedingly aloof, deeply unstreetwise Newhouse. Indeed, if you were a passionate what-next person and managed to get his ear, you were in the chips. Newhouse's what-next forays included investing in *The Face* in London and, later, *Wired* in San Francisco as well as buying New York's downtown fashion magazine, *Details,* which, in a turnabout, he grafted onto James Truman's what-next idea for a young men's Gen-X magazine.

As *Details* grew and seemed to thrive under Truman's editorship, he became Condé Nast's what-next prince. In him, rock and roll mixed with fashion sense mixed with Englishness mixed with sexual ambiguity (a kind of upper-class Englishness) mixed with Chance the Gardener crypticness and added up to a strange, compelling authority that appealed most of all to the equally delphic Alexander Liberman. It was Liberman, at age 81, planning his retirement as editorial director and as tutor and confidant to the company's chairman, who made the match between Newhouse and Truman. Liberman and James had a mutual appreciation of the court life— who was in, who was out—at Condé Nast. Liberman was the Machiavelli of the organization, with James always amused by this

Machiavellianism. The twosome of Liberman and Newhouse become a threesome. And while it was necessary that James get along with Si, James was also chosen for the job because Condé Nast had a pop-culture problem—it was out of touch. James Truman was a rock journalist, perhaps the only rock journalist they had ever met, and they believed he was in touch with what they didn't understand.

To be the hip pilot fish, the harbinger of things to come, sounds like a better job than it probably is.

Indeed, all the problems of what-next-ness—e.g., that you almost always guess wrong when you're trying to guess—unfolded at *Details*. Truman's vision of the magazine as a modified downtown-nirvana-slacker-what-are-we-going-to-do-and-what-are-we-going-to-wear-when-we-do-it youth-culture magazine was almost immediately eclipsed by bull-market-hip-hop-Internet culture. (Hence, the decision to buy *Wired* in 1998—although Condé Nast was perhaps the least wired of all major media companies.) After the fading of Generation X, *Details* became—in a process that was nearer a long, horrific struggle—a magazine about work and entrepreneurship, then a magazine about Frank Sinatra–Rat Pack–style cool, then a paler version of *Maxim,* the successful soft-sex men's magazine, and on . . .

Truman, uncoupling himself from *Details* in time to avoid the fate of its next three editors, managed to get the classic be-careful-what-you-wish-for promotion.

He became the editorial director of Condé Nast and the confidant of Si Newhouse, the most powerful man in the most superficial business in America.

"With both of them," in a picture a Condé Nast editor once painted for me, "birds fly north and birds fly south in the middle of a conversation. They do this halting, tentative, incredibly polite stuttering thing as they try to guess what the other is thinking. It's like two vacuums facing each other. If you have a problem with awkward silences, you will never have that problem more so than with Si and James."

The close but unclear relationship of James with his patron seems to have both increased James's power and confused it. His power, in some sense, is maintained by doing nothing.

Indeed, everybody seems to turn into a novelist when it comes to trying to describe his role:

"He is a mysterious, fey, ephemeral figure."

"He has a weird kind of Zen cryptic authority."

"He has exquisite, impeccable, faultless taste."

"It's all about how he wears his clothes—which he does like no one else."

To me he is a sentinel postmedia figure.

He is, possibly, a brilliant magazine talent—possessing humor, stylishness, audacity, cruelty, verbal originality—but he believes that magazines as a genre, as a business proposition, are over.

This is because nobody reads anything anymore (and even though magazines have become shorter in the things they write, their audience still largely remains the people at this ICP lecture), because there's too much media for magazines to compete with and counter, because magazines are too slow in a fast-information culture, and because the demands of a huge and consolidated company, like the one where James works, are inimical to the eccentricities of a good magazine.

Still, James makes, by all accounts, about a million a year.

I once tried to interest James in leaving his job and getting involved with an independent magazine—to own something. It was clearly only partly the Condé Nast money that held him. I really didn't think he believed that there was a business, much less a purpose, for the old idea of the smart magazine.

It was not that there wasn't talent to put out such a magazine (although there might not be that either) but there wasn't an audience that would be receptive to the voice of an independent magazine.

It was something like poetry—and what clear-eyed person would want to be a poet?

What James had done most recently, at Condé Nast, was to create a nonmagazine magazine. This was his very successful project called *Lucky* ("the magazine about shopping"), which was really a magazine in which the editors produced advertisements, which, in itself, attracted other paid advertising.

It was a very smart nihilist's idea of a very smart magazine. It was a joke that James was making. (Interestingly, as James was creating *Lucky* he had become more and more immersed in his own personal spiritual issues, going on semireligious retreats for extended periods of time.)

Anyway, as I was outlining my concept at the ICP of media = shit, and the collapse of the culture from which media has heretofore emerged, and the attendant egoization, or, by any other name totalitarianization, of the media, I was suddenly seeing James as one of the lonely figures of the business, even with his million dollars.

Everybody here at the ICP, affluent and serious and middle-aged people, with their earnest interest in the artistic possibilities of photography, had been sidelined by the media culture.

But James was, oddly, sadder for understanding the irony.

I rushed through the conclusion of my talk—the part in which I describe how the consolidated media business inevitably falls apart—and took a few questions. Then I finished and went over to see James.

"I love your idea that all these people are crazy," he said. "They're all psychopaths and sociopaths." He giggled.

I giggled too.

I wasn't sure if we were giggling at the audacity of saying this, or at the condition of living like this.

"And what about yours?" I said, meaning Si Newhouse, James's psycho- or sociopath.

"Oh, yes!" James said, but it was not clear exactly what he was agreeing with, if anything.

I said, "Are you coming to this Foursquare conference?"

"Should I?" James said in that strangely open way.

"I'm doing Murdoch," I said. "One on one on stage."

"Are you going to torture him?" James giggled again. "Oh, I want to come!"

"Come!" It seemed suddenly much less interesting if James didn't come.

"Are you really going to go after him? Oh no, I forgot. You love Murdoch."

"I'm having lunch with him today."

"Where?"

"In his office."

"What's his office like? I would love to know. How interesting."

3
MY DINNER
WITH RUPERT

I confess: I had something like a crush on Rupert. Where before I might have thought of him as one of the certain bad guys of the age, I'd had dinner with him in the spring and . . . well . . . you shouldn't discount a certain mogul irresistibleness.

At another conference—Richard Wurman's Spring 2002 TED in Monterey, California—I'd grabbed the PR diva Pam Alexander one evening for a drink. As soon as I asked her, she began looking over my head (she towers over every room) with her eagle social eyes for someone else to add to the party. Why socialize with one person when you can do a multiple schmooze? Having a drink is a scalable pursuit.

Pam, in her midforties, with a Leni-Riefenstahl-althete-like figure, followed the conference circuit—in some ways she had helped create the conference circuit.

The PR firm she had founded, Alexander Communications, which had become the most influential firm in the years of the technology boom, and which she had sold to WPP, the international advertising and marketing conglomerate, for something upward of $50 million, and of which she was still chairman (although a peripatetic chairman), had pioneered the breakthrough perception that conferences were themselves a kind of media. That being at the right place and at the right time and gaining introductions to the right people was worth not only the $5,000 or so it would cost to go to a conference, but the $40,000 a month that Alexander Communications might charge to get you to the right conference and position you at the right cocktail parties at the conference and seat you at the right dinners.

There was even a further iteration to this analysis in which it was not only conferences that were media, but *relationships* that were media—quite as though you could imprint relationships (who you knew and who you knew who knew someone else) with the message that you wanted to disseminate and distribute to your specifically targeted audience.

This is, obviously, one of those notions that's both brilliant and bullshit at the same time. It's the essence of how mediocrities promote other mediocrities. It's the back door to the meritocracy. And it is, of course, a fancy way of saying who you know is what counts. The media is a country club. You campaign to get in and we only let in the people we like—or who suck up to us. Or, as possibly, the notion was much less grand than one might be tempted to think, and was in fact just a way to make friends in an ever-increasingly fractured and disconnected world.

At any rate, I had become exceedingly fond of Pam.

"Who else can we get?" she wondered aloud, scanning the clusters of people in the lounge area outside the conference-center auditorium. "Do we want Kurt?" she asked, or rather calculated. Kurt Andersen, the writer and occasional media entrepreneur, was sitting in a comfortable chair, watching on a monitor the session in progress. The session, a dull one, was about the design of the

Airstream trailer. "Go ask him," Pam instructed. "I'll be back. Just stay with Kurt, don't leave."

"My family had one of those," Kurt said about the Airstream trailer on view on the flat-screen. I had a brief and affectionate mental picture of Kurt, a chilly ironist and world-weary mediaist, as a sunny fifties kid.

Kurt and I watched Pam move through the room, aware that she could as easily drop us; the bubble may have burst, but the impulse to network continued. She could trade up, we knew (for Deepak Chopra, possibly, or Amazon's Jeff Bezos or DreamWorks' Jeffrey Katzenberg or Yo-Yo Ma, who were all at Wurman's conference).

Indeed, suddenly, in a turnaround athletic in its speed and grace, Pam went from talking to the middlers (people she might invite for a drink, but only if there was no one better to invite) to, somehow—and I didn't catch the exact microsecond of the transition—talking to Murdoch.

Proximity is the drug. The closer you are, the higher you feel. We proximity crackheads have a biological response to those we want to be closest to. At TED, it was Murdoch.

It was not just that Murdoch was the biggest mogul at the conference. There was this other thing: Part of the cleverness of the TED conference was having unlikely people in the mix (e.g., Naomi Judd, Courtney Love). Murdoch represented no small challenge to the liberal sensibility here (Richard Dawkins, the biologist, lectured the conference on the importance of atheism), but now here he was, in the fold.

I felt a short blush of bashfulness—even though, it seemed to me, I might be responsible for Murdoch's being here.

After last year's TED, I had introduced myself to Murdoch at another conference, and after I'd awkwardly talked to him for a few minutes about conferences themselves ("Do you come to many conferences?" I believe had been my pathetic conversational gambit), Murdoch had expressed polite interest in TED. I'd relayed this interest to Wurman, who had then besieged Murdoch for the better part of the year.

In fact, Murdoch, earlier in the day, had been at my lunch table, with Naomi Judd (James Truman had been right next to Judd. "What am I going to talk about with her?" James had asked me; eavesdropping later, I heard them talking about God) and *Simpsons* creator Matt Groening (*The Simpsons* are perhaps Fox's greatest single asset, but Groening was pretty grumpy about Fox) and the (slightly worse for wear) digital guru Nicholas Negroponte (who was bending Rupert's ear about computer networking). But I demurred, rather than grab my turn with Rupert.

In the past, I had written many unkind things about him, all of which I found myself helplessly regretting now. Had he read them? Did he remember them? Would he hold them against me? (Indeed, at the lunch table, I'd been seated awkwardly between Louis Rossetto and Jane Metcalfe, the founders of *Wired,* who hadn't spoken to me since I'd written unkind things about them several years ago.)

Now, as Kurt and I moved tentatively toward where Pam had buttonholed him, Murdoch seemed not only unaccompanied but alone. He had no handlers or retinue. He was clutching his bag of conference swag, including a Tellme Networks teddy bear ("Revolutionizing how people and businesses use the phone"), which he didn't seem to want to let go of. His face was wrinkled and expressive (definitely no work done on this face). I realized he looked like my grandfather—I could have hugged him.

And finally, there was the competitive thing—someone else would surely talk to him if I didn't.

Pam, I thought, was unsure how far she could go with him, and seemed almost about to disengage. I caught her eye and made appropriate semifrantic gestures, and suddenly Pam took action: "Rupert," she said, trying out his name, "we're going for a drink"— she maneuvered around him (Pam was much taller than Murdoch too; we were, I realized, Rupert and I, the same size)—"Why don't you come with us?" He wanted, I thought, to be taken in tow.

And so suddenly we were walking along outside the conference center, making conversation with the evil emperor himself. Not only that, but trying to cordon him off, physically close out any other greedy conferees from getting a piece of our kill. Kurt was on one side, I was on the other, Pam was riding shotgun. It felt, in a small but satisfying way, as though we'd kidnapped him.

We were, however, very respectful kidnappers. We were giddy with respectfulness. We were the sycophants; he was the sage. It was very Zennish. We were fast approaching a higher plane of understanding—after all, Murdoch had created, at the very least, the media universe.

There was the sense that any question would be answered—all you had to do was think to ask it. The man with all the answers was here, entirely accessible. And amiable. A mensch, it turned out. He talked not just without airs but without filters. There was the sense that what he was saying to Kurt and to Pam and to me was what he would say to Peter Chernin, the COO of News Corp.—or to any waiter or passerby who asked.

The man, it was clear, just liked to talk. He liked to talk—pretty much nonstop—about business (one of the reasons, I don't doubt, that he was on his third marriage).

He didn't think, he said, that the caps on cross-media ownership that the courts had just removed would result in mad buying of television stations. They were good cash-flow producers, but on the other hand they were, he said, a pain to run—the smaller the station, the bigger the pain. (Of course, Rupert, the nation's largest station owner, was probably not going to advertise his intention to scoop up new ones.) He went on about the DirecTV deal, seeming wounded but stoic about his apparent loss (in the spring of 2002) to EchoStar. He told the story—with a good sense of frustration and irritation—of the series of ultimatums and extensions in the negotiations and how finally, after one last extension, he'd walked away from the deal he'd worked on for two years and, in a sense, bet his company on. (I felt tested: Would I have walked away?) Then he told the story of selling the Fox Family Channel to Disney—of running into Michael Eisner at Herb Allen's Sun Valley conference and of how much Michael wanted to do a deal. Apparently any deal.

We wandered into an open bar at a nearby restaurant in Monterey where one of the TED dinners was to be held that night—but there was no bartender. Still talking about the Disney deal, rehashing the billions he'd gotten, Rupert slipped behind the bar and started to open the wine. "I had to let Peter Chernin do the deal," he said, "because I couldn't keep a straight face."

Then a *Forbes* reporter waiting in the bar, a voluble young man, forcibly interposed himself between Murdoch and Kurt and me. (Pam was trying to get us some service.) We gave him ground because he seemed to be willing to ask the ruder questions.

"You just said you're too small," the *Forbes* guy said, grabbing on to Murdoch's passing analysis about who might buy Disney. "Are you saying it's over for News Corp.?"

"We're fine," said Rupert, with a shrug that may or may not have been meaningful. (He was so expressive and so unguarded that you began to read nuance and ambivalence into all his gestures.) Then the *Forbes* reporter began telling Murdoch what he thought Murdoch should be doing, while Rupert listened with great patience, it seemed to me. "Do something," I beseeched Pam, who cut in on the *Forbes* guy, steering him off.

Rupert kept talking. He grew more expansive, more conspiratorial, even (although it did seem like he'd conspire with anyone), his commentary more intimate. We proposed that he come with us to the dinner we were scheduled to go to—the literary agent John Brockman's billionaires' dinner, a TED ritual.

Was he dressed all right, he wanted to know—his shirt, he said, was $11 from Wal-Mart.

"Don't go anywhere," Rupert said when we arrived at Brockman's dinner. "I just have to pee."

I had to pee, too, but there was a moment of shifting and reformatting around the tables in the restaurant, and I didn't want to give any ground. Pam shooed away some interlopers and Kurt anchored an area of seats. Then, when Rupert returned from the men's room, Pam moved him into a captive position against the wall. Geri Laybourne from the Oxygen Network held him on one side; Walt Mossberg, the *Wall Street Journal* columnist, was on the other. I was across from him and Kurt was next to me. Only Pam, in some extraordinary act of selflessness, moved out of direct contact (she did ask me a few times later in the evening if I would switch seats with her, but I wouldn't budge).

Mossberg lectured Rupert about a new sort of viral connectivity (it was the same lecture Rupert had gotten from Negroponte at lunch). And Rupert listened patiently ("I'm interested in this," he kept saying, although, probably, not very). I talked to him about kids' schools. My daughters go where one of his daughters had gone.

There is, of course, however passing, the moment when you panic about having taken the proximity drug. *How could I? Why did I do it? What damage would it do?* But that is, in a second, swept away. You're high, after all.

You surrender.

It didn't seem like there was anything Rupert was holding back on. Offer him a name, and he'd give you the skinny. "What about Sumner?" "What about Messier?" At one point, Geri Laybourne was surprised enough at Murdoch's openness to ask him about it.

"I am," said the mogul, obviously enjoying himself, "as big a gossip as anyone—bigger."

I could tell you many things about what my friend Rupert told me about his fellow moguls—except that, when high on proximity, you don't necessarily remember things too well.

4
THE
REHEARSAL

Gary Ginsberg is Murdoch's go-to guy.

His name is everywhere at News Corp. He's the check-with person. He's the interpretive person. If you wanted to know what would Murdoch think about something, you ask Gary. He's known not just in the organization, but all around the media world. He's often spottable at Michael's. Murdoch himself is a remote presence—spectral even. Ginsberg is the reality. He has a high title, executive vice president. But his relationship with Murdoch often seems more intimate than corporate. In some sense, his functions are quite lowly. He's an aide. A shadow. The guy at the shoulder. He spends a lot of time observing. It's his job to know the lay of the land, to pick up on the subtleties. It's more emotional than businesslike.

He's early-forties and boyish with a full head of hair. There's a famous picture of him without a shirt playing football with John F. Kennedy Jr. Ginsberg is a lawyer who did legal work for Kennedy and then went to work for Kennedy at *George* magazine and has become something of a keeper of the JFK Jr. flame (he worked in the Clinton White House too).

Murdoch and JFK Jr. might seem like an odd set. But they're both larger than life, and they both have seemed to possess great secrets—to know things that mere mortals would not know. To a degree they are both abstractions, carrying more symbolic weight than actual weight. For someone who has worked for JFK Jr. and acquired the skill-sets for dealing with a man who is not like other men—a man who is imbued with so many sun-god attributes—it is no small stroke of brilliance to realize that one of the few people to whom these skills would transfer is Murdoch.

In this, you can partly see why Murdoch is not hopelessly tarred with the right-wing brush, why Murdoch himself has not become here, as he has in the U.K., a political issue. This is because of the transcendence factor. Murdoch may be politically retrograde, but that doesn't define or even describe Murdoch as much as it becomes a detail of a grand and unknowable strategy. Indeed, who doesn't believe that if his politics ceased to serve his strategy, his politics would change?

Ginsberg, for instance, is a perfectly liberalish young man—even with some political ambitions perhaps—who is able to over-look the Murdoch politics and ideology because he sees a much larger thing. Politics for Murdoch is a subsidiary holding—which could be sold, or spun out, or refinanced at any time. Media, Murdoch knows, and Ginsberg has come to appreciate, is so vastly larger than politics. By that same token, Murdoch, better than virtually all other media executives, has understood that you play politics in service to larger media ambitions.

Murdoch is certainly smart for having someone like Ginsberg. You would, in fact, assume that Murdoch would be more Mafia-like—that his capos would be more or less official guard-dog types, regimented, and opaque. In the style of dictators everywhere.

Ginsberg, however, is just the opposite. He's the outsider who's been put in the insider role. This means that he still has the credibility (although, of course, some people question that) and, more important, the language to talk to outsiders (the language restores the credibility). His thing is to be as surprised by, and impressed by, and fascinated by, and appalled by (this is implied rather than stated) Murdoch as anyone. The only difference is that he has more information and more insight by which to explain the man.

Ginsberg comes off as something of a biographer rather than a PR guy. It's as though he's hanging around Murdoch to write the story. He doesn't seem at all like a toady; in fact, like a biographer, he doesn't even, necessarily, seem like he's being paid—or that he's even doing anything. He just seems to be there, assessing. And what he gets out of it, instead of a salary (although, I imagine, his actual salary is high six figures), is this incredible opportunity to see the operation transpire and unfold. It's access of an undreamed-of kind. Of course, it's access of such a high order that they will have to kill him—or bind him up in vast and intricate nondisclosure agreements—before they ever let him go to tell this story (hence, the reason they have to pay him the money).

I always feel with Gary that he wants to tell you something— and in fact he does tell you a little, he always imparts a detail—but there are great underground reservoirs that you'll never get to.

He called me to say there was a wrinkle.

Actually it was gauzier than that. Ginsberg phrased everything in the conditional. There was some talk that . . . Was it your understanding that . . . ? There was interest . . . discussions . . . we had indicated we might be willing . . .

Here's the thing with any conference: The big guys are always pulling out at the last minute. The bigger the guy, the greater the likelihood that he will, if something better comes up, pull out. It's a triage world. And, at any conference, in the days preceding there is always a series of negotiations and threats and basic, undignified begging.

It's part of the conference imperative: to have, among the speakers, such a critical mass of peers that it becomes significantly more difficult to pull out. If you do, your peers will think you're a drip.

But with Murdoch, no matter who the other speakers are, it's hard to bind him—in other words, he has no exact peer.

What's more, with someone like Murdoch, it's not really his capital that's invested here, but, rather, it's Ginsberg's; nobody's ever going to blame Rupert himself.

You can imagine how this goes: Heilemann and Battelle and maybe even Rattner approach Ginsberg (there would be no way to directly approach Murdoch, no language even to discuss this with him; Murdoch would not even have in some sense the authority to discuss such an arrangement about himself), who would equivocate, take it under advisement, and then, in probably not-so-direct ways, take it up with Murdoch himself.

It would be more a thesis than a question: Rattner and his new investment group are doing an Allen & Company–type conference in the autumn, it might have good people.

Ginsberg gauges Murdoch's response: from no response, to merest acknowledgment, to neutral expression of interest, to positive expression of interest, to real, unexpected interest.

And then Ginsberg evaluates the larger agenda.

How public has Murdoch been of late? How much more or less public does he want to be? Is there a reason to be public? Is there a message to deliver, shape, reinforce?

And then, what of the conference itself? Organizers are always promising that Jesus and Lincoln will show up, but, as often as not, the final lineup is a steep falling-off. You don't want to be the best piece of real estate on a fading block.

And, as likely, meanwhile you've had a better invitation. Or in Murdoch's schedule, as complex and negotiated and as far-flung as any in the world, it just might be, last minute, that the conference piece falls out. Which then becomes Ginsberg's job to handle.

Hence, the wrinkle.

Rupert was going to be in London on the day and hour of his prospective appearance with me on the stage in New York. But they could do it as a live-link satellite hookup—Murdoch did, after all, own one of the largest satellite broadcasting companies in the world.

But Rupert didn't want to look like a god, or monster, being beamed down to the conference.

Also, Rupert was worried about the satellite delay.

And too, Rupert didn't want to be in a room all alone looking into a camera.

It was impossible to tell if this was Rupert's vanity and stage fright at issue or if Ginsberg was simply doing his job—trying to anticipate the problems of a satellite Rupert and trying to jockey for the best suitable staging situation. In the end, if Rupert looked bad, Ginsberg would get the guff.

Would I, therefore, come to London and do the interview with Rupert, which would then be beamed back to the conference in New York, Ginsberg said Rupert wanted to know?

At the same time, I guessed that the other variable was the state of

Rupert's DirecTV deal—and that Ginsberg was weighing Murdoch's availability against whatever might transpire on that deal front.

While the DirecTV pieces finally fell into position, Murdoch might want to keep a low profile. Or it might be that exactly at this point Murdoch would want to begin an extended victory walk.

At any rate, I didn't especially want to go to London—assuming even that London was a legitimate issue, and not just some smokescreen to temporize or get Rupert out of having to do the conference and this conversation with me.

I thought it was slightly creepy, too. Showing up in London to interview Murdoch had a *Lifestyles of the Rich and Famous* aspect to it. Interviewing the king in the palace. It's an unseemly bending-over accommodation to make.

On the other hand, I said, of course I'd go to London. "Whatever it takes," I said to Ginsberg, which is what you say.

"You can come in the morning. Go to sleep for a few hours and then come to the SKY studios where we'll do the interview. Rupert says Rattner should pay," said Ginsberg, which, as soon as he said it, made me realize the likelihood of this happening was small—the etiquette of the arrangement wasn't going to be easy.

"I can only do it if I go first-class," I emailed Heilemann, knowing that this would likely be the capper. I wasn't worth an extra $8,000 to anyone. Also, you could count on a passive-aggressive standoff between the two rich men—especially over a first-class ticket.

The issue went away. Rupert would sit alone in a room, and I would speak to him from the stage in New York, via satellite.

This was our rehearsal lunch just before Rupert left for London and two days before the conference began.

As office towers go, the News Corp. building on Sixth Avenue and 47th Street in Manhattan is something of a downmarket affair. Fox News broadcasts from here (the Fox studios have a fabled tawdriness—with a green room where no reasonable person would eat the Danish for fear of food poisoning) and the corporate offices are upstairs—it has a living-above-the-store feeling. Likewise, the *New York Post,* removed from its storied headquarters on South Street, operates out of a corner of a floor here, a great metropolitan newspaper reduced to a back office.

You clearly get the point at the News Corp. building that one of the virtues of tabloid journalism is that it's cheap—there isn't any pretense. Part of your economic advantage as a tabloidist is that you're never putting on the Ritz (unlike more Tiffany-esque news organizations).

Ginsberg came and got me in the lobby. He seemed sheepish and amused. This was partly about the London go-round, but even more generally was the implicit understanding that us—that is, reasonably intelligent, liberalish, savvy media guys—being here, at the heart of the Murdoch empire, was one of those things. Strange bedfellows.

Upstairs too the News Corp. headquarters was inauspicious. It could have been housing any number of workaday businesses without airs—law firms, accounting firms, ad agencies of third or fourth rank.

The temporal, physical, real estate world was clearly an afterthought for News Corp. Murdoch wasn't building any literal monuments to himself.

A young man of some obvious stylishness—he was the first suggestion of any overt fancy stuff here—came down the hallway to escort us. At first, given his youth and careful presentation, I thought it was a Murdoch assistant. In Hollywood, where of course

Murdoch also resides, moguls are always surrounded by young, good-looking, perfectly turned-out assistants. This would have been an understandable, if slightly out of character, accoutrement for Murdoch. But it was, on second look, and then confirmed as we shook hands, not an assistant at all, but Rupert's son and the theoretical heir to all this, the 31-year-old Lachlan Murdoch.

He was, really, amazing-looking. Actor amazing-looking. Male model. He slightly gave the lie to Murdoch's apparent lack of interest in appearances.

"We're listening to the DOJ news conference," he said to Ginsberg.

Then we were joined by Chase Carey, the chief operating officer and number three in the company behind Peter Chernin (who was in Los Angeles) and together we all went into the small conference room which doubled as a dining room.

Murdoch was at the table. The conference room itself was purely nondescript—office furniture ordered from a catalogue. He was bent over a speakerphone with unimpressive audio quality. He acknowledged me and shook my hand without breaking his concentration.

Everybody took seats at the table—it was already set with lunch places—and fell into listening with him. It was a quiet room except for the fuzzy voice from the speakerphone.

As inauspicious as this seemed, it was the pivotal moment.

The Department of Justice was announcing that it had decided to file an antitrust suit against EchoStar in its efforts to acquire DirecTV from General Motors.

The deal was dead, in other words. It couldn't happen now.

The litigation that the Justice Department was commencing would tie up the deal for years.

There was no recourse here.

EchoStar was out in its bid for DirecTV.

This was exactly the outcome that Murdoch had wanted. It was one of those moments of everything going exactly right, of getting everything you might have dreamed of. The kind of thing that doesn't happen to ordinary people.

Everything now was a foregone conclusion. There was, simply, no deal. Filing an antitrust suit against a pending merger was as close to a government fiat as you could get in a democratic society. There was just nothing you could do—no way to fight it. Except to fight it, but the act of fighting it would mean you couldn't do it. It was over. Murdoch had won. All of these guys were listening with Murdoch, straining to hear this news conference, just to savor all of the details of the victory, no matter how anticlimactic.

But finally I got some attention and Lachlan told the waiter he could serve the lunch.

I wasn't entirely sure how much Murdoch remembered me from our dinner in the spring. There wasn't a lack of recognition, but he wasn't turning to me as an old friend either. So with some contortions I endeavored to reconnect the bond: "The circumstances are so different with EchoStar and the Direct deal now from when we had dinner and were talking about this last spring. Who could have figured? Would you have thought this would be where you'd end up?"

"We always thought if any deal was going to have antitrust issues this one would," Murdoch said with finality.

"So in the end this is really about the incompetence at General Motors. EchoStar has been able to learn everything about its competitor and leapfrog over them during this period, and you'll be able to get this deal, if you want it, for much less money than it would have cost you a year ago. So GM is the total chump."

"Ya," Murdoch nodded. "They might sue Ergen." (Charlie Ergen, EchoStar's CEO.)

There was a little talk about who would likely sue whom.

I had that feeling again of the intimacy of strategy. There was this sense with Murdoch that he lived in a warm bath of complex scenarios. And that you were invited to step into the warm water with him—and stay forever.

He was, by both temperament and circumstance, I think, removed from the world. He was shy, reserved, suspicious, overly analytic. Then too, he was Murdoch: his wealth set him apart from normal human comings and goings, and so did the way he'd polarized much of the places he'd occupied. Few names have been so evocative as Murdoch's. Maybe only Nixon. Only in the U.S. had he found some respite from the demonization that followed him. In Australia and the U.K. he was to many an Antichrist; whereas in the U.S. he was tolerated as an exceptional figure, a media mogul.

Anyway, the strategizing and the working out of who might do what to whom, with what effect, and countereffect, was, for Murdoch, a way to occupy an amount of normal space—it was a way to interact with the normal world.

His son joined in, proposing some new wrinkle on who might sue Charlie Ergen or who he might sue. You had to wonder if strategizing was his connection to his father too. He seemed not just deferential, but full of awe. He sat next to him and you could powerfully sense the son's sense of the father. He touched his father often.

It seemed unnatural, in a way, that the son in business with the father would not want to insist on a clear line of demarcation, on physically demonstrating that he was his own man, that there would not be a natural division of space, even something of a clash.

I had a second's envy for the way Murdoch's son treated him, knowing my children would never treat me like this.

Ginsberg suddenly began to reintroduce me. This seemed strange because it would be odd for me to be here already this long if it was unclear why I was here. In some way this was one of those formal, get-everyone-on-the-same-page moments that people in business are so fond of. But in another, I had the feeling that Ginsberg could not be sure what Rupert kept in his mind, or retained, or focused on.

Ginsberg basically ran through everything again: the conference and its general point and purpose; Rattner, and Quadrangle, and that involvement; Heilemann, Battelle, and the going back and forth about London and the satellite transmission and up until the issue at hand—which was how I meant to deal with Murdoch.

This was not a small point: Why were they even talking to me? How come I was here?

Outside of the rigid left wing, I had been as negatively nattering about Murdoch as anyone—I must be among his more persistent gadflies.

I had, little more than a year before, given the Alternative Mac-Taggart Lecture at the Edinburgh Festival, among the higher cultural moments in the U.K. media calendar—Murdoch himself had given the speech before—and delivered a mocking screed against Murdoch.

Murdoch's other son, James, had, in an interview—much to the delight of my own son, who repeated it around our house—called me "an obnoxious dickhead."

There existed the very real possibility for Murdoch that I might embarrass him publicly, and, for Ginsberg, that I might, by embarrassing Murdoch, endanger his job.

Indeed, I'm not sure I trusted myself not to try something. Even without the intention or desire to embarrass him, even with my semicrush on him, I would not, given the public opportunity, trust myself.

Of course, there was this book, which exerted pressure on the situation. If I made an enemy of Murdoch that could obviously have direct and painful repercussions—on the other hand, I already had their money, and, having made myself into a greater and more public Murdoch bête noir, other publishers would likely seek me out.

Perhaps Murdoch just liked the way I talked. In the end, there couldn't be too many people as insistently focused on the far-ranging microevents of the media industry as Rupert and I. And to the degree that Rupert was probably not too interested in much beyond that, I was an obvious and good playmate for him. Undoubtedly he regularly exhausted all his other playmates.

But all of this was likely much more in my head than on their minds. Quite possibly they could not have immediately summoned what I'd written or said in the past about Murdoch. However hard to fathom, they really might not have been familiar with the substance of my Alternative MacTaggart Lecture.

Rather, it was probably just the case that I had, through my own wiles, promoted myself into the position of Murdoch's interlocutor and now here they were engaged in some modest effort to make sure that what I would say was not going to be too annoying.

"Here's my point of departure," I said. "In the modern era you have held power longer than anyone else in America."

Murdoch looked at me, either embarrassed or uncomprehending.

"Seriously, look at it: You've been a major presence in this country since 1976. There's nobody—I've gone through this—who's had influence on the level that you have had for that long a period of time. Who else? Really."

"In a sense, it's true," Lachlan said—appreciatively, it seemed.

"You're not going to say that, are you?" interjected Ginsberg with some obvious alarm.

"You don't want me to? Do you disagree?"

"I don't know if I disagree, but I think if you say something like that with Rupert on the big screen kind of floating and looming in front of everybody . . ."

My guess, though, looking from Ginsberg to Murdoch, was that Murdoch didn't mind it so much—that I had found a soft spot.

"What I want to do," I said, "is look at the greater breadth of the career, the greater meaning of the career. I don't want to make this just about deals. I have this theory that in the quarter century or so that we're talking about, to a large degree business figures, and most prominently media business figures, replaced politicians as the psychic leaders of the country."

"I'm not sure—" Ginsberg started.

"I could talk about that," said Murdoch. "The importance of business," he said, shifting the focus to a less interesting and provocative footing, but giving me my question.

"Within that too, I'd like to pursue this thing I see that you are the reason that the media business is the way it is. That you came to the U.S. and started to see the media business in this fundamentally different way than everyone else saw it, save for perhaps Steve Ross—"

"And John Malone," said Murdoch.

I couldn't tell if he was making a point about Malone's pre-science and strategy or if he was just being polite to his largest shareholder. In fact, I didn't think Malone was quite relevant to the point I was making—but I gave it to him. "And Malone . . ."

"And Sumner," he added, including the Viacom chairman.

"And that all these guys in the U.S. media business saw what you were doing and freaked out and started to do what you were doing without knowing exactly what it was that you were in fact doing. In the land of the blind . . ." I added, before I realized that this was not exactly flattering.

He said something about debt structure, which I missed. He spoke in a low reflective voice anyway, with something of an older man's negligent mumble, and that, together with the slurred Australian accent, made entire sentences incomprehensible.

It was one of the things that you went back and forth trying to evaluate, or guess at: How old was he? Really how old. How aged? He was soon to be 72, which was either not that old, or it was noticeably getting older, or it was soon to be very old. The question was, which line was he near and which had he stepped over?

This was the elephant in the room. Of course, no one would ever bring it up—that would be not just rude but frightening.

His handsome, very young son by his side lent him a lion-in-winter look—both kingly and decrepit at the same time.

"And I would love to spend some time," I said, "talking about newspapers. Among all of the men who run great media empires you are the only newspaperman. There aren't many of us left in the media business who are from newspapers," I added, pleased to make this about me too. "And for that matter, you're the only newsman in the whole mogul bunch. You are the only person who runs a major media company who knows how to write a headline."

I was, I felt—and was slightly worried that he would sense this—buttering up the old guy.

In part, I had no other motive than that he was old, and there was the natural and generous and self-protecting desire to want old people not to feel too old when you're around them. But obviously my other motive was that if you wanted to make a connection, bank a relationship, get in good, with anyone in a station above you, well then, you had better engage in some flattery.

On the other hand, this was at war with the bright-boy thing in me, too. Rupert, I was sure, would respect me if he saw how smart I was. (It was hard to escape the bright-boy compulsion, and I'd long ago given up trying to.)

"At the same time," I said, turning the point, "newspapers are all but dead." It occurred to me I shouldn't say "dead" so emphatically around someone who must have a heightened awareness of his own mortality. "You have this background in a business that functionally no longer exists—"

"Well, newspapers are hardly dead—"

"And, in fact, I think you can make an interesting case that everything you've done, every expansion you've made, is all in an effort to be able to keep doing what you're doing while understanding that the basic way of doing it is over with. That you've been outrunning some inevitable obsoleteness."

The issue of why I was saying such a slap-in-the-face thing was at war with the feeling that I was making a very good point.

Murdoch brought up the *New York Post*—the one paper he had left in the U.S. I thought he might be doing this because that was one of Lachlan's key areas of responsibility—Lachlan was the publisher. He was including Lachlan here. He was the expansive and attentive father.

Also, I wondered, trying to contain a surging sense of my own importance, if he wasn't bringing up the *Post* because I had written that he would surely be closing it soon.

The *Post* has been the sentimental heart of News Corp. in America. Undoubtedly, it reminds Murdoch that he's a newspaperman. But my guess had been that Murdoch was not *that* sentimental.

I was figuring that tough times, which these were for any media company, tended to be especially tough on Murdoch. The last time advertising dried up and the media economy hit the skids—in the early nineties—it almost took News Corp. down with it. What's more, it counts on growth and expansion as the essential tool of its financial engineering. News Corp.'s position as the largest owner of television stations in the nation in a rapidly deteriorating advertising market doubtless put the company in an ever-tightening squeeze. And, if he were to have any hope of doing the DirecTV deal, I doubted if he was going to be able to waste another nickel on the long-indulged *Post.*

What's more, Murdoch, who faced bankruptcy during the last recession, has always been a forceful and unsentimental retrencher.

In other words, it is one thing to support a paper that loses, say, $20 million a year (the consensus number among industry observers) when the rest of your operation is healthy and growing. It's another thing when the rest of your operation is facing a dramatic downturn, to support a paper whose losses, in the midst of the most difficult media-market conditions New York City has ever faced, will exponentially increase.

But I was all wrong. Way off.

Hence, the point I was now making. Unlike other media companies, there *was,* counterintuitively, a feeling heart to News Corp.—Murdoch really seemed to love the *Post.* (He had had to give up the *Post* once before in order to comply with government regulations allowing him to buy television stations in the U.S. market—indeed, he had to give up Australia to buy those television stations—and had then fought his way around those government hurdles to reacquire the paper.) And, likewise, there was something unreasonable about News Corp. (which is the thing that frightened many people), as indicated by his stubborn ownership of the *Post.* Still, if the Rosebud *Post* was this sentimental thing that existed to remind him about what he was, it was also, I think, useful in reminding him what the company wasn't. The *Post* was the irrefutable reason the company did the things that it did—expanded willy-nilly into all kinds of new media forms and *platf*orms. If it didn't, the alternative was just being the *Post.*

But we weren't talking on this level.

Murdoch, right away, was talking about the weaknesses of the *Daily News.* To hear him talk, you could only assume—you'd almost become convinced—the *Post* was a thriving business.

"You know," I said, just in case he didn't know, "that just a few months ago I was pronouncing the *Post* dead."

"I know," he said, but not meaningfully, nor with any kind of humor. If I had been teasing him with my theory about the *Post,* or flirting with him, it had been hopelessly one-sided.

"What I'm trying to get at," I said, "is that instead of talking about this moment in the media business, or the minutiae of this moment, or the present business trends, I'd like to get you to talk about"—I gestured largely and inarticulately—"the thing. The whole big thing."

"Like what?" said Ginsberg, trying to helpfully prompt me into greater specificity.

What I was saying, with a first-date inarticulateness, was that I wanted him to reveal it all. I wanted to know how he felt.

Business, like politics, the other primary public language, provides all sorts of opportunities to avoid the real subject. To create a parallel world. The business and political worlds are expressed in increments, by process, producing a mock order, and an uninteresting one at that.

There are many businessmen and politicians so inculcated in this language that they don't have a view beyond it. But I was sure that Murdoch did. That was the interesting thing about being with him. He was surrounded by emotion.

I think it was his age—and a sense he had of the terrifying and disordered world without him. This is, in some sense, the ultimate narcissism: *after me the deluge.* But there wasn't that coldness. It was more bittersweet. And there was the sense of loneliness too. There were these people around Murdoch but they were all clearly unlike him—even his son. The size of the experience and the accomplishment just made him too remote from everyone. In most companies, the divide isn't so great; people have just worked in the company for longer or shorter periods of time. Even in Jack Welch's GE, Welch was replaceable; people rose up through the ranks. That's no small point of a modern corporation—in a sense, it's even why they exist, to perpetuate themselves in an orderly way. But Murdoch, of course, wasn't replicable. And he seemed even more lonely for understanding this. The thing with Murdoch was that you felt not just that he was unique, but that he knew it. And he carried this around with him. He shouldered this burden.

"If I am right that you have held power in America longer than anyone, this is not something small. I would love to be able to get you to discuss that kind of perspective. This context of your experience. This sense of what you felt. This thing that has divided you from everyone else. The thing that has let you understand something about this business and this country and this time that nobody else has understood."

Everybody else around the table looked pretty dubious. But Murdoch looked quite pleased and up for it.

5
THE OTHER
PANEL

Compared to Murdoch, this other panel I was doing felt a bit like being relegated to the children's table. I was the older kid who had to entertain the younger ones.

Among my charges was Terry Semel, who, in an unlikely career turn, had become the CEO of Yahoo, and who before that had been the longtime cochairman of Warner Bros. and, arguably, the most powerful studio executive in the movie business, and an untoppable power within Time Warner until Jerry Levin had finally toppled him in 1999.

Then there was Peter Chernin, who was Murdoch's number two at News Corp. Being Murdoch's number two was, of course, not like being anyone else's number two (and came without the assumption that you might ever be number one).

And then there was Jeffrey Bewkes, who had been running HBO—possibly the most successful media company in America, despite the fact that it was part of AOL Time Warner—until, in another frantic dislocation at the company, he had been elevated by the departure of Bob Pittman to the two-man office of the COO. Bewkes now oversaw the entertainment and cable side of the company. Don Logan, who had run the other top-performing segment, the old Time Inc. magazine group, also promoted into purgatory, was the other half of the COO job, running publishing and the online division.

Semel, Chernin, and Bewkes were smart operators—as fair a representative group of the guys who actually made the trains run on time in the media business as you'd find. The panel we were doing together was called "Media Conglomerates—The Burdens of Scale." They would certainly know about the burdens.

Still, I had to summon my energy to want to talk to them. They were, in mogul terms, small-time. Worse, they were small-timers who you had to treat like big-timers. They were permanent government types—bureaucrats, jobholders. Like you and me, just with more entitlement.

Of course, this is just from the perspective of having come from lunch with Murdoch. From the other perspective, in which one could never hope to become a mogul of the generation of real moguls, they'd done just about as well as you could do (each of these men would certainly finish his career worth hundreds of millions).

Still.

We were knocking elbows at a different level.

I called Semel's office to chat about how I saw the panel shaping up and his office had a PR person call me back. I said why don't you have *him* call me. The PR person said why didn't I first supply a little background so the PR person could adequately prepare *him*. I said I tended to like to work in a more ad-hoc, free-associating way than that. Couldn't I give just a little background about what the panel was about? the PR person wheedled. I preferred, I said, to have this thing emerge contextually, so *he* should certainly call me at his convenience.

At this level, it was always about who could be the bigger prick.

Semel called me from an airport.

The difficulty with Semel would be to get him to shut up. He was, in the Hollywood style, a famous gasbag. And, even from his mobile in the airport, he went on at quite some length. He had many views about consolidation; the vicissitudes of consolidation (that is, Jerry Levin consolidating his power over the consolidated companies that made up Time Warner), after all, had helped him lose his job, but, too, he was obviously, for want of any other real option, hoping to consolidate Yahoo.

Gary Ginsberg, on the other hand, easily offered Chernin up—there wasn't really any level of pretense of mogul-level treatment for Murdoch's number two. "Do you want me to have him call you?"

"That would be great. Have him call *me.*"

Indeed, comparatively, there was an egolessness, an affability to Chernin. And, as with Ginsberg, you could bond immediately in a shared interest in Murdoch. Murdoch was the Grand Canyon and the people who worked for him were the National Park guards and rangers chatting with the tourists about the wonders of the natural monument.

As for the subject at hand—the perils of consolidation—Chernin was going to be deeply unforthcoming. What could he say? That there was a flaw in Murdoch's vision? Or, no flaw with Murdoch, but a flaw with everyone else?

If I was going to get something from Chernin, I would have to trick it out of him. No matter. Compared to Murdoch, the canny Chernin seemed nearly guileless—I started to think that tricking him might even be possible.

Bewkes, who on the surface had a fraternity-style convivialness, was likely to be the most interesting of the three.

Simply put, everything paled before AOL Time Warner.

There was just no argument—no spin. It was one of those rare business situations in which the businesspeople couldn't really lie. You can get such a situation in a company that's over with—in liquidation, or under indictment. But you seldom have a situation in which the people in a going concern can't hide. In which everything is known. In which everyone has somehow grasped failure, incompetence, hubris, and even plain ridiculousness as part of their corporate identity.

Indeed, all anyone did at AOL Time Warner these days was confess. They weren't even looking for forgiveness. It was just everyone getting it off their chests.

Embarrassment too was a prevalent feeling. If you were from AOL Time Warner you were from the company that had done the worst deal in business history. You had not just been fooled, you were a fool.

You just had to accept this.

Shame had given way to a kind of humor about the situation.

Bewkes was going to have something to say—he was going to have to say something.

"We're either going to be talking about consolidation or we're going to be talking about breakup," I said to Bewkes.

"Let's talk about breakup," said Bewkes, with a sudden, strange laugh.

Every panel needed a desperate character.

Bewkes was going to be my guy.

6 THE FIRST DAY

The conference setting ("the venue" as they say in conference talk) was the Grand Ballroom of the Regent Hotel on Wall Street. The Regent was a new hotel which occupied the former headquarters of the 19th-century New York Customs House. The Grand Ballroom was, next to the floor of the stock exchange itself, one of the greatest public rooms downtown. On the other hand, one look around the place should have told you that the sound was going to be terrible.

To spend, conservatively, $500,000 to stage an event that people won't be able to hear very well must mean that you have some higher purpose for being here.

That was the Wall Street point. The presence of the conference downtown was, in theory, about September 11 and a vote of confidence in renewal. But it was also more pointedly about Wall Street—that is, about money, or the nature of a certain kind of money.

Behind the scenes, the relationship between Heilemann and Battelle and Quadrangle had begun to shift.

Surely the media business was ripe for engaging in some deeply emotional encounter session, some massive family therapy, even some Maoist act of excoriating self-criticism (after which several cadre members would be taken out back and have a bullet put through their heads).

If there ever was a time for something large to emerge, some fork in the road to be created, some existential business moment to be seized, this was it.

In order for this to happen, Rattner and Quadrangle would have had to be the silent producers, or even more remotely, the silent investors, and Heilemann and Battelle would have had to be great provocateurs.

But in this, as with virtually all other media ventures, the money is never silent. It's opinionated, anxious, demanding, aggrieved—desperate for reassurance.

There is nothing more neurotic than money.

And Quadrangle, being itself a new and insecure business (and Rattner being a new and insecure would-be mogul) that had never before staged anything so publicly, much less staged something before the very people who would make or break their business, was especially neurotic.

A series of accommodations to Quadrangle's insecurities began.

Both Heilemann and Battelle rolled the eyes, grimaced, shook their head, indicating vast long-suffering conference calls over the many months since they had first contacted me. It was an elemental issue: Is this an independent congress or one in service to the Quadrangle business? To the degree that an independent congress might make money for Quadrangle, independence might be worth it; to the degree that it became more and more apparent that making money in the conference business was elusive, then Quadrangle, perhaps naturally, wanted some other tangible thing out of it.

A tonal shift occurred between the first discussions among Heilemann, Battelle, and Rattner and now. The orientation moved from media and chattering class to Wall Street. From creators to financiers. Indeed, this is the most basic divide in the media business.

You could suddenly see it physically.

The room filled up that first morning with many faceless men. In lackluster suits. With traditional haircuts. These weren't people so much engaged in the media business as people waiting for the dénouement of the media business. They were bettors at the horse race. Or ambulance chasers. These were the people whose own funds might invest in Quadrangle's funds, or who might invest alongside Quadrangle in a deal, or who might pass a deal to Quadrangle. These were deal-flow people. These were not media people at all—they had nothing to contribute, except money. They were onlookers. By the nature of their business, they were disengaged.

These people, no doubt, reflected Quadrangle's divided nature: to be mere profit takers, or actual players?

The other element of the Quadrangle influence was a general business sense of requisite good tidings. Business, after all, is a generally optimistic discipline. If you're not optimistic you're not in the game, and even if you don't feel optimistic, you had better act it. (As a child, my advertising business father once frighteningly told me: "You're not bankrupt until people know you're bankrupt.")

Nobody seemed angry, or out of sorts, or eager to lay blame. Sangfroid ruled.

Judging by this genial complacency, you might even have reasonably concluded that the media business was a pretty healthy one.

The opposite, and hardly extreme, position—that the U.S. media business is in about the same fix as the Japanese banking system—was not at all part of any discussion. This was no surprise: If there was such a crisis, then the people here—both on the stage and in the audience—would have been the people who created it. It was therefore not likely that they would now be confessing guilt, or proposing radical overthrow.

This was business as usual—naturally.

There was, finally, a lately imposed gag order. The Quadrangle people had insisted that the conference be formally placed off the record (of course, it was almost impossible to say what that meant, or who it applied to, or what enforcement methods were behind it). There was a hastily drawn-up sheet of paper handed out at the door spelling out the rule.

Media industry people are almost always more neurotic about the media than anyone else.

Indeed, Heilemann, obviously frustrated by the gag rule, constructed some elaborate rationale for me about the circumstances in which, actually, Quadrangle would like to be written about which so attenuated the basis of the gag rule that I felt determined to slip its bounds.

There was a mountain of Danish pastries and bagels in the back of the soaring room. There were sentinel coffee urns and pitchers of orange juice.

Above the rows of banquet chairs, there was an elaborate phalanx of lights. Behind the stage was the magnifying simultaneous-video screen.

I sat down in the first row.

Shortly, Pam Alexander arrived and made some Wall Streeters move aside to make a place for her.

Even understanding all of the constraints, and all of the biases against self-expression, and the general reluctance at any business conference for anyone to truly speak their mind, and the difficulties of getting the people who broke the Japanese banking system to talk intelligently about how to fix it, I was not without expectation.

It did not seem possible to entirely avoid or evade the monumental crisis we were in.

This was as substantial a gathering of moguls and would-be potentates and true overlords as you were going to find.

The occasion had to be revealing.

What's more, it was Election Day—the Zeitgeist was surely turning.

7
THE MISSING
(MEL AND SUMNER)

Sumner dropped out.

There had to be one. He was in London meeting with Tony Blair, Heilemann announced—but he wished he could be here. (The spin was that only a meeting with Tony Blair could have pulled him away, and that it was only for the sake of protocol and propriety that he did not give Blair the dump for the conference, which was so much more happening.)

The truth is that there probably never was much of a chance that Sumner Redstone would show up—or that he would be allowed to show up. Cooler and more practical heads at Viacom would have headed him off.

You didn't really want to let the 79-year-old Sumner out in public.

With a striking head of orange hair, the Viacom chairman is a vainglorious, old-school egomaniac who has an operatic personal life that has been largely kept out of the media—undoubtedly because he controls so much of it.

He benefits from an odd tolerance on the part of investors and bankers that lets a media company, more so than any other type of company, function as a hybrid between a public and private entity; Redstone's Dedham, Massachusetts–based National Amusements owns a relatively small amount of Viacom (CBS, MTV, Paramount, Blockbuster, Simon & Schuster, etc.), but nevertheless has a lock on Viacom's voting shares.

Which means he gets to treat the company as his alter ego.

"Viacom is me. I'm Viacom," he told *Fortune.* "That marriage is eternal, forever."

Even if the prospect of Redstone running Viacom for, as he's suggested, another fifteen years is unlikely ("I know I don't look my age and I don't act my age and therefore I will not accept that age," he's pronounced), shareholders are stuck with him for as long as he wants to hold on.

The outlandishness of the conceit makes it almost endearing. ("I am on a high-protein diet," he told an interviewer, spelling out his plan for longevity. "It's a way of life. People don't realize it, the culprit is not fat. The culprit is sugar . . . I am an expert nutritionist, by the way.")

Surely, we like our moguls to be over-the-top.

But then there is Viacom's CEO Mel Karmazin—the mogul-in-waiting, and Redstone's would-be successor—who, in fact, would have been the more likely representative from Viacom, but who would have purposely and smartly fobbed off this gathering on Sumner (it would have stroked Sumner's ego to do the conference, and, doing it would make him look foolish—two birds with one stone).

Karmazin is the opposite character from Redstone, and even from most other moguls. He has seemed to discourage his own publicity—or at least the publicity he has encouraged is as someone discouraging his own publicity. His career, in which he has deposed a series of executives above him, has been a rear-guard action against the more puffed-up class of moguls.

The Messiers of the world, or minor-league Messiers, have been Karmazin's *amuse bouches*—he eats them happily and without much thought.

And yet there are keen similarities between Redstone and Karmazin, who, in a Faustian deal, entered mortal mogul combat at Viacom.

For one thing, they are both small-timers in the big time. Redstone spent most of his career running a chain of movie theaters in New England, then, at 63, got lucky when MTV, the fledgling cable channel that was part of his acquisition of Viacom (itself a fledgling enterprise), made it big, allowing him in 1994 to buy Paramount. Karmazin was a radio-spot salesman, and then a station conglomerateer, who was able to trade his way up (first he got control of the radio network Infinity Broadcasting, then merged it with CBS, where he pushed out management and took over the whole shop) because he owned the cash cow Howard Stern.

What both Redstone and Karmazin do very well is topple others.

Their decision to merge CBS with Viacom in 1999 was as potentially damaging to the company as, say, Enron deciding to park a lot of debt in its dubious partnerships: Karmazin and Redstone became one another's secret liability—a massive problem they'd each have to deal with soon or later. Both almost certainly knew one would have to kill the other. (They also knew that it would cost the company—and how do you account for that on the balance sheet?)

But both thought they were up to it—both, likely, enjoyed the prospect.

This is, after all, another key mogul attribute: a blood instinct for internecine war. To strike before being struck—that's the talent.

Both guys were doubtlessly sure: *That toppler isn't going to topple me.* The logic of this was certainly on Karmazin's side. While Sumner had mischievously gotten rid of his last several anointed successors, still . . . come on. . . . *He can't hold on forever,* Mel must have sensibly figured.

Certainly for Sumner, getting rid of Karmazin at this point would be the grandest of indulgences. It lacks any sort of business reasonableness. And yet it seems logical too. To be expected, even.

It's a primal gesture: *I live!* Which is probably the point, because what's it all for, what's it been worth, if you can't keep control?

And yet—to try to impose some logic here, being aware that this would be the cost—why would anyone do such a deal as Viacom-CBS? Why would other people not have challenged the deal? Why didn't anybody say this is an obvious mess—a catastrophe afoot? That at any minute, at the least insult, or cross word, or sidewise look, it could blow up.

This is to the heart of the matter. The mogul and the deal— or how can you tell the mogul from the deal? (A mogul is, after all, just the deals he does.) And why does the mogul do these ridiculous deals? (Aren't there any nonridiculous deals?)

There are three key aspects of a mogul deal. (1) Actually doing the deal itself—the bigger the better. (2) The kind of awe you inspire for having done the deal—the bigger the deal the more awe you inspire. (3) Making the deal work—or at least surviving the deal you do.

Point 1 is obviously elemental (no deal, no mogul); point 2 is how the legend is made (no legend, no mogul); and point 3, while not just an afterthought, is existential in nature. *The future,* a mogul assumes, *can be adjusted.* What's more, a good mogul is a lucky mogul.

Now, understanding or celebrating a megadeal—dissecting the true nature of the deal, the possible permutations of the deal, the further implications of the deal—has become a mainstay of modern journalism.

The kind of second-guessing and scenario-playing that used to go into political maneuvering and cold-war geopolitical alignments now goes into reporting and analyzing the great business pacts. And nowhere does the media become so enraptured with the epoch-shaping portent of mergers and acquisitions as when it's the media itself that is combining or engulfing.

The *Times'* three-column front-page lead and almost five pages of inside coverage of the $80 billion Viacom-CBS deal in the autumn of 1999 was the most prominent play it had ever given to a merger agreement (until, four months later, AOL and Time Warner announced their merger).

The nature of the coverage (not only in the *Times* but across the business- and entertainment-news spectrum) of the Viacom-CBS deal was noteworthy, too, because the actual details of the combination—an uncomplicated stock-for-stock trade—could be stated in a paragraph. (Add another obligatory paragraph concerning who first made the proposition and in what hotel, restaurant, or corporate dining room, and you have all the known facts.) Everything else is breathless speculation. What component pieces might be sold? Which heads will roll? How will Wall Street respond? How will two kings coexist in one kingdom? Will there be the slightest peep from Washington? What's the next merger to come? Reporters, in other words, get to indulge in some of the speculation that speculators engage in. Well, why should speculators have all the fun (as well as the profits)?

Part of the effort here is certainly an honest journalistic impulse to impose a logic on the transaction—to uncover the thinking, to find the strategy, to nail the *vision* of the deal. In some sense, journalists seem to demand a much more exacting and immediate rationale for a deal than Wall Street, which accepts a certain randomness and even senselessness in any deal (there are, after all, more stupid deals than smart ones). Journalists are literalists. They tend to assume that because a deal has happened it must have been well thought out—that by the fact of it happening it must have happened for a reason. And in that belief in intrinsic meaning, journalists tend to supply the rationale and to elevate the people who made the deal, as well as the deal itself, to levels of historic importance.

Within hours, for instance, of the announcement of the CBS-Viacom deal, we were all interviewing one another, playing at being knowledgeable industry insiders and men and women of affairs. Charlie Rose (who took care to point out that he's on the CBS payroll, although he did not point out that his longtime companion, Amanda Burden, is the stepdaughter of CBS founder William Paley—which may be a more nostalgic than strictly relevant note) hunkered down with the *Times'* warhorse Geraldine Fabrikant, who has covered the media business for a quarter century; the *New Yorker's* Ken Auletta, always on hand when the subject is media moguls; and David Londoner, one of a handful of Wall Street media analysts always quoted by the media. The deadly earnestness of the conversation, suggesting at the very least some alarming shifts among the nonaligned nations, teetered back and forth between journalists talking about journalism ("There will be fewer voices," said Fabrikant, who also pointed out that there were now no newsmen running the networks—causing Rose to madly search his mental Rolodex for any newsmen who had ever run a network;

"Edward R. Murrow used to sit with Bill Paley," added Auletta) and journalists talking like investment bankers about duopoly, asset values, the "product," distribution vehicles, synergy, and, of course, branding.

"Is it a win-win?" Charlie asked his guests.

It is a particularly striking and weird sensation when you know how little the experts being interviewed for a story actually know about what they're talking so expertly about. Indeed, it is a pretty unsettling point about a journalism career today to realize how far removed (way down the food chain) we are from what the companies we work for actually do. What do we know, finally, about what makes these companies run?

It's partly this, our own insecurities, that I think causes us to adopt the language of investment bankers as a real analytic framework—we don't seem to understand that investment bankers use investment-banking jargon mostly as sales talk. This language seduces us (that's its purpose, after all: "He seduced us," said Viacom's Redstone about CBS's Karmazin) into thinking that there is not only a grandness but a grand strategy to these deals. Someone, we believe, really knows what's going on. Someone must be Bismarck.

Accordingly, in the aftermath of the St. Regis news conference where the two masterminds announced the marriage, there emerged a wide range of authoritative, albeit contradictory, formulas for understanding the merger.

Viacom needed a television network to provide an outlet for its television programming. (Spoilsports rushed to say that Disney had thought it needed one, too, when it acquired ABC in an unhappy deal.) Contrarily, CBS needed to minimize its reliance on the television-network business, which is why it sought the merger with the more diversified Viacom.

Or CBS needed an affiliation with a movie studio, although,

conversely, Viacom needed to minimize the position of low-growth, low-margin Paramount in its overall portfolio.

Or both companies were mired in low-multiple assets (Wall Street pays more for some businesses than it does for others—television networks and video retail outlets are downers; television stations and cable networks are uppers), so what they really had to do was create a critical mass of high-multiple properties.

Or content is king, which is why you would want to put together Viacom's strong programming arm with CBS's traditional network distribution model.

Or content is a *zhlob,* and distribution is the reigning monarch, and in the end what this deal is about is what media deals are always about, which is how many eyeballs you can gather together and sell advertisers access to.

Or the then 76-year-old Redstone needed a successor, and by buying CBS, he bought the hottest media CEO of the day; or not, and what we'll have is an inevitable showdown (Redstone, after all, is one of the great sons of bitches in this business of great sons of bitches, a strictly "Jump!"–"How high?" kind of executive).

Pick one of the above.

Or conclude that the media's capacity for blather, especially about itself, is unlimited; or that what we have in this, as in most mergers and acquisitions, is an absence of logic and quite a pure example of chaos theory; or even that there are secret forces, unknown agencies, hidden cabals that will get the real benefit of the deal ("some stuff in the fine print we don't know about," said Auletta).

Or try my theory.

There was no plan—moguls never really have plans.

There's only the *roll.* And Mel was on a roll.

He used to hang around my dad's ad agency in Paterson, New Jersey, 30 years ago. Mel sold radio time. My dad bought it (or did something to get it; there was a lot of trading—for several years running, in a great childhood humiliation, all my clothes were paid for with radio spots).

There is something about radio that seems to be at the heart of what's happened here. Real men were in radio; fancy country club Waspy, or would-be Waspy, guys (William Paley/Frank Stanton sort of guys) were in television.

Certainly, a subplot of the coverage of the deal was the story of the Redstone and Karmazin careers. Redstone spends 40 years humping a chain of movie theaters, until at 63 he buys a cable company called Viacom, then Paramount, now CBS (Redstone, however previously humble, steps easily into the role of media mogul and major pompous ass; "We are indeed staggered by what we have wrought," he said after Viacom nailed the Paramount deal). Karmazin, out in the boonies, puts together a bunch of radio stations, gets bought by the Tiffany network, then takes over the Tiffany network from McKinsey-trained swell Michael Jordan (Jordan had been the CEO of Westinghouse, which had bought CBS from the Tisch family) and seems to stay a pure suburban mensch—a pure suburban mensch ad-space salesman.

Now, it is no secret that the secret of all this is share price. You're successful in the eyes of your board, your shareholders, your employees, the media, and probably your family too if your share price is going up. You're wearing a *kick me* sign if the price goes down. What makes one company a plotzer and another a Wall Street darling became, somewhere along the way, less about balance sheet and more about what is called "story." The story is what turns fund managers into fans.

And every good story has got to have a good character. The greater the character, the greater the story.

The humper becomes a visionary. (All visionaries were once humpers—and many visionaries return to being humpers; Sumner Redstone was a humper, a visionary, a humper again—and now a visionary once more.)

Of course, a visionary—a modern business visionary, anyway—isn't a single-minded soul pursuing his lonely vision. He's a salesman, a consummate salesman, and something of a quick-change artist, willing and able to do whatever is necessary to be what my dad used to characterize as "an operator."

And so Mel got on a roll.

The fund managers and the analysts began to like what they saw after Karmazin deftly took CBS from Michael Jordan (that was very sweet). That set his roll in motion. The Karmazin roll translated into the CBS share price—indeed, they are extensions of each other. And when your share price is high, you've got to do something with it—obviously! It buys you more today than it will tomorrow. And trading is your job. So you buy—or sell; you act. Foolishly or not. When you're on a roll, you go with it.

And later, when the roll stops, with any luck there'll be enough legend attached to you that you'll make it to when the next roll starts.

I was sorry I wouldn't be seeing Sumner at the conference—the grand and ridiculous are exactly the things that make a gathering memorable.

8
CHARLIE
AND MICHAEL

Charlie Rose, the *60 Minutes* correspondent and the host of the Charlie Rose show on PBS, has a casual yet elegant Eurotrash style. It's mock aristocratic. Chic and yet conservative. It's a Gianni Agnelli thing. The head of Fiat, famously, and eccentrically, never buttoned his sleeves or collars and wore his watch outside his sleeve. Charlie doesn't bother to button up either.

Network correspondents and anchorpeople of high stature often mix with the men who run the media companies they work for. Edward R. Murrow had a long and fraught relationship with William Paley. Likewise, Walter Cronkite was on the CBS board. Dan Rather often schmoozed with Larry Tisch when he was running CBS. Tim Russert was on the phone exchanging Washington gossip with GE's Jack Welch. There's a certain mutuality here: Businessmen get to be friends with some of the biggest celebrities in the nation, and the celebrities themselves get an added measure of job security.

But even in this after-you-Alphonse world of self-congratulations, Charlie Rose is unique.

Men of power are his metier.

Moguls especially move him.

They like him too. For a mogul to be on the Charlie Rose show is a kind of vanity—to be taken so seriously, and to have your eyes stared into so deeply.

While Charlie has, of course, been accused of slavish sucking-up, he's obviously on to something too—he may have the keenest understanding in American journalism of relative power and importance. (Not only is his girlfriend the stepdaughter of William Paley, she's the former wife of Steve Ross.)

Charlie may be the real Walter Lippmann.

More than any other journalist (this does not seem like the right moniker for Charlie, but there is no other formal designation—"celebrity interlocutor" is not widely accepted), he has managed to transcend the usual preoccupation with politicians as power symbols and identify and cozy up to the financial-technological-media-social elite. Nobody really big is going to elude Charlie for very long—and, almost certainly, Charlie is going to have managed to know them before they've gotten really, really big.

As is the case with Michael Bloomberg, the unlikely mayor of New York, who joined Charlie on stage for the opening discussion of the conference.

Charlie has known the mayor since not only long before he was mayor, but long before anyone but the most socially tireless knew the mayor—indeed, when all the mayor had was money. But Charlie got to know him and, in some relationship of great convenience, even began to broadcast his show from the Bloomberg studios (of note too, Steve Rattner is a benefactor of Charlie's show). Long before anyone knew the future mayor, Bloomberg was appearing on the Charlie Rose show and getting the Charlie Rose treatment.

(There is surely an argument which goes: You can't get to be truly anointed if you haven't done the Charlie Rose show and gotten the Charlie treatment.)

The two of them, Charlie and the mayor, on stage now, side by side in easy chairs, in an intimate discussion for the benefit of the three hundred people close enough to the center of power to be invited here, suggested a cat-who-ate-the-canary kind of triumphalism. Who was the cat and who was the canary was not really the point.

Now, I too had been onto Bloomberg. But where Charlie, with some greater mogul sense than mine, had understood the Bloomberg power, I had dismissed it. Charlie understood that moguldom was an artful illusion, whereas to me, mistakenly, it was measurable. Michael Bloomberg was a fake, it seemed to me. A Wall Street guy (not even! A database salesman—what did he do besides collect bond prices and retail computer terminals?) with a dirty mouth, and a mean spirit, who had pathetically tried to reinvent himself as a media mogul.

True, there were no studios quite like the studios in the television-radio-publishing company that Bloomberg set up (alongside his real business of pushing his data and his terminals) just in time for the business-media boom and the information revolution of the late nineties. CNN in its cramped and dreary quarters on Eighth Avenue near Penn Station, CNBC out in Fort Lee, Fox News in the basement of News Corp., all smacked of hard times in the television business—whereas Bloomberg was something like Oz. In city after city (there were 82 Bloomberg bureaus worldwide, with some 1,200 reporters and editors), he built movie-set versions of television studios—spiral staircases, wraparound news tickers, and the fabled and spotlessly clean tropical-fish tanks, along with open kitchens, coffee bars, and a bounty of free food.

The only thing is, nobody was really seeing Bloomberg media—actually, few could watch. While Bloomberg had constructed what appeared to be a global-media juggernaut, he had never quite gotten his network, in any substantial fashion, onto the airwaves. Despite his theoretical billions, he was, it seemed, unwilling to pay the price or to make the deals necessary for getting wide pickup by the nation's cable systems. So, along with all the fanfare, what he created was a media enterprise (TV, radio, books, magazines) with revenues probably no greater than $30 million to $50 million, which is hardly anything at all. It was a minor business-news company in the guise of a powerful and visionary media empire. It was, in other words, an illusion.

Rich guys, of course, are always trying to buy themselves into the media business—and profitability is often the least of their concerns. They write their losses off against the stature they gain from owning a bully pulpit and having an audience. But Bloomberg appears to have more finely parsed his desire: Mogulhood was clearly what he was after—having an audience was much less important. Certainly, Bloomberg's illusion seems to have paid off—or created a reality. He's become a much-vaunted media player, an information-age visionary, not only interviewed by Charlie but invited to speak on industry panels and to confer with his fellow moguls in Sun Valley (which would not have been the case if he were just a financial-data vendor).

This, it turned out, was political genius. Again, the illusion is the thing. When he began to think about running for office in 2000, the illusion that he owned an important and powerful media enterprise was integral to perpetuating the illusion that he was a credible political candidate; this worked by getting the media, which deeply respects and fears media moguls (certainly more than it respects and fears politicians), to treat him very seriously—not at all like a pretender or flake, or eccentric or naked emperor. It was illusion on top of illusion—a personal Ponzi scheme.

Boredom, restlessness, the need-for-validation thing, the desire to be taken seriously, to be recognized and fawned over by people who don't work for you, often bring men from unglamorous businesses into the media business and into politics.

After all, Bloomberg's business—his *real* business—is a deeply boring one. It's an old-fashioned, single-function, almost idiot-savant-type business. Twenty years ago, he managed to monopolize data relating to the bond market. There's no ticker for the bond market; there's no SEC-like agency that files information about bonds. Bloomberg, with a vast database operation in Princeton, turned himself into a repository of prospectuses for the fixed-income marketplace. That's his business—that's why most of his nearly 160,000 clients lease his kludgy machines. The overwhelming share of his company's $2.5 billion in annual revenue derives from the need for his bond data. That's his advantage. It's his annuity—and like most annuities, it's on autopilot.

No doubt it's a little stifling. The database business is the modern equivalent of an assembly line. What's more, every other part of the financial-information business is a tough game—Bloomberg tried to get a bigger piece but without much success. To have substantially grown, he'd have to take on big debt or go public and buy some other big financial-information or media company—and risk, or at least complicate, his safe annuity. (Bloomberg was in the increasingly anomalous position of running a private company, unhampered by public accountability; certainly he wouldn't have been able to run for mayor if he had to run a public company.)

In a way, because of the boredom and the autopilot nature of making the money, the company became a two-tier enterprise. There were the people who actually processed the data and sold the product, and then there were the people who tended to and marketed Bloomberg himself—his personal handlers and advisers, the company's real powers.

Bloomberg, the man, conceived and packaged as a separate Bloomberg company product, came to market shortly after his marriage broke up in 1993. There was an *I'll-show-her* aspect to his sudden reinvention. (She, apparently, left him.) It started with a concerted effort to move into big-time philanthropies—from the Central Park Conservancy to Lincoln Center to the Metropolitan Museum—then involved a stagy social life (a date with Diana Ross) and the move into radio and television.

It was a rebranding program.

There was an implicit sense that a recognizable Bloomberg with $2.5 billion in revenues was worth more than an unknown Bloomberg with that same $2.5 billion.

"Radio and television provide our company with instant visibility," he writes excitedly in his book, *Bloomberg by Bloomberg*. "The media like nothing better than writing about themselves. The more exposure Bloomberg has to the Fourth Estate, the more they'll promote us to the general public."

He's making a knowing point. The media gets the attention of the media. Getting the media to take you seriously is the campaign.

Bloomberg people are always speaking of this hustle—and of its great success. *The Mike York Times,* Bloomberg people call the paper, because of its reliable, respectful, business-page coverage of Bloomberg. (Bloomberg was also providing the Bloomberg financial news service free of charge to the *Times.*)

But why politics? He's not personable enough (he may be among the least charming people ever to have run for office), or charismatic or even interesting enough, or ideologically motivated enough (he was a Democrat; then, taking advantage of the easier field of play, he became a Republican). Certainly, he isn't politically talented enough and doesn't seem particularly interested in learning how to *be* politically talented. And even if he were all of the above, he'd still need that fluke circumstance that allows a Republican to get elected in New York City. What's more, his résumé is fraught with the kinds of things—sexual-harassment suits, for instance—that don't exactly help a fledgling politician.

But running for office, if you don't care about being elected, and if you can easily cover the amount of money it will cost, may be a really smart money play.

If publicity is the currency of our time, running for mayor of New York could very well raise your personal value substantially. And if you're as uncharming as Bloomberg, running for office might actually make you seem more charming—ramp up your Q rating. What's more, by seeming to go after the average voter you reach your real constituency: reporters, celebrities, hostesses, titans of business, customers, possible dates. Running for mayor is an in-crowd play ("The social set in New York has discovered him," Barbara Walters told the *Times* during the campaign).

Indeed, sometimes selling *yourself* is easier than selling your business. A telling element of the Bloomberg pitch—*I'm a good manager; therefore, I should run the city*—was that, in fact, the real forum for having your management skills voted on is the public markets, which he's avoided. Most companies the size of Bloomberg's that decide not to go public do so because the process would reveal they're not too profitable and not all that well managed, hence depressing their value. But Bloomberg, by running for mayor, a process with fewer disclosure requirements, was able to trumpet his management prowess—go public with it—without having to prove it. We took his word that he's good at business; in fact, we took his word that he's worth billions.

That's the illusion he's marketing, and, even if we didn't vote for him, the one we're buying. Bloomberg wasn't really running to be mayor; he was running to be some different, enhanced, illusory version of Michael Bloomberg.

But then he won, surprising nobody as much as himself. And confusing everyone else.

Bloomberg as mayor is so odd—not necessarily unattractive, just without precedent—that you look at him and find yourself thinking, especially if you're in the media business, especially if you're a mogul or would-be mogul type. What does this mean? What does Michael Bloomberg signify?

It's a paradigm shift.

We haven't ever elected men who've made a ton of money—not megamoney, not robber-baron money. Even in a nation where "self-made" is the greatest title, there have always been those few who are so self-made, so singular, that we haven't considered them to be part of the same striving experience. We haven't, at least in the past, liked people to be that unique—that independent.

Who would trust such men? That kind of money—unlimited, unimaginable amounts of it—naturally breaks the popular connection (and who does not hold the Capra-esque belief that such men are the poorer for it?).

That a great crime lies behind every great fortune has been a basic American sentiment. Where there's great profit, somewhere else there's been great loss. (You were a financier who'd stolen money from widows or orphans, an industrialist who'd made it off other men's labor, or a monopolist who had bought off politicians—or all three.) Such men had made their deal with the devil. The more money they made, the dirtier their business—hence "filthy" rich. They had blood on their hands. They were capable of anything (out of such omnipotence, conspiracy theories were born).

Their all-powerfulness (they would certainly have been as insulated and as pampered and as fawned over and as flattered as any aristocrat ever was) necessarily made them undemocratic, to say the least. And autocratic and authoritarian. Chosen. God, J. D. Rockefeller said about his money, had given it to him.

On the occasions when we elected their children to high office, it was because they'd made a public break with business, with the act of making money. Public life was an act of contrition. To whom much is given, much is required, the Kennedy and Rockefeller heirs went around saying.

But now the bar against electing outlandish, unimaginable, otherworldly wealth has been lifted. In fact, staggering sums of money, and the freedom and power (not to mention lifestyle) such sums give you, become a political virtue.

In the past, rich men or the heirs of rich men have run or flirted with running, but, in the manner of rich men, have often turned cheap in the process. Even old Joe Kennedy once said he didn't want to pay for one more vote than he had to. That is not the spirit now. Not only is the calculation different, but the act of spending, of being able to outspend what has been spent before and to inflate the underlying cost of the entire process, is a kind of demonstration of your willingness to give it your all. Cheapness is not a political virtue.

Obviously, this new tolerance and admiration for the superrich has to do with the ethos of the time. In the nineties, so many people *seemed* to be on their way to becoming among the richest people who have ever lived, that the idea that this was a special, or weird, or even monstrous status went away. Getting to be this rich even made you seem like something of a Boy Scout. You worked long hours, had a head for numbers, gave people what they wanted. Warren Buffett is rich, we believe, not least of all because he is a mensch.

Even the recent dramatic reversal—the undoing of many of the theoretically rich—has buttressed the reputations of the genuinely rich. It turns out to be so hard to hold on to money or to turn paper wealth into the cash stuff that the singular men who are real, no-shitting-anybody gazillionaires deserve special recognition.

Here is something else: The really rich used to run from publicity. They didn't want to inflame the envy of common people; they didn't want to expose themselves to muckraking scrutiny; they didn't want to endanger the security of their families. But in the current age, when publicity has become a clear and monetizable asset, the really rich went after their due. They sought celebrity status and were eagerly granted it. They demystified themselves, packaged themselves. They became as real to us and as attractive as, well, other celebrities (which has enabled their daughters to pursue modeling careers).

This is now part of the contrast-gainer effect. We compare these sun-god-like rich men with their special celebrity status to their opponents—mortal, earnest, cheap-suit, government-issue politicians.

On the one hand, we have rich men who have demonstrably accomplished something—they have gotten amazingly rich. (We no longer think of the very rich as takers, but rather as creators—wealth creators.) On the other hand, we have politicians who, we believe, have clearly accomplished nothing—that they would actu-ally be content not to get rich makes them doubly suspect (they are the takers).

For lots of people who work in corporate America, a smartly dressed, business-jargon-spouting, occasionally charming, often despotic rich man is much more familiar and comprehensible than a civil servant, with his bureaucratic style, policy-laden conversa-tion, and wonk aesthetic. Of course, there are an enormous num-ber of civil servants working in government warrens who must find the corporate-mogul aesthetic unsettling. These two camps may define the opposing sides of the future.

Certainly, the former group seems to believe that the skills for building immensely valuable, cutting-edge businesses can be ap-plied much more successfully to the running of government than the skills acquired in a career of working in government.

He's a "good manager"—the more money you've made, the better manager you are. Notably, people speak of "management" now the way we used to speak of politics. Management is about un-derstanding human nature, having keen people skills, being able to inspire, motivate, manipulate. Management, rather than politics, is the art of the possible.

It's reasonable, surely, to ask what's in it for the rich man. Oddly, we seem to believe the rich want less than the nonrich. That the man who needs the job is less trustworthy and necessarily more of a self-promoting phony (he needs the job, so he'll say anything) than the man whose whole career has been about selling and amassing and self-benefit.

Indeed, while the financial-information business is in generally bad shape, there was said to be a $10 billion postelection offer for Bloomberg L.P. from Thomson, a Canadian financial-information concern; the Bloomberg people, however, reportedly let it be known that they thought $20 billion was more in order. Bloomberg, after all, is a pretty fabulous brand name now.

So this was surely an issue this audience was attentive to: What had Michael Bloomberg gotten out of all this for himself? Was running for office a valid return-on-investment strategy? How much did it enhance the value of personal and corporate brand?

Moguls are nothing if not competitive with each other. (Just before the election, Murdoch's people were confiding that the *New York Post* wasn't going to endorse Bloomberg because Rupert didn't want another media guy to compete with him for mogulissimo status.) *If* he *can buy that,* I *can buy that,* the rich reflexively conclude. There is a whole class of billionaires who have made their money in the last twenty years and who are now at the age when people run for high office. Mort Zuckerman, Donald Trump, and David Geffen obviously come to mind. (Does Trump feel like a chump for not being more serious about his own political plans?) I know a bunch of young technology guys who made out like bandits who could easily drop $100 million on a race—and who have nothing much else going on in their lives. I think we can expect to see them on the hustings soon.

There is also—although it would go unmentioned at this conference—the Berlusconi factor.

The nexus of media and government is a vital and powerful one. The Italian mogul and head of state, Berlusconi, had pursued this strategy and articulated this imperative more coarsely and extremely than any other of the world's media titans. Indeed, as media titans go, Berlusconi may be the world's most successful precisely because his strategy of media and government has led to the world's most complete media monopoly—which is, at some not-too-removed distance, what this is all about.

It is the central question being pursued by everybody here: how to achieve a more complete monopoly.

You needed government to do that. (Indeed, the next speaker, after Charlie and the mayor, was Michael Powell, son of the secretary of state and chairman of the Federal Communications Commission, the body without whose support media monopolies would not be possible.)

Now, the general feeling about the Bloomberg crossover, I think, is that it is quixotic, and, even for a media guy, narcissistic—but you couldn't just write it off. The political sphere, for a media mogul, was a key play. Murdoch was the other most cogent example of mogul as political figure—not only was he a brilliant lobbier and bureaucratic player and influence getter, but he had turned his news network into a fearsome and profound political voice.

Indeed, if you were anything more than just small-time, you recognized that politics and media had to a greater extent merged—that politics did not exist without media. Therefore, if you were anybody, you wanted to get some benefit from that synergistic and symbiotic relationship.

You wanted to figure out, if you were here, what the next play was, the next step in how this all worked. Where should you be standing to get the advantage?

Now, this was not the discussion between Charlie and the mayor. Charlie and the mayor were discussing the budget crisis. The idea was that the media bigwigs would get some insider's insight into the political future—and knowing more about government would be able to make better business decisions.

And while that was not without some value, the real focus was on Bloomberg and what he was up to and how he was performing.

MICHAEL WOLFF

It was not only what advantage he had gained by his strange and unexpected crossover to political office, but something else—something possibly more profound.

You had to ask yourself: Was he running away from moguldom?

Had he made billions and positioned himself in the mogul limelight and found it all . . . unsatisfying? Was politics his escape?

Did Michael Bloomberg here, on the stage, with Charlie Rose, talking about the fate of a great city, shame everybody else here? Was everyone else here, compared to Michael Bloomberg, just so small-time? If you were in the media business, the Zeitgeist was ultimately your play. It was important to know then, insofar as being a mogul was concerned, if Michael Bloomberg had redefined it.

One more thing that, I know, everyone was evaluating: How odd was he?

He is odd, certainly—a strange, distracted, disconnected, imperial (say in the Franz Joseph style), self-conscious, unglamorous figure. Michael Bloomberg was a heavy dose of reality. So how much did this reflect on other businessmen and moguls? How bad did Michael Bloomberg make all other businessmen and moguls look?

This was a difficult moment, everyone knew.

The bursting of the bubble, Enron, AOL Time Warner, Martha Stewart. Oy.

The PR wolf was at the door.

Did odd Michael Bloomberg help or hurt the cause?

What was his role?

9
MORE
MICHAELS

The other way that conferences make money is through sponsorships. Companies that want to be associated with the conference or want to expose their logos and such to the people who attend the conference will pay high fees for certain VIP privileges, including signage, and bulk tickets, and speaking opportunities.

For $150,000 the international consulting firm McKinsey & Co. was a sponsor here. For that $150,000, the head of its media practice, a rabid self-promoter annoyingly named Michael Wolf got to interview Michael Powell, the FCC chairman, in the second discussion of the morning.

Consultants have become very big in the media business not least of all because so many people have gone into the media business who know nothing about the media business and so many media businesses have bought other parts of the media business that have no relation to the specific skill-sets of the businesses that they have heretofore been in that it has been necessary to hire people who say they know what you don't know (no matter if they in fact know it).

And so, often, the person hired has been this other Michael Wolf(f). As a gnat feeding on the carcass of the media industry, he's been, possibly, even more ubiquitous than me.

Our names and mutual media interest have thoroughly linked us. I get his mail and telephone calls and get asked to make his television appearances. People I don't know call me in the hopes that I will tell them how they can turn their businesses into media plays. We shoot daggers at each other across the dining room at Michael's, but people still confuse us. We may, of course, be helping each other—each expanding the other's brand. Once, when I unraveled the confusion on one television show—that it was not me they wanted but the other Michael Wolf(f)—the producer said I would do anyway. A McKinsey competitor took me to lunch to suggest that I ought to work with them because then we could get some of the business that the other Michael Wolf(f) was getting, which would be fair because he was getting business because people thought he was me.

Are we the two Darren Stevenses of the media world?

This other Michael Wolf(f)—he is Michael J. Wolf—has even written a book titled *The Entertainment Economy: How Mega-Media Forces Are Transforming Our Lives.* In it, he decrees that the economy is driven by fun, by the pleasure principle—the "E-factor," he calls it. People won't buy your services or products unless you entertain them, he maintains.

As it happens, his book is ghastly—unfortunately for me, or perhaps fortunately. (Would I feel better or worse if it were good?)

"Hilfiger realized it's not about clothes; it's about being cool" is one analysis he offers.

"Case had seen the future, and the future was online," he says in an effort to explain the foresight of the AOL chief.

Most characteristically, he has never met a mogul he didn't like.

"Like the conquistadors of the Age of Exploration, the heads of the major media companies are planting their flags everywhere," he tells us.

Now, I suppose, that while a world based on entertainment doesn't sound like such a bad thing, as it happens, his version of entertainment is the singing chicken at Stew Leonard's superstore supermarket. He confuses kitsch with entertainment—a common but fatal mistake.

"I had a blast trying out a mountain bike on the 470-foot biking and hiking trail," he says about a store he visits in Seattle (I have been to this store and you have to wait on line, and the salespeople would obviously rather you not try the mountain bike).

Describing Ralph Lauren's flagship store on Madison Avenue, he says: "When I visit that store I feel as if I'm making a visit to an exclusive British club, that somewhere between the underwear counter and the neckties I might bump into the cast from *Upstairs, Downstairs* or *Remains of the Day.*" It obviously cannot be true that he feels this way (the store is in fact a rather creepy, depressing, and fetishistic place). It's just PR talk. He is marketing the marketing. Indeed, he doesn't seem to distinguish between marketing and entertainment.

While this is certainly not a book that anyone has ever truly read, it has nevertheless become important and influential by virtue of the author's client list, which has included Bertelsmann's now former-CEO Thomas Middelhoff (Bertelsmann owns Random House, which published his book), Pearson chief Marjorie Scardino, Virgin king Richard Branson, Hasbro chairman Alan Hassenfeld, Universal president Ron Meyer, and a host who need no introduction: Ted Turner, Rupert Murdoch, Sumner Redstone, and Barry Diller among them.

Am I envious?

I am certainly curious about what it takes to get along with so many of these guys. What is he whispering in their ears? What megamedia strategies is he cooking up? What's the nature of the flattery he must engage in?

Figuring that we were in an awkward situation—two people with the same name in the same business, but him extolling the virtues of the great moguls and testifying to their inevitably greater successes, and me excoriating them and predicting their inevitable failure—I called him up sometime before the conference and proposed a friendly meeting.

A PR person returned my call and invited me to breakfast at Lespinasse in the St. Regis Hotel to meet my double. This is not, they seemed to assume, just a friendly meeting—but a press meeting.

In the consultant-banker-CEO world, breakfast and where you breakfast are significant. The choice of the heavily brocaded Eurotrashy Lespinasse suggested to me that he was a serious Hollywood type—or saw himself in that role. (He says in his book he's in L.A. at least once a week—he goes to Mortons on Monday nights, he says, when everybody's there.) A kind of business-school Jon Peters (Barbra Streisand's hairdresser-turned-mogul) was what I was thinking.

But Hollywood doesn't at all describe him—no flash, no chains, no charm even.

Rather, he's a small man with rimless glasses, parted hair, white shirt, and tie, accountantlike.

He is, in other words, a suit. Except for the Nurse Ratched PR person by his side, he seemed remarkably unassuming. (Why would he bring a PR person? Was she there to protect him or monitor him?) He seemed like anyone's father; he's 40-ish, but could easily pass for an old-fashioned 50. It is kind of a visual joke that this is the person who has written a book about entertainment.

He didn't seem to want to dwell on the weirdness of the name thing (maybe he's above it—or, like a schoolboy, embarrassed by it), so I dove straight into the conversation, which instantly became an interview (we can't escape our roles): "I'm interested in the argument you're making in your book, it seems so . . ."

"Entertainment," he dove in and restated crisply, "is increasingly having an impact on business." He gave the example of McDonald's and Happy Meal premiums.

"Haven't banks been giving out toasters for years? What's the difference?"

"Now consumers," he said proudly, "are making choices based on entertainment."

"Can we talk about the implications of an economy based principally on entertainment, or, even more to the point, on hype?"

He hesitated over his scrambled egg whites. "Everybody," he said, "has tried to copy Disney, but only the highest-quality products are successful." In addition to not being particularly responsive, this is also surely not true—God knows my kids have had U-Hauls full of toys that instantly fall apart.

"Consumers," he said, "are looking for fun in all parts of their lives."

I couldn't help wondering how much money this sort of worldview commanded. I'd guess partners at big consulting firms are in the million-plus range.

But I suppose that's not the point. His real job is to get along with moguls and their lieutenants, which takes, obviously, a rarer talent. The consulting business is a business about "validation." When the CEO is about to do a ridiculous thing, a prideful thing—

like going into the media business—he needs the cover. McKinsey is completely behind the move, the CEO tells his board. McKinsey (or Booz Allen, the consultancy Wolf used to work for) says anybody can be in the entertainment business—and everyone should.

I tried to engage him in a discussion about the instant obsolescence of plush toys, the fading of the major television networks, the expansion of the cable dial, and suckiness of movies. (This is the only time the PR person says anything, to heatedly defend the movie industry.) I threw down the gauntlet: Here we are the two of us, in the same business, not to mention with the same name, but whereas I believe this spread of media into all walks of life is absurd and debasing, you believe we are in the Camelot reign of the mogul kings.

He said no, he doesn't really think we are so far apart in our thinking. In fact, he said, he reads my column all the time and enjoys it immensely.

"So what is it that you do, actually?" I asked. It is, of course, my real question, and, I suspect, the source of my envy, that he has found the way to get big money out of all these opinions we trade in.

"My firm," he said, "works with the seniormost managers of the largest entertainment companies to help them with their most important strategic decisions. How they should compete. How they should sell their products. And who their partners should be."

But who and what and how, he won't say.

"Can you tell me about a big success you've had?"

"I'm afraid that would not be appropriate."

But before I departed he offered a significant crumb. He told me he knows why people are consuming more media. "They're sleeping less," he said. "I have studies that prove it."

No doubt, he is just another guy with his hand out in the entertainment economy—any doppelgänger envy I might feel is misplaced. He doesn't know more about the media business than anybody else. Oddly, I find myself thinking: Why would he be writing a book if he really had valuable things to say? Wouldn't he be selling his secrets for a lot more than $24.95?

Still, I know that whether he is whispering sweet nothings or brilliant windfall business strategies into the ears of CEOs, he has clearly articulated an average business guy's yearnings: Everybody wants to be in the media business.

To me, the entertainment economy represents the banality of fun, the homogenization of culture, the commodification of creativity. (As the other Michael Wolf(f) says, "Consumers who are already well acclimatized to multitasking in their business and professional lives will look to products and services that include entertainment content as an additional part of their offerings.") And I'd argue that in the end, it's bad for business, too, that the entertainment economy is run by people who aren't entertaining.

But that is obviously naïve. The new world entertainment order is also clearly about bland and unfunny guys who want to do some strutting. (Once, an airline analyst explained to me that the industry was ruined by an influx of businessmen who knew nothing about airlines and flying but who liked stewardesses.) And it needs other bland and unfunny guys to tell them that it's okay to be in the media business. That it's just business after all—complicated, hard-nosed, heavy on the M.B.A. theory, rather than just an obvious vanity play.

On stage, a mousy Michael Wolf now sat close by an immensely puffed up Michael Powell.

Powell, a Bush appointee, is certainly the latest in a succession of lynchpins of the entertainment economy—which is, by another name, the vast, hapless, consolidation of the media industry.

It is only fair to point out that in this vast consolidation the Clinton Democrats are as culpable as the Bush Republicans.

The Democrats allowed incremental consolidation because it was in their interest to be nice to the media business—not only are media business power brokers pervasive in Democratic politics (and, of course, big contributors too), but the single most powerful force in politics is media. What politician would be so dense as not to realize that if you alienate the lawyers and executives and big shareholders of media enterprises that it will come back to bite you harshly?

The media is of course as courted and as accommodated and as sucked up to as any other big industry. What's more, the Clintonites had special reason to bend over backward for the media— hence, they began a significant cutting back on long-standing media regulation, and took a tolerant position when it came to media antitrust enforcement.

The Republicans, on the other hand, more honorably perhaps, but more frightening too, seem wholly to have bought the rationale for consolidation. Consolidation, they do truly believe, is good for you—really good for you. An excellent adventure. That's the mantra.

Consolidation is "proconsumer."

It's nicely Orwellian.

Without consolidation there will be no more "free" television.

Consolidation protects choice.

Michael Powell is a happy believer in the absurd, and ironic, and unreal—without knowing that what he believes in is any of those things.

Perhaps because of his father, Colin Powell, the secretary of state, and growing up an Army kid, he has the kill-for-peace attitude.

There's no piercing the contradictions.

There's a benighted self-satisfaction about him too. The arrogance of the military without having had to be in the military. A banana republic dictator thing—and, indeed, there is some eerie (and I fear, unmentionable) Baby Doc aspect to him.

He's enormously confident, confiding to the other Michael Wolf(f) that consolidation is the way to protect a free media.

It's easy to suspect that he's an ideologue because he doesn't seem too bright. But his extremism may also come from a certain amount of impatience. The alternative in a job like his is to weigh and sift each element and request and petition—better to have some sweeping approach.

It is, too, arguably a technology thing. He is a technocrat. And, in that vein, you do see that technological growth and enhancement almost always depend on consolidation. On single standards. On research efficiencies. On massive investment. On building infrastructure.

It was a frightening but lackluster discussion that he was having on stage with the other Wolf(f). The consultant, who certainly had no interest in ruffling the FCC chairman's feathers, and indeed had every interest in smoothing them, fed him a series of eager-to-please questions.

Their assumptions were shared and embraced:

Big is destiny.

Big is powerful.

Big is what powerful people want.

Because powerful people wanted big, big is what would happen.

Big is the universe and if you don't accept the universe, well, there's no place for you in it.

Big is our business.

At the moment of the Foursquare conference, almost every media mogul in the country had lawyers petitioning Powell and the FCC for the further—indeed, nearly final—dismantling of media-ownership rules, of any protections which existed to prevent media monopolies and single-source information control.

It was easy to close your eyes and imagine the penultimate spasm of consolidation in which there were only two media companies left standing—one strong and one less strong. This is inevitable, you find yourself concluding, because it's what everybody but the most marginal wants—it's where the big money is.

You have to slap yourself to realize that this isn't true—or at least that two parallel realities neatly exist.

On the one hand, you have the mogul class that is continuing to lay the groundwork for a further paroxysm of media mergers and acquisitions.

But on the other hand, you have investors who are shunning these companies, and managers who are eager—even desperate—to unhitch themselves from their troubled overlords, employees who hate their jobs, and consumers who continue with increasing speed and perturbance to abandon and reject the products offered by these companies. Indeed, it would be almost reasonable, on this side of the reality chasm, to conclude that virtually everyone in the media business, save for the very topmost people running the consolidated media enterprises, has come to question the ideas of consolidation and synergy—even to accept the likelihood that the great media combines will imminently be shaken apart.

In other words, what we seem to have is a generation gap.

There are the grandees of the business with ever-greater dreams of bigness-as-usual, and then a restive, younger media class using AOL Time Warner, Vivendi, and Disney as punch lines.

It is, in fact, worth asking what happens when the older generation, the mogul generation, dies; that might have been the better debate to have before the FCC (or now, up on the stage).

This is part of the analysis often performed by investors and business students: What happens if the top dog gets hit by a bus (not to speak of being eliminated by natural causes)? In other words, how dependent are these companies on the idiosyncratic forcefulness of their mogul leaders? And in what new direction do they evolve without them? Can they even exist without some brute ego holding them together?

Both AOL Time Warner and Vivendi are helpful here, because they have offed their leaders—moguls-in-chief Jerry Levin and Jean-Marie Messier.

These deaths were by palace revolt instead of accident or attrition, but they highlight the fundamental divide: The men who invented these companies are egomaniacs and fabulists; the men who took them over are managerial rationalists.

Which prompts the question, what does a rationalist do with an irrational enterprise?

This conundrum may account for the caught-in-the-headlights look of both Dick Parsons, now the CEO at AOL Time Warner, and Jean-René Fourtou, who is running Vivendi. In neither instance can you imagine these men creating or envisioning the kind of companies they now are responsible for—hence their palpable sense of uncertainty and even, it seems, despair.

Indeed, the theme of virtually all great consolidations is the complexity of the financial schemes that created them (the better the deal, the more difficult it is to understand). But Parsons's managerial credo at AOL Time Warner, a company built almost entirely out of confounding transactions, has been a pledge of "no more complicated deals."

His most significant move as of the autumn of 2002 had been to try to untangle AT&T's (soon to be Comcast's) investment in certain AOLTW properties (you don't want me to explain this deal—no one, really, has ever been able to explain it). Parsons's proposal was to pool the company's cable assets into a separate public company. So although AOL Time Warner would still be running this new company, it would have a fiduciary and legal responsibility to maintain an independent relationship with its sister divisions (which, come to think of it, may be even more unwieldy than the former arrangement). In any event, in a stroke of rationalism (or at least attempted rationalism), Parsons, if he can accomplish this untangling, will have undone all possibilities of synergy, the shibboleth upon which the entire foundation of media consolidation has rested. In fact, by spinning off the single largest part of AOL Time Warner, Parsons will have taken what is obviously a clear step toward breakup.

Fourtou, for his part, is also in retreat from complexity and entanglements. For Vivendi, at this point, it is all about negotiated retreat and undoing the ties of empire. Of course, Fourtou and Vivendi are in the humiliating position of having someone from the mogul generation as the local strongman. Barry Diller was not only running Vivendi Universal that autumn but—because he, a real mogul, bested Jean-Marie Messier, Vivendi's would-be mogul, in their initial, and vastly complicated, mogul-to-mogul arrangement—had effective control over whom the company can be sold to (i.e., him—if that's what he wants). Fourtou, no doubt, wished the bus would run over Barry.

Now, moguls believe that other moguls will die or be eliminated, but not them. This is one of the reasons the remaining moguls were petitioning the FCC. The prospect of the end of AOL Time Warner, Vivendi, and Disney meant good pickings. According to business mythology, all industries reach a point where, in a final spasm of consolidation, there is a last man standing.

Murdoch? Redstone? Diller?

But what happens if the bus heads their way?

It is certainly reasonable to believe that with Murdoch still safely in place, a whole new dimension of consolidation is in store for his company. What—or how much—might he want of a disaggregating AOL Time Warner, Vivendi, and Disney?

But what happens without Rupert? His son Lachlan is faithfully by his side and is, one would suppose, getting a thrilling education. And there are numerous loyal executives who would step into the breach. And yet, after Rupert, is it even necessary to argue that News Corp. will be a more realistic, less adventurous, even gentler place?

And then there are Mel and Sumner at Viacom.

Which one will the bus hit first? Or, more to the point, who will be driving the bus?

And then there's the 60-ish Diller, whom I find I am reluctant to kill off. I just can't forgo the spectacle of watching whatever it is he will do.

This is the problem with my dead-mogul analysis: We know that the media world is teetering near collapse and will inevitably be divided and administered by more modest men. And yet, for better or worse, so many of us have this helpless mogul worship (or fixation). It is hard to escape the thrall. It is hard to believe that all of this—big companies as well as big men—will pass. That this generation is done. (Once, when asked about Murdoch's brush with prostate cancer, Barry Diller described the extraordinary steps—stake through the heart, deep-excavation burial, concrete reinforcement—it would take to kill him and keep him dead.) Especially because this generation is so much larger, meaner, more heroic than the one coming next—which will be dealing with all the problems caused by large, mean, heroic fathers.

I have seen Michael Powell, who is meant to restrain these men and their companies, laughing dreamily and schmoozing delightedly in the presence of moguls. He can't escape his awe. You bend to the larger power, the bigger ego.

Even now, on stage, it was striking, and almost embarrassing. The smaller Michael Wolf was bending to the larger Michael Powell, who in turn was rationalizing why he was going to bend to the greater moguls.

I wonder if anyone believed the words here—the clinical distinctions between this apparent monopoly which wasn't one and that apparent monopoly which wasn't one either. Or if they were even listening. The body language was so much more compelling. Powell flexing his arms, shooting his cuffs, crossing his feet at his ankles, ennumerating his issues on his fingers. He understood his power. His power was in giving other people power. He sucked up.

10
KEN AND STEVE

Before Ken Auletta and Steve Case, the most awaited interview of the day—the train wreck moment—there was a strange interlude at a sluggish moment in the afternoon.

Heilemann sat on the stage with Jim Barksdale, the former CEO of Netscape, now on the board of AOL TV, and with John Doerr, of the venture capital firm—the most successful venture capital firm of all time—Kleiner, Perkins, Caufield & Byers. Each man balanced half-awkwardly on a stool.

There was a self-conscious listlessness or what-me-worry sheepishness about Barksdale and Doerr. And, too, an arrogance—they were in the dock, but they weren't contrite. Although, God knows, there wasn't much question of guilt.

These were two of the most successful men of the epoch, and yet, from this early 21st-century perspective, they really hadn't done much right. Or, even more to the point, what they had done, what bets they had made, had often turned out to be largely wrong for everyone else but themselves.

They were vastly rich, but the great majority of the people

who had invested with them were now significantly poorer. What's more, it had been the pronouncements of these two men which had fueled much of the great Internet bull market—so there were, far beyond their own companies, a multitude more who had lost money because they had believed what Barksdale and Doerr had said.

Hence, their sheepishness.

Now, of course, they would not have entirely subscribed to this indictment—no matter how sheepish they appeared. But, no doubt, in the dark of night, in their fabulous homes, and their carefully decorated bedroom suites, Barksdale and Doerr must have had moments of wondering if they weren't charlatans, too.

Barksdale was a clipped, no-nonsense, no-bull, western sort. He was Reagan-esque in a way, but clearly not dumb. When he spoke, with great practicality and some humor, he carried the day. Doerr—mild, pale, fragile, cryptic—was the nerd type. At the top of the boom he had been eerily charismatic; now he was just eerie. Very Martian-like.

These were Heilemann's goombahs. Heilemann had spent the better part of the boom and now several years beyond trying to get their story. Part of the problem now may have been that he knew them so well, and they knew him so well, that they didn't much have to say what was on their minds. It was very muted, even private, their discussion now—opaque gestures which might have been expressive, but which nobody else, except the people on the stage, understood. We're here because you asked us to be here but this is all a little embarrassing and everyone knows it's a little embarrassing, even a little ridiculous, so we're not going to pretend it isn't, but on the other hand, we're not going to give a big wet confession either. The world is as it is.

Shit happens, was their basic demeanor.

They'd lost money too, they both said with some large degree of insensitivity.

This is capitalism, was the subtext. If you can't take it, get out of the kitchen.

Better to have made money and lost it than never to have made it at all.

This was, quite likely, the most sympathetic audience that could attend them, and yet you could feel the steam rising. In the end, nobody was ever going to excuse you for losing them money, and, surely, there was a special place in hell—a leper colony all your own—for people who lost other people's money while they made money themselves.

Indeed, the class of people who had escaped the carnage of the boom was not an enviable one.

For the better part of a generation, money—having money, making money—had involved pretty uncomplicated emotions.

Money was good.

We understood money in the Calvinist sense: if you had it, you deserved it; God had given it to you.

The election of Michael Bloomberg might have been the high point of this pure and uncritical sentiment—even possibly its last gasp.

You could, here, on this day on Wall Street, if you strained, sense something else. A resistance. A clarity. A rising irritation.

An air of judgement was in the room.

The strong desire—and certain pressure—for everyone here to identify with Barksdale and Doerr had passed.

What was left was a much stronger imperative to find the points of differentiation—of why we here in our seats were not like these two guys, who, while they might be financially independent, were also, as clearly, adrift, separate, without a country.

People began looking away.

Also before the Steve Case interview, there was a panel on sports. Jim Dolan, the CEO of Cablevision, was on the panel. In no sense coincidentally, Rattner and Quadrangle had just, that day, announced the acquisition of a minority stake in the cable company.

This was, in other words, all very keiretsu-like. Or the dream was that it should be all very keiretsu-like. That everyone here should be engaged and cross-collateralized with each other.

Finally, Steve Case, the day's main event.

The issue was not so much what he would say, but how he would present himself. Like Barksdale and Doerr, Case had gotten away with something. But what he had pulled off was larger than what even Barksdale and Doerr had pulled off, and more audacious. What's more, there was yet very little distance between Case and the unfortunates whom he'd screwed. He was the wholly discredited leader still hanging around. He was the despot on the eve of exile. He was a disgraced person appearing in public. The pariah of the moment.

We were all here as voyeurs.

It was exciting.

The choice of the *New Yorker*'s Ken Auletta as the interlocutor was a good one. Auletta has done as much as anyone to invent the idea of the modern mogul. He was the mogul biographer. He had spent time with each of the moguls. He had long since passed the point of mere journalism and become in status and in demeanor and influence a mogul associate. He was the mogul artist.

Ken was always very tan and very fit and very well dressed and had a sense of agelessness, but he had been a part of the modern media era as long as anyone. He was an aide to New York's mayor, John Lindsay, in the 1960s, then part of the launch of *New York* magazine; and later had gone to the *New Yorker,* which lent business and moguldom a formal cultural cachet.

Indeed, a mogul is not just a businessman, not just a rich man, is Auletta's underlying point, but a seeker, and adventurer, and hero for our time.

Likewise, by this measure, Steve Case might not be a mogul. Almost from the beginning of Auletta's interview with Case on the conference stage, it seemed like this was Auletta's point: to show not just that Case was the agent who brought down a great American company, but that he was not even the real thing. Indeed, his early question, which went largely unanswered, was about what Case did, how he filled his days.

Auletta, I thought, who had created the new mogul paradigm, was articulating a new analysis of the AOL Time Warner debacle. In a sense this was the view on the street, that the AOL Time Warner guys—Levin, Case, Pittman—were inflated egos. But I sensed the analysis move a bit further here: that there was not just hubris at work, not just vanity, that this was not just a wild gamble that had failed, not even just a moment of profit-taking by some at the expense of others, but that this mess was the product of men who were just not large enough to pull it off. They were less than moguls. *That* was the AOL Time Warner fatal flaw.

Case's baby face seems scrunched from both above and below— the effect is to focus you on his eyes, which seem darting and furtive. He was here, clearly, to save himself. You could imagine what his handlers were saying backstage:

"You're going to have to get out there, Steve. Make it clear that you're not going anywhere. You have to show ownership. You have to occupy the leadership space. They—Wall Street, the press—have to know that you're in the game."

But Auletta's point was well taken: It was hard to see Case as a player, much less a survivor, much less triumphant.

Now, it is true, and Case took pains to remind everyone, that he had triumphed continuously against long odds. AOL, which was counted out so many times before, had survived to dominate the industry.

Well, yes.

But you couldn't escape the luckiest-white-boy-in-America look about Case. Nor, if you knew anything—and clearly the point was that the people at AOL Time Warner did not know anything— you would not have failed to see that AOL's survival was not so much about making it out of the onrushing river, but merely making it to the next rock. And that it had triumphed, such as it had, not by its own strength, but by the benefits of more pervasive weakness. More basically, it was a company built on a certain order of short-term lies. This is an old-fashioned business strategy, and, in the scheme of things, a necessary and not even all that dishonorable one: It's the check-is-in-the-mail strategy. You're trying to create a series of bridges to solvency and safety. Your job is to keep balls in the air. That was the sort of place that AOL was; the greater problem was that Time Warner mistook it for something much more than that, and believed that Case was swimming mightily instead of treading water.

Case, defending himself now with Nixon-like implacability and negative credibility, had always been a very strange fish.

He was the Procter & Gamble marketer—an indication of good-old-fashioned white-bread American corporatism, rather than darker, vastly more interesting, Machiavellian mogulism.

Then he was the front man, the get-along guy, and the whipping boy for a bunch of last-stop money trying to recover cents on the dollar at the early AOL.

Then, he became, rather by pure happenstance, the clean-cut front man for a modest porn enterprise: AOL, by the early nineties, was accommodating in its chat rooms a growing stream of online dirty-talkers at $6.95 an hour.

Then, in the mid-nineties, succumbing to the temptation of many an unimaginative executive before him, he fell in love with his company's PR person, precipitating a personal crisis and transformation. So just when the company began to grow hugely, Case stopped working. As potential moguls go, indeed as perfectly run-of-the-mill CEOs go, Case might have been the most disengaged in America.

He was in love; indeed, he divorced his wife and married the PR person.

What's more, he may have sensed a greater truth: There was no real way to guide the company. The growth and the direction of AOL depended on two things, which it was almost impossible to control.

There was the technology factor. Could the never-before-accomplished be accomplished? Could you get a million (and more) people online at once? For a long time, this was not really answered. There were a series of stopgaps and kludges and jury-rigs which might have, at any time, collapsed. Indeed, at several times they did. Here were the limits of the company. You just couldn't know if it was going to make a breakthrough that would allow it to grow, or if, at any moment, it would fall to pieces.

Then the next unknown and uncontrollable element: Once you had these people online, would they titillate each other?

Here was the rub—and here was another reason why Case might have absented himself: If you fully engaged in the business you were running, you were engaged in porn. Or you could disengage, and not think about it, and let it do what it did on its own. If people wanted that, if they created it, if they got off on it, so be it.

If a mogul is defined as some order of preternaturally aggressive, pathologically motivated control freak, Case was the diametrical opposite, a very passive, and apparently quite satisfied, modern executive, wholly accustomed to accepting whatever happened to him.

This was, in some sense, the theory he was propounding now to Auletta. Sure things were all fucked up now, but it was a long race—all kinds of other things, better things, possibly great things, would happen in the future if everybody just had a little patience.

He tried to talk about what needed to happen to put AOL back in business. But this was a hard discussion to have because you still could not really talk about what AOL's business was.

You would not have Case admitting that AOL had depended upon and continued to depend upon the sex business, and you wouldn't have a writer from the *New Yorker*—Auletta was nothing if not gentlemanly—pursuing such a thesis. Nor would the guys at Time Warner ever even understand that this was the game.

But in a turn of vast social consequence, seeking sex on the Internet had become, in the three years since AOL and Time Warner had agreed to merge, no longer weird or shameful behavior. Across the Internet, dirty talk had become a progressively more developed social form—even a social norm. In fact, it is quite possible that everybody of a certain demographic profile who is dissatisfied with his or her current romantic prospects is experimenting with meeting someone online.

Even John Podhoretz, the very conservative and highly un-with-it columnist and former editorial-page editor at the *New York Post,* much interested in family values and opposed to anything that suggests moral relativity, showed up recently with a wedding announcement explaining that he'd met his wife-to-be on matchmaker.com. (The site where a couple meets is becoming an element of respectable wedding and engagement announcements.)

What's more, the matchmaking business was growing in a way, and producing profits of a sort, not seen since the advent of eBay. (Among the largest dating businesses is Barry Diller's match.com.) Indeed, logically, why wouldn't every lonely heart try a dating site?

Given the reach and the efficiency of Web dating, there would be only two things reasonably holding you back: embarrassment and technical difficulties. But if John Podhoretz was doing it, the embarrassment factor was obviously dwindling—it had become a perfectly decent, unremarkable, squaresville thing to do. And with dating sites throwing off lots of cash (the more you want to know about a possible date, the more you pay, seems to be the basic model), the technology for online courtship rituals—searching, profiling, chatting, photo uploading—had become really nifty.

Meanwhile, in contrast to the new, slick, and easy-to-use hookup sites, AOL had started to look like a bus station.

In the early nineties, AOL had succeeded in creating a simple, orderly, largely text-based chat client—the first to work effortlessly. Next, AOL developed the Instant Message (IM), through which you could talk directly to anyone else online; then it offered a searchable database of fellow chatters that grew to vast proportions, in which any interest (or kink) was immediately searchable; and it introduced the Buddy List, through which you could monitor the comings and goings of anyone who interested you (or whose kink interested you). This simple technology—nontechnical people really couldn't chat anywhere else online—was the engine of AOL's wild growth. And finally, AOL extended its chat range with the AIM applet, which could be used from outside the walls of AOL to chat with other AOLers (and other AIMsters).

Then AOL rested.

It could afford to. Not only did AOL have better technology, it had what nobody could reproduce without great luck and limitless money, which was a critical-mass audience—chat doesn't work unless, at every moment of the day, you have loads of chatters. Across the Internet, there were lonely chat rooms (where the chat function didn't really work, anyway) and, at AOL, rowdy and randy crowds ("Are you hot?" "Yeah! What are you wearing?").

Meanwhile, the AOL guys were refining their story. A great American brand could not appear to be in the sex business. So what AOL focused on was getting the dirty-talk audience to buy things. From sex to commerce was the conversion it was attempting. (This is the conversion that cable television managed with infomercials in the mid-eighties.) Certainly, Time Warner believed in conversion (the people at AOL used the word *community* as a euphemism, but the people at Time Warner used the word for *real*—as though imagining little shops and churches and schools).

The result of this confusion or obfuscation about what AOL really does, as well as the ensuing cutbacks, recriminations, and dismissals that came with the AOLTW merger, meant that development in most areas at AOL stopped—for two years, virtually nothing!—just at the time when easy-to-use chat was breaking out all over the Web.

Everybody with any connection speed is locating and targeting and qualifying possible mates with great ease in well-designed, mall-like settings, while back at AOL, it's still a creepy, anonymous, low-class world. (AOL's weird censorship policies, in an increasingly tolerant world, somehow seem to add an extra measure of tawdriness.)

It's a demographic nightmare: If you are still signing on to AOL to chat, there is, ipso facto, something wrong with you.

From the beginning of the merger, I thought this was going to be an interesting cultural problem. The AOL guys had always managed to keep the dialectic finely in play—encouraging dirty chat by encouraging family values. Profiles to foster "community" and multiple screen names for family use and parental controls to create clearly marked areas of menace (otherwise, it was hard to find this stuff) served its porn business as well as its family image.

But this is not something you would have explained to the Time Warner guys.

I'm pretty sure nobody from AOL ever sat down at a Time Warner boardroom table and spelled out the workings of the auto-eroticism business.

And count on it, the Time Warner people, those uptight guys, didn't ask.

What's more, I think the higher-up AOLers suddenly, given the opportunity, didn't want to be in the sex business anymore either. They'd all made hundreds of millions—now they wanted to be respectable.

Classically, nobody was minding the store.

Now, AOL's problems are always blamed on the AOL people—they were the flimflammers who got everybody into trouble. And they certainly *were* the flimflammers—playing a bit of bait-and-switch, cooking the books a bit.

But the Time Warner guys were not only the guys who got duped but the guys who couldn't even see the real value of what they had: a monopoly on dirty chat. Possibly the greatest growth industry of the age.

Indeed, by the autumn of 2002, most of the core AOL executives had departed (save for Case himself, whose picture still appeared on the AOL opening screen, exhorting the faithful), leaving the Time Warner people, with all their inhibitions, in charge.

It is unlikely that the Time Warner guys had spent much time in the Long Island Swingers chat room in the Special Interests chat area, or given much thought to building a business to cater to those special interests—that is, pursuing the business that AOL created and until recently dominated.

Instead, the Time Warner guys, in some remarkable demonstration of human and corporate steadfastness, have announced that they are going to save AOL by transforming it into a business that sells Time Warner content. For a premium, you'll be able to read *People* online! (Forgive me . . . ROTFL.)

Poor passive Steve Case, trying to hold on to his lousy job, was in the hapless position of having to defend and expound upon this strategy now, while elegant Ken Auletta gracefully took him apart and held him up to the great ridicule of the crowd.

11
MORE MICHAELS
AND MORE
DINNER

Pam Alexander maneuvered me into a seat at the banquet at the end of the first day next to Jim Wiatt, the head of William Morris.

I believe this was for my own good. Agents were one of the formal nexi of media power. The heads of the three major agencies—ICM, CAA, and William Morris—were like party whips. They knew where the votes were. Or, like Michael Ovitz—and before Ovitz, Lew Wasserman—they were in a position to become party leaders and ultimate kingmakers. So to have a relationship with one or more agency heads was to have access and insight into the true operation of celebrityhood and pop culture and entertainment commerce in America.

Indeed, media conglomerates would surely come and go, media moguls would rise and fall, but talent agencies would always be making money.

I should reach out to Wiatt, I thought. I had tried in the past.

But I always found him too literal. And too suspicious. And too scary. Unlike Ovitz, who had many moves and a vast range of charm, Jim Wiatt seemed unsubtle and unreconstructed. He held power; that's what you were aware of. When he dispensed it, it wasn't in dollops and increments.

He didn't give out information either. The Ovitz way, and, indeed, the general method of media power people, is to be able to spin a hierarchy of information. To know what you need to give to someone to keep them interested but at the same time to reveal as little as possible. This is the gossip chain. Gossip that offers mere titillation at the bottom; gossip that you can turn into big money at the top.

Jim Wiatt must gossip—there would be no way to survive in the media business if you didn't, and no reason to be in the media business if you didn't want to. But there didn't seem to be a lot of subtlety in his hierarchies. I was outside, so therefore he was locked up.

I was the press; he wasn't talking—except in chamber of commerce–type bromides.

Still, you work your sources.

From Jim Wiatt, I wanted the Michael Eisner story. While there were other Disney people here, Eisner wasn't. He couldn't be. He wouldn't, and couldn't, expose himself—everybody knew that.

It was the ongoing weird act of the media business. Michael Eisner was a sort of corporate Michael Jackson. He had held on to Disney even though everybody knew everything had long since become too troubled, and problematic, and embarrassing for him to continue running Disney—or even for Disney to continue. (The question of who might buy Disney was always a subtext to media merger-and-acquisition gossip.)

Indeed, it was his holding on, rather than his dysfunction, that had somehow come to define the state of the business.

Michael Eisner was Franco.

When, by the late nineties, it appeared that nothing could get worse at Disney—fleeing executives, share-price collapse (and this was during the boom), dismal results at ABC, and a CEO involved in a bitter, costly, and very public lawsuit with a former subordinate—Jeffrey Katzenberg, since decamped to DreamWorks—I wrote what could not have been more obvious: Michael Eisner's extraordinary reign at Disney was coming to an end.

Well, not long ago, some media bigs I knew were out for a little retreat at Herb Allen's place in Sun Valley and, over drinks, put together a friendly pool about whether Michael would last the year.

When I dismissed Eisner, I not only got it wrong but missed the story; likewise, the media bigs in Sun Valley betting against Michael were falling into the same trap.

The point we missed is that Michael Eisner had perfected the art of survival—nobody was going to make him go anywhere.

It may have just been a matter of management priorities: Do you focus on share price, market reach, product quality, kicking ass, or, just as strategically, your own entrenchment?

A key mogul challenge is to create a company that can't get rid of him, in which he can survive any mistake he makes (and if what he cares about first and foremost is his own continued existence, he's going to make a lot of mistakes), in which he is guaranteed to be the last living cockroach.

Of course, this is not so easy to do. Even in the now-done age of the exalted CEO, we live in a highly disposable corporate culture.

When the tide turns against you, you're usually finished. Shareholders, like team owners, are very fickle.

There is, however, the mogul exception. It's similar to the French "cultural exception." Market forces alone are not allowed to rule. By general consensus, we have agreed to subsidize the unique institution of the media mogul. By which I mean not mere manager-moguls (like Jean-Marie Messier or Thomas Middelhoff or Bob Pittman) but a true creator-of-worlds mogul, with vast control of his (theoretically) public company.

The Eisner accomplishment, and the insuperable bulwark his disgruntled shareholders were up against, was that he transformed himself from a mere manager into a being virtually synonymous with Disney itself.

He may be the only mere manager ever to have successfully elevated himself from hireling to fully vested mogul (unlike Mel Karmazin at Viacom, who has been on the losing side of such an effort). What's more, with some screwball irony, Michael Eisner was hired at Disney in 1984 precisely because he was a nonmogul, a nonvoting-class owner-operator, an outsider who would do the bidding of shareholders against entrenched interests.

But what happened is that he consumed the company from within. He ingested it—and it became him.

To understand the extent of his grasp, you have to look to the larger mess. That is, since the acquisition of ABC in 1995, or since the death of Eisner's number two, Frank Wells, in 1994, or since the departure of Jeffrey Katzenberg six months later—everybody has a favorite precipitating event—Disney had become weirder and weirder, more and more dysfunctional, a bizarrely isolated place.

Even during the good years—when Eisner, Wells, and Katzenberg remarketed the Disney assets (helpfully, the video revolution was at hand) and relaunched the animation studios (coincident with a boom in family entertainment)—there was what people call "the Michael thing."

There was always the good Michael and the bad Michael. The good Michael was the no-Hollywood-jive, drooping-sock Michael, the faithful-to-his-wife Michael, the decent, goofy, puppy-dog Michael. The Michael played by Tom Hanks.

Starting in 1984, the good Michael took Disney—a company with a fading brand and sclerotic management, a nonplayer in the media and entertainment business—and turned it into the most powerful force in the industry, creating the model of the media merchandising-licensing-branding juggernaut. For his troubles, he became a billionaire as well as one of the most prominent chief executives in America. (For fifteen years, in my family, we've been watching a tape of *Mary Poppins* in which Michael Eisner glides down the cable car at Disneyland and like a folksy Dad—a Jewish Walt—and introduces the Disney classic).

But at the same time, though it was mostly hidden from view while the company was doing well, there was the bad Michael: controlling, vindictive, dissembling Michael. The avaricious Disney-is-too-small-and-no-company-is-too-big-for-Michael-Eisner Michael.

In contemporary Hollywood mythology—a mythology partly authored by Eisner himself in his autobiography (written with Tony Schwartz)—the loyal and unflappable Frank Wells, before his death in a freak helicopter-skiing accident, acted as buffer, counselor, mother. He was the producer handling the tantrums and ego excesses of Eisner, his difficult star. In Wells's production (it was, in fact, Wells who brought Eisner to Disney), Eisner is genius, leader, statesman, one of those unique executives—Gates, Henry Ford, Walt himself—who personify their companies.

If Frank hadn't died . . . is the preface to almost every rumination on the part of Disney observers and insiders. If Frank Wells had lived, the thinking goes, Eisner would not have had his fight with Katzenberg. DreamWorks would not have started and ruined the economics of the all-important animation business by paying animators vastly more money. (In this model, Katzenberg might have left anyway, but would now be running an independent animation studio financed by Disney.) Michael Ovitz would never have been hired as the next heir apparent—and hence the huge and costly embarrassment of firing him would never have occurred. Most of the executives who have departed Disney over the past few years would have stayed. And, not least of all, Disney would not have bought ABC.

There is, however, another interpretation of the Wells myth, which, in essence, paints Wells as the great enabler. Because he let Eisner look like a statesman, a CEO of archetypal proportions, a Jack Welch type, everybody got fooled, including Eisner himself. He started believing he was actually a godlike corporate manager instead of an impulsive, immoderate, hands-on (as likely to be idiotic as brilliant, as likely to be dismissive and cruel as he is to be charming and charismatic) showbiz guy without basic knowledge of, or an innate head for, the fundamental details of running a massively disaggregated modern corporation. Eisner has, in this scenario, the classic attributes of the turnaround guy and entrepreneur—who should be kept away, as far as possible away, from running the whole shebang.

Certainly his successes—at ABC in the sixties, at Paramount in the seventies, and at Disney in the eighties—all had to do with taking dispirited also-ran enterprises and rolling up his sleeves. (At ailing Paramount, for instance, he picked up films by Warren Beatty and Jack Nicholson and gave them offices on the Paramount lot just so people would see them arriving every day.) Accordingly, he continues to believe that anything he becomes personally involved in gets better because of his involvement.

In the mid-eighties, the Disney brand was something like an abandoned mine that, with new technology, could still yield up a bit more gold. But brands are not infinitely renewable resources.

The innocence and novelty wear off. Disney crapola inevitably becomes less interesting than other, newer crapola. When you get to 500 Disney stores, it's not so easy to envision 500 more or even 100 more or even 10 more. If your synergistic food chain is built on incredibly expensive animated feature films generating theme-park attractions, live-theater events, video sales, plush toys, publishing properties, and on and on, you're screwed if your animated movie isn't boffo. And boffo was no longer what Disney produced.

So Michael Eisner bought ABC. (There is a part of Eisner that has always remained a sixties network guy—his confidence is the confidence of a man who grew up in one of the great easy-money games of all time.)

You might be able to justify this $19 billion purchase, because it included the lucrative cable properties ESPN and Lifetime. But Disney got a network too—it yoked itself to one of the world's most highly visible businesses, one with dwindling market share, exploding costs, and a rapidly deconstructing paradigm. It was a sucker's deal. Eisner thought he had bought the most powerful component of the media business—one of the three major networks—only to find he had acquired an anachronism (like going long on the American auto industry in 1973) that would sap Disney's energy, resources and reputation.

It is against this background—the limits of growth, the whiff of corporate mortality—that Eisner, in 1999, frustrated and furious, tries to reach out and throttle Katzenberg, the little midget, who was, annoyingly, trying to claim more space, more notoriety, more brand identification (Katzenberg, after all, was Mr. Animation, which was what Walt was), than Eisner could temperamentally ever let him claim.

The Katzenberg-Eisner thing was so weird, so extreme, so on-the-sleeve, so futile and unnecessary and just not done (among the most intractable business rules: the one thing that a CEO must never do is engage in a public fight with a subordinate) that it made sense only as a form of corporate suicide. It was not just the billion real dollars *Variety* estimated Katzenberg's departure would cost Disney and not just the incalculable value in corporate goodwill that was squandered, but the cost to Eisner himself of looking like a fool, or, much worse, Moushwitz Commandant and fool. The bad Michael—the raging, maniacal, stubborn, vindictive, for all practical purposes sociopathic Michael—went public, and didn't care who saw.

What's more, as would soon become evident, it was a trap.

In a town of serious enemies, Eisner's were more serious. Michael, people would say, just cannot be trusted. (This is notable—and preposterous—because no one in Hollywood can be trusted.) It is not just the thirty years of double dealing (everybody in Hollywood double deals). It is the sense that only Michael Eisner, over thirty years, had not had his comeuppance.

The fight with Katzenberg was supposed to be the Disney machine against the midget Katzenberg, but it turned out as much to be Hollywood—in the form of the mighty David Geffen and Steven Spielberg, among others—against Eisner.

The whole town was rooting for Jeffrey. Shortly before the trial opened, the trades were filled with display ads of the we-love-you-Jeffrey variety; Katzenberg had just, coincidentally, been given an award by the American Jewish Committee.

What's more, Disney had *already* paid Katzenberg $100 million as part of his settlement. In other words, Katzenberg had 100 million dollars of Disney's money with which to pay lawyers to inflict incalculable humiliation on Michael.

This was pain and humiliation that Michael invited on himself; he wasn't just sadistic (which he surely was), but deeply masochistic, too.

All conversations about Disney, and, for that matter, many other merely idle conversations in Hollywood, end up being about the psychopathology of Michael Eisner. He's the opposite of the powerful emperor whose nakedness nobody wants to acknowledge—rather, he's constantly, and savagely, picked apart.

It's near impossible to convey the way people talk about Michael (almost everybody in Hollywood calls him Michael, oddly, with a deep intimacy)—the quality of the invective, the depth of the bitterness. It is not just the thirty years of perceived betrayals, but that he's stayed in power so long, and against so many unlikely odds, that nobody can imagine a world without him—it's this frustration of being stuck with him that's so infuriating to so many people. He's ingrained, omnipresent. He's just a standard of evil (and when you're the standard of evil in Hollywood, that is really something). The discussion is so extreme that it may partly explain why he stays: There is no place for him to go. Without his position and power, he would be ripped apart by the crowd—like Michael Ovitz.

This is, of course, a very fitting place for Eisner to end up. Ovitz, the most powerful man in eighties Hollywood, and, not incidentally, Michael Eisner's best friend, went to work in 1995 as Eisner's number two, until, in short order, Eisner turned against him. Out of power, Ovitz, in a lesson that Eisner must replay every day in his own mind, was over and over again—until he ended up in tears in *Vanity Fair*—ritually crucified.

But as it turns out, if your goal is just staying in power (unlike other moguls who, foolishly, see being loved and admired as an equal priority), this—the paranoia, the isolation, the denial, the fact that you've worked yourself into a corner that you won't and can't come out of—may be a good management strategy.

Here's the insurmountable hurdle Eisner had to surmount: He did not own, nor could he afford to buy, voting control of Disney—as Murdoch has at News Corp., or Redstone has at Viacom.

There is, I should mention, a corollary to the mogul exception—if you haven't gained such voting-class control of your stock, you will surely be overthrown. Pretty much everybody had been except for Michael.

But Michael created a third way: He couldn't control the voting shares, but he could obsessively control every other detail and every other person in the company. He could turn Disney into a closed kingdom.

The elements of this entrenchment strategy involve, for one thing, longevity itself. Indeed, he had been there so long, and had been so amply rewarded (his package of cash and options in 1998, for instance, was worth as much as $600 million a year), that he became Disney's third largest shareholder (no small feat for somebody who joined the company owning no part of it at all).

Then there's the isolation. The flight of several generations of Disney's senior executives, which is reasonably thought to be a downside of Eisner's management, also had a positive effect for Michael—it dug him deeper in. Nobody could really challenge him. Nobody had the standing to reason with him. (If the people you trust tell you you have to go, then you have to go—but if you trust no one, you can stay.) And, most clearly, nobody was there to replace him. (Few people saw his would-be heir, Bob Iger, who was promoted from ABC after failing to fix the network, as a true alternative.)

There were, too, the yes legions. Over time, Eisner managed to pack the Disney board with his personal retinue: his lawyer, his architect, even the principal of his children's elementary school.

And there was the vastness of the operation itself—not just the vastness but the dysfunctional vastness. The problems at a failing network (and now at the former Fox Family Channel, which Eisner bought from Rupert Murdoch for $5.2 billion to rerun ABC shows), at a declining animation studio, and with exhausted product lines (every time Disney needed a bump in earnings, it flooded the market with backlist releases) were so deep and intractable that nobody would want to fight you for your job.

Then, not least of all, there was the absolute knowledge, on everybody's part, that there were only two ways that Michael Eisner would leave Disney: if he was escorted out or carried out. And nobody was brave enough or big enough to pull that trigger.

There was, finally, the length of the Disney slump itself as an odd, almost sobering virtue—everybody was used to it. After all, Disney wasn't in anywhere near the final-days shape of AOL Time Warner or Vivendi. What's more, it was certainly true, as Eisner constantly repeated, that ABC was—as is always the case with network television—just one hit away from a turnaround. There might always be another *Who Wants to Be a Millionaire?* (which made ABC and Disney look good before the network's slavish, and amateurish, four-nights-a-week dependence on the show made all concerned look very bad).

But it did seem that Michael Eisner, as dug in as he was, was surely now up against it.

Board member Stanley Gold, who represented Roy Disney and

his Shamrock Holdings (one of the company's biggest shareholders) and who led the overthrow of the former Disney Establishment and helped install Eisner in its place, was after him. Then there was a rebel group of shareholders preparing a fight against him. And, indeed, a lively conference topic was the idea of Mel Karmazin as Michael's replacement.

At a hush-hush autumn 2002 Disney board meeting, there were reports of various ultimatums. Among them, the board had to be more independent (although, in something of an Eisner victory, Stanley Gold lost his job as sole chairman of the important governance committee—he now shared the spot with former senator George Mitchell). There were rumors, too, that the board had drawn a line in the sand: Eisner had to name his successor (not Iger) and specify a date for the succession.

And everywhere, there was the rising dust that precedes other moves. The sports teams were on the block. ABC was suddenly serious about merging, or at least about talking about merging, its news division with CNN (although this would come to naught). There were even rumblings of a Disney sale (rumblings that met with the perplexed question "To whom?").

It did seem like it could, really, truly, and finally, be the autumn of the 60-year-old quadruple-bypass chief executive. Or maybe next year.

"I think Michael is fine," said Jim Wiatt, without equivocation, as I tried to politely interrogate him over dinner. "Disney is an asset-rich company. Its issues are its issues, but the company obviously has the resources to overcome those problems. Relatively speaking, Michael is in a strong position."

"Come on," I said.

"Seriously."

"Do you really believe that?"

"I wouldn't say it if I didn't believe it."

He was hardly defending, but he wasn't capitulating either.

It struck me: The weaker everybody else is, the stronger the agents are. Duh.

12
KURT AND
HARVEY

Harvey Weinstein is, oddly, a sentimental favorite in New York. He is far from a mogul—his company, Miramax, is a Disney division; he works for Michael Eisner—but he has wildly exaggerated mogul attributes.

He is obese and grotesque, with a W. C. Fields nose, pockmarked face, and menacing eyes. He's a thug too—he's threatened all kinds of people. He's thrown punches and grappled with people in public. He's a tsunami of PR agents. He's always trying to buy off reporters with favors and charm. He's a great and gross manipulator.

On the other hand, he is generally thought to have good taste. In a world of prefabricated, plasticized movies, Harvey's (*Shakespeare in Love, Gangs of New York, Chicago,* etc.) are, well, less plasticized—less overtly Hollywood.

So the fact that he is not a corporate mogul—not one ounce of boardroom slickness—but rather a street mogul, and that he's ethnocentrically New York, and that he makes movies that recall the days of Cinema, endear him to many people, especially those who don't have to deal with him.

He's a kind of kitsch.

Kurt Andersen was his interviewer over dessert after the first day's banquet dinner.

I believe that this involved a certain sort of irony on Kurt's part—that he might appear to take this lug seriously—but a further part of the irony is that he would never admit to it.

Kurt had been one of the creators and editors of *Spy* magazine in the late eighties. *Spy,* being in the somewhat scabrous and satirical tradition of the British *Private Eye,* had, as much as any publication, identified and ridiculed the behavior and mores and customs of the mogul class. It had seemed, like *Private Eye,* to have occupied an entertaining and, for various powerful people, dangerous cultural and political space.

Spy was certainly among the more emblematic magazines of the era and yet it failed—through a combination of bad luck and too-large ambitions.

Its principals did not, however, fail with it. Kurt became a heavyweight member of the media and cultural class in the city—running *New York* magazine for a period, writing a cultural commentary column for the *New Yorker,* publishing a very long novel about the media industry, and becoming the confidant of moguls, including Barry Diller, for whom he worked as a consultant.

Kurt truly knows everyone—and you would be nobody too important if you did not know Kurt.

One of Kurt's other partners at *Spy* was Graydon Carter, who, in a vast, strange, postmodern-type reversal, became the longtime editor of *Vanity Fair,* the publication most attentive to, and most central for, the mogul class.

Kurt and Graydon, who, before *Spy,* were protégés of Walter Isaacson at *Time,* certainly have a major position in the creation of the modern mogul myth. They helped create it by opposing it, and then by joining it. From radicals to conservatives. Communists to anti-Communists. They were media neocons in a sense.

But not without some self-consciousness.

It was impossible to tell, really, if Kurt respected Harvey Weinstein or was making fun of him.

And because he was maintaining that fine line, it was impossible to build a case for him having sold out, or for all of us having capitulated to the strength and overbearingness and big money of these guys. Kurt had an ineffable way of maintaining his distance. It was a model that many people followed.

We were all just locked in our orbits around each other.

It was raining by the time the dinner finished and there were no cabs on Wall Street. I had to negotiate a ride home in a big white limo.

13
TERRY, PETER, AND JEFF

Steve Rattner was presiding in the green room on the second morning, while Brian Roberts—who, with his father, Ralph Roberts, controlled Comcast, the cable giant—was being interviewed by Charlie Rose on stage, and while the members of my panel congregated. Rattner was a collegial and convivial presence. All the relationships were seamless. Rattner along with Terry Semel and Jeff Bewkes and Peter Chernin all seemed just like guys at a businessman's breakfast.

Semel and Rattner were talking about Brown University, where Rattner had gone and where Semel's daughter was going (it was de rigueur for Hollywood royalty kids to go to a good eastern college—ideally, an artier one).

Everybody was talking jocularly about doing business together and buying each other. And everybody was joking about not knowing what we were going to talk about, which masked some anxiety.

Certainly I would be looking for some public breach, some way to channel through to the unbusiness-like sense of dread and confusion that I knew they must feel. They must.

This was a big opportunity—and I hoped not to waste it.

On a practical level, if the media business lost the confidence of guys like this—the ultimate and real managers—the façade would really start to crack. And I had no doubt that beneath it all they were no longer confident—except now what had to be done was to get beyond their habit of putting on a suit every day and showing up at the office and having great perks along with the moment-by-moment *joie de vivre* of running things.

I had to appeal to what I suspected was, for each of them, an innate sense that they could run these companies more reasonably than the moguls they had had to work for.

Bewkes—like everyone else at AOL Time Warner—surely felt this.

Semel, the longtime head of Warner Bros., had been fired by Jerry Levin—and undoubtedly felt done in by mogul spite and incompetence.

And even Chernin had to harbor some normal person's antagonism to Murdoch. (Indeed, Chernin contributed to Democratic candidates.)

On the other hand, as career employees (although Semel now was, in his retirement years, finally running his own show), they must have a large measure of complacency. That would be hard to shake. Indeed, the "burdens of scale," which undoubtedly gave these guys an amount of daily grief, also gave them their jobs.

Still, I could try to move them—or get them to reveal how far they themselves had moved—to accept what more and more people inside and outside their companies were saying was plain and incontrovertible: that synergy was alchemy. That putting companies together and making more money because these companies could do business with each other—the very concept—was asinine. Relatively speaking on the level of spontaneous generation or cold fusion.

The problem with approaching this head-on was that you were asking people to say in public they had been duped, or that they were dumb. Also, and this was the even trickier point: they *were* dumb. They had many virtues, but the capacity for abstract thought was not one of them.

We lumbered out onto the stage—me leading the way, Chernin in a dark suit and tie, Bewkes slightly less somber, and Semel in sleek salt-and-pepper hair, rimless glasses, and open-necked shirt. The four of us uneasily lined up in mock easy chairs, and then were magnified on a large video screen behind us.

"I have a personal interest question," I began innocently, as though there weren't three hundred people in front of us waiting for the answers to their deep business questions. "Do you guys, like, have TiVos?"

This was my set-up question. It was always interesting to get media producers to talk as media consumers—to see if they would have the same complaints as everybody else.

But they all looked at me vaguely. They were somewhat aware of having TiVos at home, but on the other hand the larger truth struck me that they probably didn't spend all that much time at home.

"I have one," said Semel, with some uncertainty.

"I have one," said Chernin, putting up his finger.

"I haven't hooked it up," Bewkes said.

"Don't you find," I said, pursuing what seemed to me to be an interesting and obvious point, "it's like fifties television again, everybody fights over the TiVo as though there's only one television in the house?"

Silence. Dead silence. Like this was a serious fruitcake sort of observation.

"Not really," Bewkes said.

"You must have a TiVo experience," I said, struck by how they had all not personalized their technology; I didn't know anyone with TiVo who didn't go on at length about how it had dramatically changed their TV habits.

"Yeah, well, we're all trying to figure out how to use it first," said Semel—who ran a technology company—about what was among the most important and unsettling technologies in the media business.

"All right," I said, like the talk-show host who's lost the laugh. "So, Jean-Marie Messier, Jerry Levin, Bob Pittman, Thomas Middel-hoff?"

"Is this a Karnak question—looking into your future?" said Chernin.

I continued: "Unlucky guys, bad apples, tragic figures, or cautionary tales?"

There were titters and slight guffaws in the audience—the comedy and nuances of failure were an unexpected and, I think, guilty pleasure for this crowd.

My panelists all tried to avoid eye contact with me.

"Each one is different," said Semel finally.

"Who is the most tragic?" I continued, knowing none of my panelists was going to talk tragedy.

Bewkes made a noise—a throat clearing—and everybody looked at him.

"I'm thinking," he said.

"These are guys—you know them, you've worked with them, possibly you've admired them," I pressed, "but they've failed, they've been written off, they're out, they've been disgraced—so what do you think? You can't just think nothing."

I was assuming some quality of introspection here, that each of these guys had seen their colleagues fall and that it must weigh heavily on them. They must be dealing with this in the middle of the night. How could they not? The burden of this must be huge, the depression unavoidable. But in fact, they all seemed genuinely surprised by the question—even baffled. It seemed almost to be an eccentric question to them.

Semel finally delivered a careful answer: "They all went down slightly different paths, not necessarily for the same reasons. At the end of the day somebody like Jerry Levin had a very long and very successful run and he believed in the concept, as I do as well, that if you're going to be in the product-making business and control a lot of forms of distribution that the idea of being together with AOL was conceptually a good idea—"

"Yes, but," I interrupted, "don't you find yourself saying if it could go that wrong so quickly for them without any kind of warning signs that it could happen also to me? How could you not?"

I might as well have been asking whether they believed in reincarnation.

I was the one who must have seemed foolish—vastly misunderstanding what business was about. Some guys got whacked, some didn't. Some messed up, some cleaned up the mess. Life went on.

The system was what it was, and you'd be crazy to overly personalize it.

"*I* don't think AOL was a good idea," interjected Chernin, hastily, to clear up any possible misunderstanding.

I pressed: "What I'm trying to get at here by evoking these guys who loom over the business—guys who were absolutely credited with knowing better than anybody what to do at a given period of time—is to suggest the possibility that none of us here know where we're going. That we're proceeding blind in ways that are really serious and ridiculous. . . ."

Unlikely, I realized, that they would all, at this moment, admit to being random elements of a kind of media chaos theory.

"I think online and media is a good idea," said Bewkes, feeling forced, it seemed, to give a brief defense of AOL and to deflect my larger, weirder question. The silence of the audience made me wonder if they too—all these Wall Streeters—might not also wonder where I was going with this weird, meaning-of-life stuff.

Chernin, Bewkes, and Semel all immediately dove in and defended some vague principle about technological convergence and the importance of distribution and the benefits of owning what you needed to own to control your business—clearly better to defend the basic order than to admit that there was no order.

"But hold on," I said. "What you're saying now isn't any different from the assumptions made by the aforementioned gentlemen who are no longer with us."

"It's a price question. We all now know the price was vastly wrong. We accept a dramatic reevaluation of the price," said Bewkes.

"So you're just saying that your former colleagues were bad deal-makers?"

"Yes," said Bewkes, resolutely.

In other words, I was seeing business as a dramatic whole, a psychological reflection, a complex community of relationships—indeed, a thing to be written about—whereas they were seeing it as, well, business. Shit happens. I was the romantic, and these guys were practical, no-frills, nuts-and-bolts guys.

I turned to Terry Semel, trying to probe his sense of the whole: "First—let me ask: Is life better outside the movie business?"

"Is life better outside the movie business?" Semel said slowly. He seemed slightly puzzled for a moment—surprised by the notion that there might be life outside the movie business, or by having to recognize that he was outside it. Indeed, he seemed to regard his move to Yahoo in 2001 as not his real life. "I love the movie business, I totally enjoyed everything I did for 20 or 25 years, but I wanted another challenge. . . ." It is perhaps no surprise that men who have spent their lives hiring people end up talking like they are in a perpetual job interview.

"So—your decision to go to Yahoo was because you had great faith in the Internet business, because you had great faith in ad-driven media, or because you saw Yahoo as a deal vehicle, a synergymobile?"

Obviously, the true answer was the last one.

"No, no, I didn't see it as a deal vehicle," he said, confirming my point.

"Two years from now Yahoo is independent or not?"

"Independent," he said, wanly, meaning, everyone understood, not independent (he hoped).

"Jeff"—I turned to Bewkes—"you've recently moved from HBO, a great company, a terrifically successful company, to managing a vast part of AOL Time Warner, a very troubled company; it doesn't seem to me necessarily intuitive why you would have wanted to do that."

I wonder if Bewkes, who was clearly self-styled as a media executive—that is, a manager of media companies, the larger the better—ever really considered staying put? Or was that just not part of the career matrix? He wasn't a pay-television executive after all—

that wasn't how he would have described himself. And, I wonder if it's really a choice. In any organization if you're called to step up you step up, or, in some way, you step out.

The effect of this, this ambition and this fungibility, is that nobody really does their thing—or that nobody has a thing to do.

The great dream of upward mobility—and a mogul, after all, is just some pathological example of moving ever upward, amassing ever more—means that everything you leave behind is a little devalued. And that, in the end, nobody knows what they are doing.

And nobody ever runs his own shop.

Bewkes started to enumerate the great virtues of AOL Time Warner—of the advantages of having all these companies together, of one being able to augment the other, of the marvelous condition of the distribution side of the company having access to the content side of the company.

"But that's synergy," I said, using the discredited word.

But he disagreed, or at least made the argument against the word. "It isn't synergy. What is synergy?"

I nodded: "That's why we're in this mess—no one knows."

Still he insisted: "Distribution is very important, and linking content to distribution is a very important thing."

I said: "I return to the gentlemen whose names we will no longer mention. This is their argument. They could have said exactly the same thing—I've heard Jerry Levin and Jean-Marie Messier say exactly this."

"Well I'm not exactly sure if they said the same thing," Bewkes replied with just a hit of petulance.

He went on: "There's scale and leverage, et cetera, and horizontal market share and position—what's less clear is vertical. There's a lot of things that can be said to work in vertical distribution."

Semel jumped in to defend the idea of big horizontal and verti-

cal companies and why some work better than others: "The difference comes down to people." That old shibboleth. "Look at
sports—they all wear similar-looking uniforms, but why can one
team get to the Super Bowl and the other team not win another
game?"

"Let me take that people issue and go to Peter," I said, redirect-
ing. "When the age of the media moguls passes, what will it mean
for media companies to be run by mere media executives without a
sense of possessiveness or hubris?"

"I'm not sure I get the real point of the question," said Chernin,
suspiciously, or defensively. "Whether Rupert is a mogul or not, he
has spent 40 or 50 years building a company from a small newspaper
to whatever it is now, and I'm not sure that's a function of hubris or
anything else—but it is a function of understanding the media business."

"So," I went on, "do you think it's reasonable to argue that there
is a difference between Murdoch and Redstone and maybe Steve
Ross and everyone else?"

"Probably about five billion dollars," said Chernin. Slight titter
from the crowd. "Rupert grew up knowing if you put a good headline on a good story the paper is going to leave the newsstand on
Sunday morning and if you don't it's just going to sit there. Same
thing with Sumner knowing somewhere deep inside that if you put
a good movie in those theaters you fill the theater on Saturday and
if you don't put in a good movie you don't."

Was the world of moguldom as banal as this? I wondered.

"It comes down to management philosophy," Semel interjected.
Semel then went on to enumerate the virtues of Steve Ross's management philosophy, with paeans to the decentralization and divi-
sional autonomy that had let Semel become a great power running
Warner Bros. studio.

"I don't think there's a lot of doubt about bigness or scale or about the wisdom of scale," said Bewkes, as though challenged at an important point of his own philosophic identity. "If you take a scale retailer, Wal-Mart, I don't think there's a question about it being too big to manage."

"But Wal-Mart and the media business—you don't see a difference?"

"If you take mixes of five to eight big businesses that are in a different though related media business, some in content, some in publishing, some in networks, some in distribution—I think that's what you're asking—and, yes, it is different from Wal-Mart and you have to have some autonomy and decentralization so that those units don't lose the decision-making capabilities."

"Scale may be a question thing, but lack of scale is a pretty scary thing," said Chernin.

I was definitely getting the idea of how it must be to talk to Japanese bankers about what ails the Japanese banking system.

"Let me just explore if you're wrong about bigness and the virtues and inevitability of scale. Let's just look at what happens if the market goes against you, if the market levies a consolidation penalty, forcing your share prices ever lower, forcing you to deconsolidate—what happens?" I was hoping for a vision of a new world.

Indeed, this is pretty much where we stood now. Over a generation, no media conglomerate had kept pace with the S&P 500. What's more, there wasn't a core business that was stronger now than it was a generation ago.

"You rethink. Do you really need to own cable?" said Bewkes.

You redo the theory, in other words.

"There comes a sense of prioritization," said Chernin. "I can't own everything."

They were, I realized, adaptable.

"John Malone," I said. "At this point in time, do we think he's smart, or . . . not smart?"

This got a big laugh from the audience—because nobody knew.

Malone, who was the greatest player in the cable business, was, I felt sure, the one person everyone here had measured himself against. You might not measure yourself against Murdoch, because he was Murdoch, or against Redstone, because he was eccentric, or Mel Karmazin, because he was always going to be better at selling ads than you, or Michael Eisner, because he was so unloved, or Levin or Case or Pittman because they had been knocked out, but you would have against Malone, because he was purely about the deal.

Out in Denver, Malone had assembled the country's biggest cable colossus. Along the way he had inserted himself into an array of strategic positions in the larger media business, including at CNN, Time Warner, News Corp. and Comcast, and as, often, Barry Diller's principal financial backer.

What's more, on top of deal-doing abilities—mainly a facility with numbers and brute stubbornness—he had the conceptual thing down. That is, he could take a set of contrarian assumptions—cable television is a powerful new force which will disrupt the broadcast paradigm, was a quixotic assumption he had in the late seventies—and project it into the future.

Indeed, these were the elemental mogul attributes: the cleverness to imagine the future, the willingness to shape it.

Everybody admired Malone.

Then, in 1997, near the top of the market, he sold his cable system to AT&T, in the person of C. Michael Armstrong, one of the greater glad-handers, empty suits, and stupids of the communications business.

It was the ultimate deal.

He sold his crummy cable system at full value. As much as sell-ing the lousy pipes, he had sold C. Michael Armstrong a vision of media and telecommunications and delivery and platforms and convergence. *Convergence* . . . yewooo! It was the same stuff that AOL had sold Time Warner.

It was certainly the thing to sell. Armstrong had no more idea than Jerry Levin what this was about.

While clever, the problem was that Malone, like Case and the AOL guys, actually, in some sense, believed it too.

Armstrong became Malone's tar baby.

He was stuck. He couldn't get out. The value of his holdings de-clined as AT&T dramatically declined. He had boosted himself, and overthought himself into what at that time was the biggest mess in the history of the media and telecommunications business.

Since then, as he was stuck in this ongoing and frustrating and hapless winding down and breaking up at AT&T (the cable proper-ties were just going to Comcast), Malone had been making efforts to repeat his strategy with cable in the U.S. in Europe. Now, possibly this was once more brilliant, and he would do it all over again, and even trade up to some future AT&T—but there was also the sense of rather hopeless recidivism. That the guy just knows one trick. And there should be some kind of benevolent intervention.

"Given that he owns 20 percent of our company he's very smart," said Chernin.

"You'd have to say very very smart. Brilliant track record. On the cutting edge, a pioneer, and financially a brilliant person," Semel said, and didn't stop. "One of the reasons I wanted to do what I did is that I always envied people who are pioneers. Being a pioneer to me is being a little patient. We can't expect all of these things to take over the world in a day or two."

"Smart," said Bewkes and then turned to Semel and said, "You're a mogul."

Among moguls, it occurred to me, you couldn't really use the word "mogul." It was either an outsider's, slightly despairing word, or it was something that only the over-the-top and immodest could claim to be.

"I'm a retired mogul," said Semel.

"Fifteen seconds," I said. "Rupert is waiting to join us by satellite."

"The story of my life," said Chernin.

"Have you guys read any good books lately?" I asked as the clock ran down.

Semel (after a beat): *"The Tipping Point."*
Bewkes: *"Biography of Ben Franklin."*
Chernin: *"Lovely Bones."*

14
THE MAN UP THERE

We followed directly into the Murdoch interview.

There was a quick shuffling and the easy chairs were removed from the stage, and I was given a stool, which made me feel just slightly like I was the host of a mid-seventies variety show.

Up above on the movie-size big screen, there was for just a second a hold-your-breath Houston-we-have-contact moment before Rupert came into view.

He was caught unaware—he was not seeing us. At his remote location, he would just be looking into a dark camera lens. Again, I had that sense of looking at an especially unexpected and revealing and affecting face.

It was the face in a way of a writer or intellectual (in addition to being the face of my grandfather). It was the face you get because you've concentrated. Because you have stayed in one position for long periods of time focusing inward. It was all about working through the puzzle. There was nothing social, or gregarious, or posed about his face.

It was true, as Gary Ginsberg had feared, that Rupert seemed somewhat godlike, beamed in from somewhere above.

"Hello, Rupert," I said, not really wanting to disturb him.

Pause. Was his earpiece working?

"Rupert?"

I could hear the satellite echo of my own voice.

Pause. The satellite delay.

"Hello, Michael," Rupert finally said. "I enjoyed listening to that conversation."

I was thinking as I gazed up at him about my thesis that he had held power in this country longer than anybody else in the modern era, and, adding to that, that he was possibly more powerful now than ever before, and, possibly, more powerful than anyone else.

Indeed, it was the Wednesday after the first Tuesday in November and the Republicans had just had one of the most astounding midterm victories on record. This was, arguably, a Fox victory.

Murdoch, through Roger Ailes, was, if not in control of the Republican Party and the conservative movement, giving it its voice. Its confidence. Its moxie.

And then there was the DirecTV deal. He had come to have a dominant role in politics in the U.S. and was now on the verge of controlling the satellite leg of the duopolistic cable-cable U.S. television distribution system.

"How is London?" I asked, convivially. "Do you have jet lag? Do moguls get jet lag?"

"They sure do." He did in fact look tired.

I jumped in, aware of the expensive satellite time (which Rupert was donating): "An easy question for you: If you were the CEO of AOL Time Warner, what would you do?"

As I asked the question, I immediately wondered why, given the vast number of mistakes that Murdoch had made in the formation of News Corp., he wasn't a joke too.

His company had come to the edge of bankruptcy and dissolution in 1991—a shockingly disordered and overextended enterprise. Murdoch had made great and painful and historic Internet blunders; at various points in the age of the Internet, Murdoch had lost more money on digital dreams than anyone else. And now, of course, he was on the verge of the DirecTV deal, which, he must late at night consider, could be his undoing also.

But he responded without equivocation or modesty. Immediately he began to contradict the point of view of the last panel—Semel and Bewkes's view of a decentralized media conglomerate.

"You need forceful leadership in knitting together all these units which have been run as a sort of federation of empires with tremendous independence. I don't see the point of having these things together if they don't speak to each other—if you can have a company with a major subsidiary, Warner Bros. studio, who can ban from the premises for five years the head of the music company"—which, if I was not mistaken, was a direct slap at Semel, who had been the head of the studio who banned the head of the music company.

"So are you saying that if Time Warner goes back to the way it has historically been run, which is as a set of fiefdoms, they might as well just sell it off?"

"Yes."

"Good." Done with that, I thought. "Start placing your bids," I said to an audience that seemed uncertain about the Murdoch certainty.

"Now, as long as I have you here in this forum, Rupert, I want to get your advice. Let's assume there's a new boy on the block—somebody with heart and imagination who is now getting ready to take advantage of what is obviously enormous turmoil and transition in the media business. It could be Charlie Ergen, or it could be a distribution guy, or it could be me, a content guy, or Arthur Sulzberger, a newspaper guy, or Steve Rattner, a financial guy—what would you tell him?

I was also asking something else. I was asking how it felt not to be that boy—to have to look at the field of play and realize you would not be on it.

Indeed, I sensed with Murdoch that it was precisely the field of play that motivated him. That part of the satisfaction was being better than the other people in the business. In fact, this becomes a kind of strategic outlook. If you can analyze and anticipate the moves of your peers, then it tells you how to move. It's a hermetic mogul world. You do things because other moguls do them, or do things at counterpurposes to the way other moguls would do them. It's very 19th-century Europe. You're caught in a very fixed, and nearly zero sum, grid.

"What's your advice? Maybe you can begin with some cautionary words."

"With due respect to Steve Rattner," he said, in a vaguely Churchillian cadence, "I wouldn't recommend that a financial guy become a media guy. Those are two different skill-sets altogether. The media guy will pay for and use the brains of the likes of Steve Rattner"—again I felt the fast air of a swift slap—"but these are different gifts. I heard that earlier bit about moguls and so on. It depends on how you describe them," he said, deviating from my question about advice and instead surveying the mogul landscape. "A hundred years ago you had the Hearsts and the Pulitzers and the Northclifts of the world; in time we've seen the Steve Rosses and Sumner Redstones and Mel Karmazins. Michael Eisner would have to qualify on this list. And others will emerge. Barry Diller is positioning himself now and with what he's about to do he will probably be a major mogul. And just five years ago, who thought that Brian Roberts was going to control 40 percent of all the cable homes in the country? And Arthur Sulzberger is clearly reaching out to do great things with the *New York Times*—make it a global franchise rather than just a national one. There are new people coming all the time and others dying off or going broke."

"Well, this current generation of media executives? What's your frustration with them? What do you think this generation of executives lacks? What talents don't they have? What inclinations do you wish they have but don't? Jean-Marie Messier, for instance."

He used a clear bit of body language—a turning away, a shaking off—to dismiss Messier.

Then, somewhat oddly, he began to make a point about newspapers. "One of my frustrations may be because I'm old-fashioned. I come out of the newspaper world. In America you really only have really good newspapermen and good newspaper organizations in a few remaining cities such as New York and Chicago. The *Times* and the *Tribune*. Across the rest of the country you only have lazy monopolies where their owners take no responsibility for the words they print which are often right out of tune with the interest of their readers. There's nothing interesting in print."

It is odd that in these kinds of public settings you often can find people who seem to be addressing large groups actually talking to themselves. Almost nobody saw the world in terms of newspapers anymore, but clearly Rupert did. There was some dying thing here that obviously bothered him.

"Ever since you arrived in the U.S.—in some sense because you arrived in the U.S. and began to run your business the way you did—the theme of the modern media business has been consolidation. Do you think that theme continues?"

"I wouldn't agree with that at all," he replied, precisely on message. "I think our record has been one of creating or maintaining competition. We created the Fox television network and we were considered mad to do that. We created the Fox News network. We fought very hard to keep the *New York Post* alive. These are competitive things. These are not market consolidators."

Of course, he couldn't admit to consolidation and monopoly. Duh. "I accept that," I backpedaled. "But nevertheless, obviously around you, in a sense to compete with you, we've had massive consolidation in the media industry. Since you arrived in the U.S. a thousand media companies have been essentially reduced to five. Is this the continuing theme?"

"I think you can argue it either way," he said, off message. "I had an argument yesterday that within two years if AOL or Disney got their act together one would take over the other one." This, I imagined, was precisely the kind of discussion that filled his days—and had now for 30 years.

"What side of the argument were you on?"

"I was just, ahhhh, listening in to it." Somehow I couldn't see him as the passive listener. "And, I don't believe that will happen. They'll probably both be there big and strong—but you can also make the argument that if they falter they are more likely to be broken up than taken over whole by anybody."

"Let's look at News Corp. itself and scenarios for the future. Does it acquire? Why won't it be News Corp. that acquires Disney? Or is News Corp. broken up? Or sold—or is there an alternative?"

If I had to read his answer by his face, I'd say he didn't know. Even, I suspected as he paused, this was the great existential question for him. The dream would be, of course, to acquire, to become one of three, or one of two—or the primordial last man standing. And yet, he had to know that was the least likely outcome. In the scheme of things, the media business was still inchoate. We hadn't arrived at a stable automotive or jet-engine design. Nobody would even be able to say, at this point, what our vehicle actually was. Indeed, each of the component technologies—television, newspaper, magazine, celluloid, recorded music—was crumbling. The last man standing was a generation off.

"Disney wouldn't interest me," he said, with another passing slap. "I'm not interested in theme parks or cruise ships, let alone the things that go with them. I think we've got a very full plate of things that we can expand and make more profitable. We can build our station group—certainly if the cap is lifted by the FCC. It's growing brilliantly right now—a great support for our network. We can expand in book publishing—either by organized growth or buying other companies." Within minutes, this statement, I was sure, would be circulating through the higher echelons of Harper-Collins. "We have just made a very advantageous deal in Italy where we are going to be the only distributor of pay television—tremendous upside, probably bigger than SKY in Britain which has to contend with government-subsidized competition and cable. You take these opportunities as they come and they create a pattern. In Brazil and India . . ." he began but then trailed off. "Well, we have a lot of fun around the world."

Helplessly, I loved the sweep of his talk. The certainty. It was hard not to beg for Rupert to buy more.

"Just about a year ago, Rupert, I argued in a column that you would inevitably close the *New York Post*—I was obviously right about that."

"Dream on."

We laughed together.

"Let's talk about the family nature of media companies," I then said, moving to the real subject, the D subject, that I would, of course, not get to. "Is there another family-owned media company that you study and which informs how you talk to your children about the future?"

"I'm not aware of the inner relationships of the other families you might be referring to," he said, seeming to get caught on the question. I wondered if he was thinking about the relationships in his own family or if he stumbled because he was, in fact, keenly aware of the inner workings of other media families. "I certainly look at and respect greatly the Sulzbergers at the *New York Times* and the Grahams at the *Washington Post*. And who knows what's going to happen at Viacom when Sumner's daughter takes over," he added as an interesting slap, I thought, to Mel Karmazin. "I'm too diplomatic to point to other companies that have been passed down where the generations haven't been much good and the companies ended up going broke or getting sold."

Bringing up the Sulzberger family and the *New York Times* lent this a poignant note. Surely, at least from the Sulzberger family's point of view, there could be no two families more inimical. Not only did the Sulzberger family represent a singular tradition of journalistic respectability and responsibility, but they were basically a one-horse operation. Murdoch had an entirely different view of the nature and uses of journalism, and had created a company at philosophic business odds with the Sulzbergers' historic view of what media was. And yet the Sulzbergers had gone on for a hundred years.

It was not a small character note that in some large sense (although one that might not override a host of business decisions), Murdoch wanted that.

"I would be curious to hear—after holding power in this country effectively longer than anyone else in the modern era—what you've learned about being powerful in America."

"You make a lot of enemies." He smiled, and I noticed we were out of satellite time.

"Rupert, our time"—his satellite time, in fact—"is up. I thank you very much and look forward to seeing you in New York."

"I look forward to that too, Michael."

And we were out of there, his face fading from the screen.

15
UNREAL
PROPERTY

Stealing stuff. This was one of the basic themes of the second day of the conference.

The stealing-stuff subject was exciting because it drove business guys into a great lather of agitation, and because it opened the possibility for absolute anarchy in the business. It was the revolutionary element.

There's an almost frightening passion in the way film and music executives talk about people downloading their products for free. It's a moral position. Their fervor is genuine. These normally pretty bland, very business-language-y guys—suits—become incredibly intense and bent out of shape on the file-sharing issue. The ferocity of their counteroffensive—in lawsuits, in government lobbying, in semidemented technological-protection schemes—also seems as personal.

This is real pain—and real fury.

The disconnect here occurs on several levels. For one thing, it is very strange to have entertainment executives—generally regarded as among the most amoral, conniving, and venal of all businessmen—taking the high ground. And yet here they are delivering heartfelt defenses of artists, and even art itself—they see the very essence of the nation's cultural patrimony at risk. And you really don't sense a phony or opportunistic note. Rather, these guys actually seem to be losing sleep over this. It's right and wrong they're arguing about here. Good character versus a virtual barbarian deluge. They believe, with feeling, that bad or sadly misguided people do this digital pilfering. Every time I get buttonholed (at this conference and at almost any media gathering these days) by both suity and formerly hip types (the formerly hip have an especially plaintive air), I find myself feeling incredibly guilty and resolve to have a word with my children about this whole downloading issue.

The other odd thing is that these guys who have built their careers and their industry on trying to give an audience exactly what it wants—no matter how low and valueless and embarrassing— are now standing with a High Church rectitude against the meretricious desires of this same audience. It is a bizarrely out-of-character role: holding the line. Censuring the public. *Suing* the public! Indeed, branding the great American mass-media audience as a craven and outlaw group.

And, personally, I find the technology aspect of the discussion funny too. Almost all of these guys now aghast at the limitless possibilities of digital reproduction are salesmen and promoters and talent tenders, with a limited grasp of the actual mechanics of the products they produce and amazingly short attention spans for most detail-oriented issues. But now, when they buttonhole you, you get an earful about encryption and magic keys and electronic watermarks and digital policing. It's mad-scientist stuff, but it's also a new, determined, almost messianic belief that the technology that caused all this trouble is what's going to save them now.

Obviously, self-interest is the driver of this new effort at radical reformation of the American audience. The music business, which ignored this consumer revolution, is in a crisis that almost no one expects it to fully recover from. It has gone from the most profitable and desirable sector of the entertainment business to the most troubled and reviled. Film executives believe that without Draconian measures, they are the likely next victim. So they're going to war—by whatever means necessary.

But it's not just a selfish crusade. Rather, they think they've seen evil of a kind. It's like Bible Belters in the face of the sexual revolution. It's the end of civilization. It's everyone's reason for being that's under attack. It really isn't *just business.*

They don't, for instance, see file sharing as just a change in the nature of the transaction: a fundamental, but not unfamiliar, discrepancy between the ask price and the bid price.

But here's the merciless trend (which obviously has big and heartbreaking implications for weakened media conglomerates): The price of content keeps falling.

This trend is sweeping and across-the-board. It's not just in music, where the bid price approaches zero. It's in cable television, where hundreds of channels and premium-programming offerings are only incrementally more expensive than the price of a handful of channels. (While the consumer often thinks he's paying more, on a per-hour-of-programming basis he keeps paying less and less.) And it's in the new market-share-grabbing retail strategy of low-price DVDs, as well as the longtime practice of dramatically discounted (indeed, nearly free) magazine subscriptions, and the relentless downward price pressure on once-expensive specialty databases. Information in all its forms gets cheaper and cheaper.

And this isn't just a simple one-cause effect.

There's the Internet, of course, which, flooded with free content, has undermined (to say the least) content value. It has also, as dramatically, altered the idea of the content package—being able to take only what you want and leave the rest has a powerful negative pricing impact. But then, too, there are the desperate or overeager music companies, which have marketed and licensed music so that it has become ever more *freely* atmospheric. Music stars, often as part of great synergy plans, saturate TV shows, movies, and advertising; in addition, since movies and television are seldom scored anymore, cuts from CDs (otherwise for sale) become incidental background music. Music itself, in other words, is now Muzak.

And then there are magazines, which, to court advertisers, have become not just cheap but are virtually shoved down your throat. And there are mass-market-media retail chains—Barnes & Noble, Blockbuster, the warehouse clubs—which have a Wal-Marting effect (as psychological as it is economic) on books and videos. What's more, the ever-falling price of consumer electronic equipment, instead of creating more and more platforms for expensive content, may also have contributed to the general sense of deflated entertainment value.

Ubiquity has become the main media standard.

So this is elemental: The more available content is, the inherently less valuable it is.

In some sense, the anomaly of music and movies is not that they are, suddenly, in free circulation, but that they have existed for so long, against the trend, as paid, premium items. What's more, that the cost of movies (at least in theaters) and music, on a unit basis, has continued to go up instead of down is, in fact, an odd and exceptional business model—which a prudent person should have logically assumed would never last.

While the movie and music people see their lost revenues as a moral issue, everyone else is feeling the pain, too, and trying desperately to buck the trend.

Much Internet business talk is now all about putting content back "behind the wall" and getting people to pay for it. Everybody is dreaming of electronic subscription services (the plan to save AOL seems to be mostly based on the idea of making it the HBO of the Internet). Alas, there are virtually no examples (except porn) of content subscription services working anywhere online. Even the *Wall Street Journal* online service, which has always been the grail of Internet paid-for content, is little more than a break-even operation—and it's had to curtail original-content-creation efforts in order to reach break-even.

In the magazine business, the most coveted number is the news-stand number, even as cheap subs (and, arguably, free Internet content) progressively erode that business. There is, too, a kind of Utopian talk about getting the consumer to pay for actual content value—but I don't know of anyone who really believes that after two generations of subsidies (and now with infinitely greater and cheaper information distractions), consumers would now pay full fare.

The great cable scheme for restoring some kind of parity between content consumed and content compensated for is pay-per-view. Indeed, on my Time Warner system, the relatively feeble pay-movie offerings are being replaced by the kind of vast, play-anytime, choose-anything-you-want system that we used to check into hotels for. The problem is that, so far, nowhere on any cable system in the U.S. has there been any meaningful use of pay-per-view stuff; even for sports it hasn't developed into anything more than a marginal business. We just don't do it. We don't pay for content.

Notably, Europeans do. They slice and dice and pay for content in droves. From the TV, from the cell phone, from the PC.

But paying for content—at least content for content's sake—

has become an un-American trait. We believe in getting it all, a bigger and bigger bundle for a lower and lower price. The flat fee rules; we don't even pay for long-distance telephone calls anymore. And a flat fee is very close in function and perception to no fee.

It's easy to understand why for the movie and music guys it's primal-scream time. They maintained a very basic relationship with the consumer—we make, you buy—which suddenly was messed up, not least of all by the media empires to which the movie and music business belonged.

The West Coast movie and music guys have always had a simpler view of the world than their New York counterparts. Indeed, their New York counterparts have always treated the movie and music guys like dimmer cousins. Just off the farm in many ways.

They just didn't understand how the whole media view came together, how synergy happened. In the empire's view, consumers had to be *made* to consume—growth depended on media being everywhere, media being transparent, a utility. And as with a utility, it was better that you not really even be aware of how you consumed the product. It would just be on and available all of the time. The way to do that was to commodify the product and to make it ever cheaper—or in the case of the Internet, to make it free—and then to figure that with a giant audience and vast brand awareness and utility-like dependency and this incredible cross-platform cross-marketing apparatus and an instant star-making and self-promotion machine, you couldn't help but make a big pile of money for the conquering empire. ("DISNEY TO PUSH RETAIL GEAR TIED TO ITS TV SHOWS," read an ever-so-hopeful headline in the *Wall Street Journal*.)

The thing that I always try to say to the movie and music executives frothing at the mouth about this stealing issue (accusing my children and, one might fairly suspect, their own) is that *everybody* can't be an outlaw. If everybody does it, it's normal rather than aberrant behavior. It's not so much the consumer who is on the wrong side of the law, but the entertainment industry that's on the wrong side of economic laws.

It's the transition from high margin to low margin that the media business seems to be having the most psychological trouble with.

For instance, the music business doesn't end, or even face true obsolescence. Rather it just becomes something like—however horrifying this must be to almost everybody in the music industry—the book business.

Hemingway, after all, had rock-star status (and even impersonators). Steinbeck was Springsteen. Salinger was Kurt Cobain. Dorothy Parker was Courtney Love. James Jones was David Crosby. Mailer was Eminem. This is to say—and I understand how hard this is to appreciate—that novelists were iconic for much of the first half of the last century. They set the cultural agenda. They made lots of money. They lived large (and self-medicated). They were the generational voice. For a long time, anybody with any creative ambition wanted to write the Great American Novel.

But starting in the fifties, and then gaining incredible force in the sixties, rock-and-roll performers eclipsed authors as cultural stars. Rock and roll took over fiction's job as the chronicler and romanticizer of American life (that rock and roll became much bigger than fiction relates, I'd argue, more to scalability and distribution than to relative influence), and the music business replaced the book business as the engine of popular culture.

Now, though, another reversal, of similar commercial and metaphysical magnitude, is taking place. Not, of course, that the book business is becoming rock and roll, but that the music industry is becoming, in size and profit margins and stature, like books, a pop culture afterthought, a nearly starless province, a quaint thing.

There'll still be some big hits (Celine Dion is Stephen King), but even if you're fairly high up on the music-business ladder, most of your time, which you'd previously spent with megastars, will be spent with mid-list stuff. Where before you'd be happy only at gold and platinum levels, soon you'll be grateful if you have a release that sells 30,000 or 40,000 units—that will be your bread and butter. You'll sweat every sale and dollar. Other aspects of the business will also contract—most of the perks and largesse and extravagance will dry up completely. The glamour, the influence, the youth, the hipness, the hookers, the drugs—gone. Instead, it will be a low-margin, consolidated, quaintly anachronistic business, catering to an aging clientele, without much impact on an otherwise thriving culture awash in music that only incidentally will come from the music industry.

This glum (if also quite funny) fate is surely the result of compounded management errors—know-nothingness as well as foolishness and acting-out (suing college kids). But it's way larger too. Management solutions in the music business have, rightly, given way to a pure, no-exit kind of fatalism.

It's all pain. It's all breakdown. Music-business people, heretofore among the most self-satisfied and self-absorbed people of the age, are suddenly interesting, informed, even ennobled, as they become fully engaged in the subject of their own demise. Producers, musicians, marketing people, agents . . . they'll talk you through what's happened to their business—it's part B-school case study and part *Pilgrim's Progress.*

Start with radio.

Radio and rock and roll have had the most remarkable symbiotic relationship in media—the synergy that everybody has tried to re-create in media conglomerates. Radio got free content; music labels got free promotion.

Radio's almost effortless cash flow and mom-and-pop organization (there were once 5,133 owners of U.S. radio stations), made it ripe for consolidation, which began in the mid-eighties and was mostly completed as soon as Congress removed virtually all ownership limits in 1996. A handful of companies now control nearly the entirety of U.S. radio, with Clear Channel and its more than 1,200 stations being the undisputed Death Star.

Radio, heretofore ad hoc and eccentric and local, underwent a transformation in which it became formatted, rational, and centralized. Its single imperative was to keep people from moving the dial—seamlessness became the science of radio.

The music business suddenly had to start producing music according to very stringent (if unwritten) commercial guidelines. (It could have objected or rebelled—but it rolled over instead; what's more, in a complicated middleman strategy of music brokers and independent promoters, labels have, in effect, been forced to pay to have their boring music aired.) Format became law. Everything had to sound the way it was supposed to sound. Fungibility was king. Familiarity was the greatest virtue.

Once Sheryl Crow was an established hit, the music business was compelled to offer up an endless number of Sheryl Crow imitators. Then when the Sheryl Crow imitators became a reliable radio genre, Sheryl Crow was compelled to imitate them.

But then, just as radio playlists become closely regulated, the Internet appears.

File sharing replaced radio as the engine of music culture.

It wasn't just that it was free music—radio offered free music. But whatever you wanted was free, whenever you wanted it. The

Internet is music consumerism run amok, resulting not only in billions of dollars of lost sales but in an endless bifurcation of taste. The universe fragmented into subuniverses, and then sub-subuniverses. The music industry, which depends on large numbers of people with similar interests for its profit margins, now had to deal with an ever-growing number of fans with increasingly diverse and eccentric interests.

It is hard to think of a more profound business crisis. You've lost control of the means of distribution, promotion, and manufacturing. You've lost quality control—in some sense, there's been a quality-control coup. You've lost your basic business model—what you sell has become as free as oxygen.

It's a philosophical as well as a business crisis—which compounds the problem, because the people who run the music business are not exactly philosophers.

"They're thugs," says a former high-ranking music exec of my acquaintance, who is no shrinking violet himself.

Such thuggishness, when the business was about courting difficult acts, enforcing contracts, procuring drugs, and paying off everyone who needed to be paid off, may once have been a key management advantage. But it probably isn't the main virtue you're looking for when you're in a state of existential crisis. Being street-smart is not the same as being smart.

In a situation of such vast uncertainty, with the breakdown of all prior business and cultural assumptions, you don't necessarily want to have to depend upon, say, Sony music head and former Mariah Carey husband Tommy Mottola to create a new paradigm.

For a long while, the management response at the major labels had a weird combination of denial and foot stamping: putting Napster out of business—then sort-of/sort-of-not buying Napster—all the while being told by everybody who knows anything about technology that no matter what the music industry does or who it sues, music will be, inevitably, free. Duh. There is, too, a management critique—perhaps most succinctly put by Don Henley in his now-famous post-Grammy letter wherein he quoted Mel Brooks in *Blazing Saddles:* "Gentlemen, gentlemen! We've got to protect our phony baloney jobs!"—that sees record labels as generally engaged in the usual practice of ripping off anyone who can be ripped off while remaining oblivious to the fact that Rome is burning.

But for the most part, denial, and even the reflex to just keep squeezing the last dollar until there is nothing left to squeeze, is passing. (Labels have even recently awoken to the problems of dealing with the radio behemoths and are frantically, and way too late, trying to find reasons to sue the radio guys and gain back a little leverage.) Acceptance is the lastest stage: We simply don't know what to do.

The truth is, there might not be anything much to do.

Here are the choices:

If you're providing free entertainment, which is obviously what the music business is doing, then you have to figure out some way to sell advertising to the people who are paying attention to your free music. But nobody seems to have any idea how that might be done. Or you can provide stuff that's free, and use the free stuff to promote something else of more value that people, you hope, will buy—now called the "legitimate alternative." (Putting video on the CD is one of those ideas—though, of course, you can file-share video too.) Or sell the CD at a price that makes it cheap enough to compete with free (free, after all, has its own costs for the consumer).

It's a spreadsheet solution. There will continue to be a market for selling music, however diminished—but it will have to be cheaper music. Margins will shrink even more. Accordingly, costs will have to shrink. Spending a few million to launch an act will shortly be a thing of the past. A&R guys making half a million are also history (in the future, they'll start at $40,000 and max out at $150,000). And no more parties.

And then there is the CD theory. This theory is widely accepted—with great pride, in fact—in the music industry. It represents the ultimate music-biz hustle. But its implications are seldom played out.

The CD theory holds that the music business actually died about twenty years ago. It was revived without anyone knowing it had actually died because compact-disc technology came along and everybody had to replace what they'd bought for the twenty years prior to the advent of the CD.

The music business, this theory acknowledges, is about selling technology as much as music. From mono to stereo to Walkman. It just happens that the next stage of technological development in the music business has largely excluded the music business itself.

The further implication, though, might be the more interesting and painful one: You can't depend on just the music.

Rock and roll is just an anomaly. While for a generation or two it created a go-go industry—the youthquake—it is unreasonable to expect that anything so transforming can remain a permanent condition. To a large degree, the music industry is, then, a fluke, a bubble. Finally the bubble burst.

But not with a pop. It's an almost imperceptible, but highly meaningful, alteration in context. Alanis Morissette becomes Grace Paley. Bono becomes John Hersey. Fiona Apple is Joyce Carol Oates. Moby is Martin Amis.

This is not so bad.

And best of all, our children—all right, our grandchildren—won't want to become rock stars.

Howard Stringer, interviewed by Heilemann during lunch on the subject of file sharing and the future of the music business, was a world-weary presence. He had come out of the news business and risen through the ranks of network television and found himself on top of an anomalous media empire as chairman of Sony America. Sony had been slated to take over the media world a generation or so ago, but had faltered when it realized it had paid too dearly for what it had bought, and then when the Japanese economy fell apart, and finally when it learned that all of this hardware-software-cross-platform synergy stuff was, relatively speaking, bunk.

Stringer had been, one might imagine, a voice of reason here, having to explain to the Japanese that most of these media sugar-plum visions were never going to be realized. Indeed, having endured the disappointments and humiliations of being an also-ran media empire, Sony America was relatively healthy now. Except for its music woes. And even here, it was amusing to hear Stringer on the irony of the company's reverse synergy—Sony, with its myriad listening devices, actually benefited from people stealing music.

Stringer, a cheerful ironist, was in some way a model for a post-media mogul. Although he too said it was a terrible, terrible thing that college kids everywhere were stealing all this stuff, and obviously felt compelled to play the stern father, he also, I would bet, got the joke.

16
THE BIG
EVENING

Something was going on that had not been spelled out. There was a bit of social underhandedness—and awkwardness.

The Foursquare program listed a reception at the National Museum of the American Indian, another impressive building downtown. But it turned out there were two receptions at the National Museum of the American Indian. One exclusive and one non.

This was it, of course: No matter how exclusive you got to be—here, for instance, you were at a $4,000-a-ticket conference to mix among the titans of the most important industry in the world—there was still, always, a more exclusive level to get to.

The hoi polloi among the elite had one event, the elite among the elite had another.

It was stunning to me that the elite of the elite had the gall to be so openly standoffish—and the precision to have so finely tuned the hierarchical distinctions.

It was equally stunning that the rung just below the elite of the elite did not immediately rise in open revolt.

Partly, they did not rise up because they had been tricked. They had not been told they were excluded or that there was any other event happening anywhere else.

We were all just sheep being herded out of the conference venue and toward this other venue somewhere out beyond. There were uniformed conveyers posted to guide us on the streets of New York. And there was special signage and even chalk marks along the way. It was very organized, even momentous. There was even the sense of this being worth the $4,000—or, at least, it not being a disappointment. It didn't seem like anybody had cheaped out.

Except that I was walking with Pam Alexander, and as we talked about where we were going, and what seemed to be going on, it became increasingly clear that we were talking about different things.

First, she tried to reconcile the apparent differences. And in her reconciliation it seemed, for a moment, that she was also going where I was going (although I had my doubts). But then in her further, somewhat obsessive, pursuit of the social details, it became hard to maintain this illusion.

I had gotten a guest list. She had not.

I was expecting dinner. She was not.

I had had to confirm several times. She hadn't even had to confirm once.

She stopped suddenly on the street. In pain. Bereft.

There was a moment, too, in which she blamed it on herself. Had she not answered an email, returned a phone call? She tried to recall something her assistant had said to her she was supposed to do.

But soon enough, and more painfully, she came to blame it on the Sisyphean struggles of life itself.

Here she was, one of the greatest event organizers of our time (well, at any rate, of the boom—and of course the boom had passed), someone who had made a literal fortune on figuring out how to penetrate to the innermost circles of the innermost conferences, a woman who would pick up Rupert Murdoch by the scruff of the neck and take him to a bar—only to now find herself excluded.

She knew the point, of course. The boom had passed and she had taken her fabulous nest egg and, well, relaxed a bit—which is a kind of suicide in the business of climbing ever higher. The price of not being excluded for a single second is eternal vigilance, and absolute graspingness, and a tireless capacity to work the phones.

And Pam had faltered.

It was a hard blow.

This wasn't pretty at all.

Here was primal social pain.

I had to get away from her.

At first chance, I maneuvered around and caught up with Steven Levy, who had moderated a panel on the future of computing which I had skipped. Levy, laconic and dyspeptic, worked for *Newsweek* and was one of the great reporters of the technology business. He had been in the business before the boom and would be here after. Indeed, he wore the boom and its aftermath like a personal burden. He was not, I wouldn't have thought, your most likely moderator.

But he was one, and I assumed the reason I'd been invited to the elite status affair was because all moderators were included.

Constrained by the social realities of having had to walk here with the spurned Pam Alexander, I suddenly relaxed with Levy, helplessly gossiping about the excluded and the included, and assuring him that we both were in this special circle.

Even as we arrived at the clearing point—young PR women behind a desk checking names and discreetly directing elite traffic one way and superelite the other way—I, unhesitatingly, pulled

Levy along with me (it is, after all, always good to have a friend when you go into a strange room and an uncertain crowd), as I headed down the long superelite corridor.

But then, just as we reached the checkpoint into this other sanctum—even on the approach you could see the dark wood of a rare and exclusive interior—a team of forceful PR girls intercepted Levy and led him off, helpless.

I had erred. He might also have been a moderator. But he was not welcome or included here.

I went into the dark, ornate, lovely, something-to-do-with-Indians room.

17
THE GUEST LIST

Ken Auletta	Staff Writer	The New Yorker
Zoe Baird	President	Markle Foundation
Jeffrey Bewkes	Chairman, Entertainment & Networks Group	AOL Time Warner Inc.
Hon. Michael Bloomberg *	Mayor	City of New York
Richard Bressler	Senior EVP & CFO	Viacom Inc.
Tina Brown	Columnist	The Times of London
Graydon Carter	Editor in Chief	Vanity Fair
Stephen Case	Chairman	AOL Time Warner Inc.
Peter Chernin	President & COO	News Corporation
Barry Diller	Chairman & CEO	USA Interactive and Vivendi UNIVER-SAL Entertainment

* Cocktails only

James Dolan	President & CEO	Cablevision Systems Corporation
Timothy Donahue	President & CEO	Nextel Communications
Michael Elliott	Editor-at-Large	Time Magazine
Peter Ezersky	Managing Principal	Quadrangle Group LLC
Dennis FitzSimons	President & COO	Tribune Company
Gary Ginsberg	EVP—Investor Relations & Corporate Communications	News Corporation
Robert Glaser	Chairman & CEO	Real Networks Inc.
Donald Graham	Chairman	Washington Post
Christie Hefner	Chairman & CEO	Playboy Enterprises
Andrew Heyward	Chairman & CEO	DIC Entertainment
Walter Isaacson	Chairman & CEO	CNN
Mitchell Kertzman	Chief Executive Officer	Liberate Technology
Andrew Lack	President & COO	NBC Inc.
Russ Lewis	President & CEO	New York Times Company
Susan Lyne	President	ABC Entertainment
Craig McCaw	Chairman & CEO	Eagle River
Mike Ramsay	Chairman & CEO	TiVo
Steve Rattner	Managing Principal	Quadrangle Group LLC
Brian Roberts	President	Comcast Corporation
Ralph Roberts	Chairman	Comcast Corporation
Charlie Rose	Host	Charlie Rose
Kevin Ryan	Chief Executive Officer	DoubleClick

Ivan Seidenberg	President & CEO	Verizon Communications
Martin Sorrell	Group Chief Executive	WPP Group plc
Josh Steiner	Managing Principal	Quadrangle Group LLC
Martha Stewart*	Chairman & CEO	Martha Stewart Living Omnimedia
Howard Stringer	Chairman & CEO	Sony Corporation of America
Arthur Sulzberger Jr.	Chairman & Publisher	New York Times Company
John Sykes	Chairman & CEO	Infinity Broadcasting Corporation
David Tanner	Managing Principal	Quadrangle Group LLC
Jack Valenti	President & CEO	MPAA
Harvey Weinstein	Co-Chairman	Miramax Films
Robert Weinstein	Co-Chairman	Miramax Films
Jon Weiss	Managing Director	JP Morgan Securities Inc.
Jim Wiatt	President & Co-CEO	William Morris Agency Inc.
Michael Wolf	Director & Senior Partner	McKinsey & Compaany Inc.
Michael Wolff	Columnist	New York Magazine

* Not yet confirmed

18
♥ MARTHA

Unconfirmed Martha was who I most wanted to see. Even more than Case, she was the pariah of the moment. But it was not just the macabre fascination that attached to her—it was some other thing that made many of us flutter.

She was nasty and brutish to many people, but never to me. I only ever got the sudden look, the laugh, the glow, the tough-tender aside. She really was quite a dame—and a pure media thing.

I can't begin to count how many times I've heard somebody say "Think of this as the Martha Stewart of . . ." or "The idea is to create the Martha Stewart for . . ." or that he or she could be "the next Martha Stewart." (Or even the subvariation—I once knew an investment banker who was always touting his wife as a Jewish Martha.) Countless people have undoubtedly thought to themselves, *I could be the Martha Stewart of . . .* (I myself could be the Martha Stewart of media criticism.)

This came to be called, in a catchphrase of the boom (and then in a derogatory sense after the boom), being your own brand. But the Martha concept went well beyond that. The idea was embodiment. Representation. Mimesis. Perfection. *I am my own worth. I am my own value. I am my own definition. I am the perfect articulation. I have become who I am.*

It was about the narrative as business. Martha was marketing the back story. If you were a non-businessperson, a non-counter-of-beans, then Martha represented true commercial hope: You could start a business, a fabulously successful business, that was not about business. Your interior life could become a commercial life. It was the dream of authors everywhere—except you could be a writer without having to write. You could be your own fiction.

Martha really is an entrepreneur—unlike those business-school wannabes. She is an independent. No organization, except her own, would have tolerated her.

She was tougher than anybody else. Going back twenty years, she started to do little deals, then put bigger deals on top of the little deals—deals everywhere; it was life as a licensing scheme.

As a rule, somebody like Martha almost always gets screwed in these sorts of deals—the kid with heart and imagination gets squeezed by deal-makers and lawyers. But Martha paid attention. She outdetailed everybody in a detail game. She never let go. (You just know when she got the call that Sam Waksal was selling Im-Clone stock, she wasn't going to let herself be screwed like that— her crime, if any, was a *fuck-him* reflex.) She gave everybody the shiv before they gave it to her. She did a deal with Time Inc. to start up *Martha Stewart Living,* then got her magazine back from Time because she was too tough, too hard-nosed, too tactical, for even the tough guys at Time.

In negotiations and in carriage, we are talking about a most remarkable control. Absolute discipline. On message. Within theme. Never missing a beat.

And then there's the business itself. It's the first postmodern media empire. The Martha business is the ultimate guerrilla-marketing strategy: using the media to promote your media. It was the mirror trick, the infinite-reflection principle. Everything you did promoted everything else you did. In an age in which media could no longer stand on its own, you had to come up with an approach that allowed you to get paid for promoting yourself (the dot-commers were always trying to be Martha, but they didn't understand that Martha always got paid to be Martha). This endless advertisement loop is the Martha monument.

And now it was being brought down.

For the prosecutors, she was a special kind of trophy. The Feds were piggybacking on her brand. Martha's sin (she did, after all, grab the money) was not their foremost preoccupation—rather the publicity for prosecuting Martha was what they went to bed at night and woke up in the morning thinking about. Who doubts this?

And then there was the Establishment's disdain. Entrepreneurs, while paid great lip service and occasionally mythologized, are seldom anybody's favorite people. They're always in the process of sucking up to somebody while alienating somebody else (sucking up while alienating down). What's more, they're taking power from somebody else. It's a zero-sum media world: If you're the flavor of the month, somebody else isn't. And so, after twenty years of Martha's striving, you had a very large group of people in the media business who hated Martha's guts. (Talk to the people at Time Inc.)

As for the rest of America, it enjoys a ritual burning.

But let's look at this through Martha's eyes. She saw this not, I suspect, as a horrifying, Joseph K.–type reversal of fortune but as part and parcel of the never-ending effort of the bastards to get an advantage over you. This was, of course, denial, a refusal to accept your own crookedness, and it's no doubt what the Dennis Kozlowskis of this world thought too.

But let's also give truth its due—it's business, and people are out to get you.

So what do you do to stay in business?

If the overwhelming amount of your equity is built into the goodwill that attaches to the name Martha Stewart, then, by definition, by the time your trials (in the press as well as in the courts) are finished, the idea of Martha Stewart, exquisitely besmirched, would be valueless.

Prosecutors—and other media—were taking Martha's equity in the form of anti-Martha equity. It's black-hole stuff.

Martha in prison: That's the picture—not just a stark one but a broadly comic one. (The laughing-at-you-not-with-you thing is very bad in the image business.)

This isn't like, say, Steve Madden, the shoe guy, whose name is on the door and the insoles, who had recently gone off to jail for various financial shenanigans. We don't know Steve. He's a pure brand—he's only incidentally a person. (Many designers, after all, continue to design clothes long after they're dead—so why not from a jail cell?)

Martha was more in a Pete Rose bind—she'd dirtied something pure. Of course, there was a lot of willing suspension of disbelief here—we didn't really believe that Martha or Pete or baseball was pure.

Martha may be more George Steinbrenner–like. In Steinbrenner, who pled to a felony charge in the seventies, you already had a quintessentially moneygrubbing, I-take-what-I-want sumbitch. Steinbrenner the felon is not that different from Steinbrenner the nonfelon. He could, therefore, after an appropriate time out, recommence his management of the Yankees.

Martha is, we know, also a moneygrubbing, I-take-what-I-want sumbitch. Susan Magrino, Martha's longtime PR consigliere, should have gotten her head around this. The strategy should probably have been to jettison the old Martha image and suggest that a felony charge and conviction are a natural part of the Martha story. That being your own brand requires a nastiness and greediness and megalomania that make prosecution always a possible outcome.

The theme should have been My Way. Sinatra is of no small relevance here.

Most of Sinatra's career was under a cloud. At several points, it seemed sure he was headed for indictment. If Johnny Roselli hadn't ended up stuffed in an oil can, who knows what would have happened to Frank.

In part, Frank was tougher than the prosecutors. But nobody can really be tougher than the Feds.

You can be more talented, though. Frank sang his way out of trouble.

Could Martha pot or darn or sauté—I'm not sure I can quite get the parallel here—her troubles away?

The point is about talent. The Feds were trying to make Martha out to be Kozlowski—just your average business crook, ever fungible. Who will miss Kozlowski? Will the world be lesser without him? But Martha is, I believe, unique. She has vast, if eccentric, talent. For presentation, for look and feel, for brandedness, for media itself. (I'd argue that it is so hard to make a successful magazine of any sort that if you do, you deserve a type of immunity.)

Hugh Hefner could be instructive here—indeed, I saw his

daughter, the iron maiden, Christie Hefner, across the room having a glass of wine.

Hef got into trouble in the eighties. It was gaming-commission stuff. His empire teetered. He lost the Playboy Clubs—the empire's jewel.

Hef was as identified with Playboy as Martha was with Martha.

In many ways, Hef and the Playboy concept are the real precursors to Martha—not only live the lifestyle, but Omnimedia-ize the lifestyle. Playboy, too, like Martha Stewart Living Omnimedia, in a moment of hubris, became a public company. This was an error—the greed factor, which is why, of course, Martha was in her present mess. Having a public company means that the world is going to be judging the monetary value of your identity instead of the quality of your talent.

What was necessary for Hef and Playboy—and what may now be necessary for Martha and her enterprises—was a period of debranding. (This may be a larger trend in an overbranded world—even AOL Time Warner was considering getting rid of the AOL.)

Playboy became a kind of generic concept of airbrushed girls rather than a heroic concept of a new lifestyle. Likewise, Martha would have to turn into a well-executed upper-middle-class design-accessory company rather than the incredible story of Martha herself.

Come to think of it, Martha, like Hef, should probably put her daughter in charge of the company. The deal she should really have tried for while she still had bargaining room was house arrest—not unlike Hef in the Los Angeles mansion.

Whatever happens she'll still be Martha—who paid the price for iconhood.

I scanned the room—everybody was looking for her—but no Martha anywhere.

19
TINA

But I saw Tina Brown. In fact, in her hapless manner—when she's on her own, without minders, which she has been more and more since her magazine, *Talk,* closed, she tends to be hapless—she had wandered into the less-than-elite-of-the-elite reception and had to be retrieved and brought back to this special room.

Many people who have taken personal satisfaction in the fall of Tina Brown, trade in hapless-Tina stories. Mine was once to have, one morning, picked up a newspaper in the lobby of the Carlyle Hotel, and, on my way out, run into a woman in an outsize raincoat, with a refugee-like scarf around her head, weaving toward me. She seemed confused, or in some distress, or so nearsighted as to make you think immediately of Mr. Magoo. She reached out to steady herself on me and, in an English accent, which made her seem somehow even more befuddled, asked, "Do you know the way to Madison Avenue?"

"You're actually *on* Madison Avenue," I replied, looking at her closely and realizing, suddenly, that the discombobulated woman was Tina Brown.

This story, which I've long dined out on, and which everyone

MICHAEL WOLFF

I've told has enjoyed enormously, is an example of backlash. You could not have told this story a few years ago. People would not have been receptive to it. It would have said more about the teller (that you were envious of, or worse, unknown to Tina). Or it would have been understood in a different way. It might have even seemed charming, humanizing (at the height of her power, people often spoke of her vulnerability).

Whereas, at this moment, everyone understood it as caricature. Belittling. Farcical. Possibly exaggerated (was she really weaving? Really wearing a scarf like that?). It fit the current thinking: Tina Brown was a lost figure who could no longer even find her way to the main thoroughfare of her life and career.

Tina, even more than Martha, may be the most vivid exponent of the media life to have been brought down—in some sense she may stand in for all of the others who the crowd secretly, and not so secretly, wishes to see toppled.

Indeed, the failure of *Talk,* launched in 2000 and dead two years later, was the most talked about thing about it.

Why did the shuttering of a magazine that never had much of a following, that couldn't ever define itself, that wasn't particularly talked about, and that by some substantial consensus was expected to fail, attract so much interest?

What an anticlimax.

You could fairly say that *Talk* magazine had been destined to close ever since its second issue was published. But I think the slow-motion, you-saw-it-coming-from-a-mile-away sense, with everyone playing a part in the debacle, with the operatic levels of denial and umbrage and soldiering-on, and then the inevitable shuttering anyway, were all part of the attraction.

While *Talk* never managed in its pages to summon the Zeitgeist, or find the tone of the time, or create the heat that its editor, Tina

Brown, was famous for creating at *Vanity Fair* and the *New Yorker,* it did manage to mirror the real thing that was happening in the culture, which was that every big-deal thing was failing. Indeed, *Talk* was launched just as all of the boom-time expectations that had been raised—the new economy, the new media, the new earnings multiples—began to crumble.

Talk became the perfect expression of these dashed expectations. The magazine, which envisioned itself as a great new vehicle of promotion and mythmaking, became the embodiment of hype de-flation. On the subject of failure and unrealizable expectations and the undoing of invincibility and celebrity, it was something like per-formance art.

Talk failed publicly and unself-consciously (it was not aware enough of what it was doing to be self-conscious), and also instruc-tively: It was a detailed primer on how not to publish a magazine.

True, it worked overtime to create the illusion of success. But unlike, say, Enron, which snookered the stock market and the media (not to mention the President), *Talk's* illusion seemed to work mostly on the people working at *Talk* (although *Talk* seemed to have snookered the Clintons—Chelsea even became one of *Talk's* name writers). *Talk* got the trickery backward. *Talk* worked its magic on the wrong people. It fooled itself.

For the rest of the interested world, it was an absolutely trans-parent enterprise. There was the thickness of the first issues and the thinness of ensuing numbers; there was the constant and well-documented turnover of the staff (writers and editors were always rolling their eyes about their *Talk* experience); there were the article miscues (a steady stream of over-the-hill or irrelevant actors and actresses on the cover); there were the damning newsstand sales (it was widely reported that *Talk* was selling only 20 percent of its news-stand distribution); there was the sniping from Hearst, a partner with Miramax in the *Talk* venture; indeed, there were the disparaging remarks from Miramax chairman Harvey Weinstein himself (likewise, the *Talk* people disparaged Harvey).

And yet, at the same time, there was the apparent belief at *Talk* that this was normal. Tina was always going on about what it takes to get it right. Great magazines require great suffering, she seemed to be saying. She appeared to have convinced herself that *Talk's* dysfunction, and, for that matter, her own dysfunction, were somehow the building blocks of success.

In fact, it was not hard to see that one of the key problems of *Talk* was Tina herself. In a logical enterprise and a rational universe, she would have been fired. Except that she was the only reason for the magazine's existence. Who would have wanted the magazine without her? She was the value proposition. All the goodwill was bound up in her. She was the asset—and she was rapidly depreciating.

There was, vividly, over *Talk's* two-and-a-half-year life, the transformation of Tina Brown from princess of the media-celebrity-market-power culture to one of its dispossessed. (At the same time, her husband, Harry Evans, the former editor of the *Times* of London and one of the most famous journalists of the era, was also sliding down the power ladder.) There was even a visual morph, from sexy, glam, high-style power babe to dowdy, bad-hair, no-style lady (she who had raised superficiality to perhaps its highest expression was suddenly complaining that she was the victim of sexist stereotyping). She began openly, albeit awkwardly, to express her hurt and anger. It was all downward spiral.

She seemed to become something other than the real Tina. She was a hoax. Or, cruelly (she is right that people were cruel to her), she started to seem like a nuthouse version of Tina Brown. She was someone claiming to be Tina—with the other patients and a kindly hospital staff humoring her.

There was a lot of pretend (and bizarre) behavior.

The *Talk* party to celebrate the Golden Globe awards, held the night before she and publisher Ron Galotti told the staff the magazine was closing, was either grand denial, financial irresponsibility (they should have been retrenching months ago—kill the parties!), or pathetic pretense: *We must put on a good face for the stars.*

Over the course of *Talk*'s two years, beginning with her famous Statue of Liberty bash, there were always the parties. Tina as media hostess. Tina as celebrity arbiter. Tina as she was when she had all that Condé Nast money and power behind her. It was Tina pretending to be who she no longer was.

Strangely, trying to imitate successful business magazines that hold conferences where attendees pay thousands of dollars, she inaugurated a series of *Talk* conferences called "Innovators and Navigators." She invited celebrities and opinion-makers and anyone who was anybody—but, neglecting the key element, and no doubt fearing she'd be stood up, she didn't make anybody pay. It was, in other words, just a costly illusion. You have a conference but not a conference business.

There was, finally, no value to Tina's ability to attract celebrities (although the *Talk* staff would desperately argue that this was of great value to Miramax—that the publicity itself was worth it, that *Talk* was a legitimate marketing expense for Miramax and its movies).

Tina has always had a reality-distortion field around her. Things became larger around her, more interesting, more important. But in the end, she was standing alone in that distortion field.

She was, by the end, more interesting for how she came to be—and what that said about everybody else and how they tried to be like Tina and how they were willing to treat her royally—than for what she was.

There was even a dreadful book about Tina and Harry—*Tina and Harry Come to America,* by Judy Backrach—which briefly was the talk of the town.

The book, which details the couple's professional, social, and sexual histories (here is a universal lesson: Whoever you sleep with will someday talk about it—plan accordingly), was itself part and parcel of the backlash—an unrelenting, not-very-nuanced indictment of character flaws, professional conflicts and compromises, and a host of other unkind social acts written for an eager, and bitterly predisposed, audience.

Still, as compelling as all these tidbits are, the more telling point about the book was that there is no smoking gun. There's no deed, or event, or betrayal, that provides a clear explanation for why the crowd would want to tear Tina and Harry apart—why they should have become such a cautionary tale. Indeed, they really have not behaved differently from most other hyperdedicated media careerists in Manhattan.

In fact, what the book outlines is a Horatio Alger story of get-up-and-go, shoulder-to-the-wheel, how-to-do-what-you've-got-to-do-to-get-ahead-in-the-media-business savvy. I'd recommend it to anyone who is starting out. It's a fine manual.

Rule No. 1: Don't sleep with just anyone; make your couplings count (Tina's college-age liaisons included Dudley Moore, Auberon Waugh, and Martin Amis, and culminated at the age of 21 with Harry Evans, a national monument in British journalism).

Rule No. 2: Learn how to give a party (which is different from learning how to party).

Rule No. 3: Cultivate the press (publicity being the currency of our time)—best done by throwing parties.

Rule No. 4: Get to know some celebrities (which takes work, but it's easier than you think) and invite them to your parties.

There is the strong suggestion in the book, and on the part of the many people I know who obsessively rehash Tina's and Harry's careers, that there is something shallow, vulgar, and possibly immoral about their way of career building. And yet there is virtually nobody who is a success in the media business (Tina and I are the same age, and I found myself, as I read *Tina and Harry Come to America*, awed by her precocity—with just a little more energy and fortitude, I could have, I think now, learned how to throw a party) who hasn't followed some of these precepts. Tina (and it is always Tina, more so than Harry) is in a terrible trap: We are enamored of her because she was such a success; we are repelled by her because of what it took to be a success. (There's surely a woman's point to be made here—a man is respected for his wiles, a woman trashed for hers.)

The media class is not usually so ambivalent about success, but success, no matter how much you've had, becomes something else when it's coupled with failure—e.g., *Talk*.

Psychoanalyzing the backlash, we're bound to get to the formulation that it's not about them; it's about us.

There was an obvious codependence. We were each other's enablers. It was an age of excess, of overweening ambition, of greed, and phoniness, and sucking up, and the glorification of strange, obnoxious, preening, uninteresting people. And Tina Brown and, by association, Harry Evans, had the misfortune of coming to stand for all this (not to mention having made us participate in it).

I wonder, too, if the backlash doesn't also say something about the general-interest-magazine business. Tina's *New Yorker* and *Vanity Fair* may have been the last gasp of the magazine as social chronicle. By spending huge amounts of money and through constant vainglorious acts of self-promotion, and by creating a subculture of editorial dirty pool (if you could help the magazine, or Tina and Harry, you were stroked; if you could neither help nor hurt the magazine or them, you were fodder), she supported a dying genre. Everyone in our business cheered her on, hoping out of self-interest that she would succeed, but when she didn't (and, I might argue, she couldn't), we all distanced ourselves from her embarrassing and desperate acts.

Likewise, she helped import to New York, and the constricting publishing business, an English sensibility. Because in the publishing world there is so little room to maneuver and there are so few opportunities, it was fertile ground for the development of a class-based, hierarchical structure, which she at *Vanity Fair* and the *New Yorker* and Harry as editor in chief of Random House reigned over. In this system, you're always kissing up to the people above you, but at the least sign of weakness (places in the firmament being so scarce), you rip them apart. The fact that she ran three magazines that competed with each other only increased the strain. Indeed, the author of *Tina and Harry* is a *Vanity Fair* writer; the perception, certainly at *Talk,* was that when Tina went down, *Vanity Fair* and Graydon Carter went up.

Then there's the Hollywood thing, which was the magic potion Tina sprinkled on a magazine (and which fit the spirit of a self-aggrandized era).

Her father, George Brown, was an English movie producer; she came of age when the movies were the hottest sector of media (and also had a foreigner's awe of Hollywood); she transposed British class hierarchies to America by elevating Hollywood celebrities. But now, as the result of various cultural transformations (for instance, new technology, which Tina has seemed really dim about), the movies have become peripheral and disposable (certainly *Talk* magazine was a cavalcade of celebrities one could care less about); it's a bottom-of-the-class business. It isn't where the heat is; nobody takes movies seriously anymore. Hollywood, which once made Tina look hip and powerful, now made her look craven and silly—and like a dumbo for not getting that it's so over with.

Ironically, Tina and Harry turned out to be bad at playing the media game (doubly ironic because they had the game fixed for so long—no one would say anything bad about Harry and Tina because everyone was on their payroll or invite list).

They had, it turns out, no appreciation of the rhythms of thrust and parry. Bad press sticks to some people (and then increases geometrically), while other people brush it off. The process of brushing it off involves a certain level of self-confidence—you have to be able to not take it seriously. Whereas Tina is always chewing over her bad clips, calling reporters and attempting to recast quotes, having friends call reporters, deploying PR agents. And Harry, while in one life a crusading journalist, is in another an enthusiastic libel plaintiff.

They wound easily. They're paranoid. They're Nixon-like. They're thin-skinned.

Worse, they set themselves up. You don't throw the party of the century to launch a fledgling magazine—I mean, anybody who knows anything about managing expectations will tell you this.

It is the self-confidence issue, though, that may go to the heart of the matter. To some degree, I wonder if this doesn't have to do with a structural anomaly of their success. Tina, especially, achieved massive notoriety of the kind associated with the biggest payday (hence engendering the most resentments). She should have been rich. She became an international brand name. But because she was, in reality, just an employee (and at *Talk,* despite her best efforts to become a mogul, *continued* to be just an employee) and because her successes, at least from a profit-and-loss standpoint, have been mostly illusory, she never made her fuck-you money.

And the money is where the confidence and the respect come from—it redeems you. Not having the money means you're just a sucker. Which is, in essence, the social rule propounded most forcefully and unforgivingly by Tina Brown.

20
AND STILL
MORE
COCKTAILS

"You're everywhere!" Tina Brown said to me, moving from the dark, ornate outer room to the inner room where dinner was to be served.

"No, *you're* everywhere," was my weak rejoinder.

Tina's estimation of me stung. I had to wonder if being here meant I'd achieved a certain carte blanche: If there was a media party, I'd be invited to it.

But, if so, why? I could be counted on to write snide and mocking things about anyone who had a measure of power in the media business. Of the nearly fifty people here in this momentous room, I'd written unkindly about half of them.

Indeed, Barry Diller, with drinks in both hands, came gliding by not a foot in front of me. "Michael," he said, in courtly fashion, "I'd shake your hand but fortunately I'm holding two drinks."

Perhaps the people here were less wounded by what I had written about them than they were amused by what I had written about their colleagues and competitors. This was the zero-sum view: Everybody was there to see everyone else fail. I was part of the failure function. I was an angel of media business death. I articulated the nuances, even the poetics, of failure. Still, you would not necessarily think that that talent would earn you fancy invitations.

I huddled in the room with the least famous and powerful: Gary Ginsberg, who was here because he had facilitated Murdoch, and Michael Elliott, an Englishman and editor at *Time,* and moderator of the closing panel on the news business, who was here for no reason that he could quite put his finger on.

Steve Case, who for many years now I had written about as a great pretender, greeted me without awkwardness.

I could only figure that to be here, to be *in*—to have made it over the social and career hurdles, to have gotten through the hierarchical gauntlet—meant you should be here. Of course, this was not so much a precise meritocratic point as a mirror trick—we accept you because you're accepted. I was one with Steve Case. I found this unnerving.

There was the further point that I was not *just* writing about the people here in withering fashion, but that I was regularly writing about the thing that they were most interested in. Not just the failure of their colleagues and competitors, but the comedy of it. I was, in my fashion, a light society writer. An up-to-date Cleveland Amory, the old patron of society and animal shelters. Or a British-style gossip or diarist. Auberon Waugh (with whom Tina Brown had had a youthful affair).

Likely, nothing so interested everyone here as our thing—*la cosa nostra*—itself. And if you were devoting as much time as I was devoting to appreciating this thing, to valuing it and therefore celebrating it, at the same time you were dissecting or deconstructing it, well of course you'd get an invitation. I was Mario Puzo.

And then you could go back to the political thing, the Walter Lippmann possibility. A column, by its constancy and ubiquity, is a weird and powerful instrument. Just by the fact that it is always there, every week, carping, hazing, reminding, grinding its axe, it becomes a piece of reality, a creator of reality. And, on that basis, everybody submits to it. And gets used to it.

Of course, the other reason I might be here would have nothing to do with having been invited, or being wanted or accepted, but with having inserted and insinuated myself.

This would, to some degree, be a reporter's accomplishment— I'd gotten up close to the most powerful people of the age. I was a successful hack: I'd wheedled an invitation to the weekend at the country house. I was *that* reporter.

The one with his face—his smarmy face—pressed to the glass.

And myriad resentments bubbling up.

In other words, I could not be sure my version of scathing criticism was not precisely tailored to be the scathing criticism that would be most appealing to the people here. I was an enabler not just of the grudges and cutthroat competition that pervaded the media business, but of the solipsistic notion that we were all inside this perfect bubble. Indeed, I helped define the parameters of the bubble, as certain Washington reporters helped define what lay within the Beltway. This was the meta thing. Meta gave both irony and gravitas to what we did. The delicious incongruity between our superficiality and our importance. The *joie de vivre* of self-referentialism. The stupendous, intoxicating power of being able to create the world we lived in—of this being the thing that executives could never discuss on pain of overweeningness and arrogance and self-parody, but which I could discuss for them.

And then there were my personal aspirations. My Zeligness.

It was a critical-mass function: If you knew enough people, were known to enough people, then you were part of the whole. Part of the network. If you're on the minds of a majority of the planners of the guest list, then, with some predictability and inevitability, you become a guest. And if you are a guest at this event, then likely you become a guest at the next event—that you become part of the idea of any event.

That was the deal.

Not ten minutes after the cocktail party began, the mayor was suddenly directly and unavoidably in front of me, short, jowly, but counterintuitively appealing. Helplessly, I began to apologize. I couldn't stop. Everything I had written about him, I dismissed, cringed about, set fire to. I went well past the point of simple social niceties.

The more the mayor beamed—even blushed a bit—the more I grandly apologized. Why not?

21
PINCH

The dinner was hosted by the two friends, Steve Rattner and Arthur Sulzberger Jr.

It was unusual to see the *Times* chairman and publisher in such a full-blown, media-honcho setting. The *Times,* for so long, had held itself out from not just bare-knuckle media games, but from the philosophical notion of media itself.

The *Times* was the *Times.* Period.

Its counterpoint was *Time* magazine. A generation ago, the New York Times Company and Time Inc. were close in size, businesswise, and in stature, culturally (although *Time,* historically, was more Waspy Republican, to the *Times'* more Jewish Democrat leanings). But Time Inc.'s merger with Warner Communications turned it into something as far from the *New York Times* as a media company could possibly be (while at the same time, interestingly, changing the company from WASP Republican to Jewish Democrat).

The *Times* maintained an almost stoic distance from the consolidation of the media world.

Arthur, though, you could begin to infer—not least of all because of his long friendship with Rattner—was more and more impatient with this stoicism. Indeed, Arthur has the thing the Sulzberger family has traditionally and conspicuously not had: executive-itis. He likes to run things. He likes to put his mark on things. He is not transparent. He does not have, nor does he have much use for, a light touch.

Change is his mantra.

Like many other CEOs, he sees the organization as an extension of his views and sensibilities and ambitions. He's a would-be Jack Welch.

Almost every story that people tell about conversations with the *Times* publisher is somehow about his bluntness or flippancy—his tone issues. About him saying this or that person is an asshole, or about how something is all fucked up, or about some other swift, colloquial, often disparaging, unmediated remark he has made.

Some time ago, when I called Arthur about doing a formal sit-down interview, he said he would think about it. When we spoke a few days later, he said, "I've really thought about it, and you know why I don't want to do it? Because I hate *New York* magazine."

Many people have conflicted responses to his brusqueness or unceremoniousness—or superciliousness.

First, it's a little scary. You have a person with such great, even august, power, apparently not at all mindful of what he says. You're afraid for him—that he might lack a certain order of self-control. Candor becomes aggression.

And then you're afraid for yourself.

What does it mean when the chairman and publisher of the *New York Times* thinks someone is an asshole? What does it mean when the chairman and publisher of the *Times* says he hates my magazine?

But then you find yourself wondering if it isn't refreshing. The point is not that he talks differently from anyone else but that he talks just like anyone else. You could be friends. Why not? He's quick and funny. He's got an open smile. Bright eyes. Great hair. Let's go have a drink.

Then it gets confusing. Because you've separated him in your mind from the *Times*—in a way that you would never have separated his circumspect and courtly father. It's not just that you've differentiated Arthur Jr. from the *Times* but that you have great trouble reconciling the two. Arthur in bearing and tone doesn't seem *Times*ian at all. He isn't earnest. He may be smart, but he isn't thoughtful. He isn't highbrow, or obviously culturally minded, or even recognizably a Jewish liberal—indeed, he gets annoyed when people assume that just because he's from one of the great New York Jewish families, he is Jewish (he was raised as an Episcopalian).

He seems, in a sense, more cut out to be a tabloid editor. He could be one of Murdoch's sons, or any ambitious upstart in the media business.

What he does not seem to be is the self-effacing steward, in a long line of self-effacing stewards, of the world's greatest newspaper.

The relationship of the *Times,* or more precisely the *Times* newsroom, to the Sulzberger family is an intricate, complex, and—despite the various books devoted to the subject—mysterious one. It is, arguably, the most successful relationship between staff and proprietor in journalism history. It's not just the relative noninterference of the family in newsroom matters, or the remoteness factor—the *Times* editor functions more or less as prime minister, and the Sulzberger family, the *Times'* controlling shareholders, as constitutional monarchs—but also the historical willingness of the controlling shareholders to see themselves as subordinated to the larger idea of the *Times.*

Nobody seems to have assumed—as you might with any corporation that gets a new top executive—that as part of Arthur's taking control, the company, and hence the paper, would naturally go in a dramatic, unsettling new direction.

The elevation of Arthur to controlling executive has been, in fact, a glacial process. As recently as three years ago, when I asked Joe Lelyveld, then the executive editor of the paper, to speak on a conference panel, he could say that seeing as how he really didn't have time for conferences, why didn't I ask Arthur? (While this was probably as dismissive as it seemed, it was, I think, an acknowledgment that Arthur likes to speak to groups, that he is outward-looking in a way that the *Times* has not traditionally been outward-looking.)

And yet it has happened. Young Arthur, as he is still persistently called (along with the belittling "Pinch"), has certainly taken charge. He has won various executive-suite battles with his father's retainers. He has won various family turf feuds with ambitious cousins. And, in the figure of Howell Raines, he installed a guy as executive editor of the paper who spoke with his kind of I-don't-care-ness in the newsroom. Indeed, Arthur may be the first member of his family to actually exert day-to-day management over the newsroom, trying to move it from its cautious, culturally insular, frequently obsessive-compulsive identity as World's Greatest Newspaper into a more freewheeling, glamorous, un-*Times*ian World's Greatest Information Brand.

As it happens, by most modern executive standards of dealmaking and decisiveness and quarterly results, the motorcycle-driving publisher is good at his job. He may well be quite a talented modern media executive.

In the media world, the business side of the *Times* has, for a generation at least, been something of a joke. Indeed, if you were in the media business and ended up at the *New York Times,* you were a joke. Even within the *Times* itself, you were a second-class citizen. The increasing stature and importance accorded to the business side at, for instance, Time Inc. and then at Time Warner did not reach the *Times* business side. After all, businesspeople at the *Times* just had to do what had been done for a hundred years—keep the paper going reasonably well. And do no harm.

But under Arthur, the business operation at the paper has steadily—and stealthily—awakened.

Four daily sections have grown to as many as eight (much more for advertising purposes than news concerns), big investment has been made in new production facilities, and a largely local audience has been transformed into a growing "national footprint." An urban paper has gone suburban.

At the conference that Joe Lelyveld had handed off to Arthur (this was in the spring of 2000), I asked Arthur about his then-rapt interest in the Internet. My question was about why the *Times* was now getting swept up in this faddishness when it had so successfully—or diffidently—resisted other media enthusiasms. "If you could rewrite your family's history," I asked, "would you have wanted the Sulzbergers in, say, 1953 to have made a big play for television?"

"You bet I would!" he nearly yelped.

Indeed, under Arthur, the *Times* has acquired, in addition to the eight network affiliates it already owns, a half-interest in one of the cable channels owned by the Discovery network.

And, in a mogul-worthy bit of business cruelty, Arthur pulled a fast one on the *Times'* longtime partner in the *International Herald Tribune*, the Washington Post Co., and gained full control over the (long-ailing) *IHT*. (This was "exactly what Ben Bradlee would have done," said Arthur, grabbing at the mantle of the *Post's* fabled and aggressive editor. Bradlee promptly responded by saying Young Arthur had "hijacked" the *IHT*, which would never have happened "if Arthur Sulzberger Sr. were still in charge or if Katharine Graham were alive.")

This new business audacity is informed by a new business language. Sulzberger is, he recently told an interviewer, "agnostic about the method of distribution"—which is to say he has no overriding commitment to a newspaper as the medium. "It's about cross-selling," he has said, embracing the synergistic vision of other media conglomerates. It's clearly the strategic view—market share, competitive positioning, franchise extension, category dominance—rather than the newsroom view, that more and more informs the direction of this international information franchise.

The *Times*, notably, *is* part of the consortium of media companies—which, as notably, did not include the *Washington Post*—that, during the autumn of 2002, was petitioning the FCC for regulatory changes that would allow them to own newspapers and television stations in the same market.

There is, I think, a denial mechanism among people in the *Times* newsroom that allows them to believe that while Arthur may be out to change the direction of the Times Company, that entity is somehow different and remote from the paper itself.

Indeed, the Times Company has always been involved in disparate, marginal ventures almost entirely irrelevant to the business of the newspaper.

And Arthur, no doubt, would be among the first to deny that corporate concerns would in any way redirect the mission of the newsroom.

And yet, everywhere you read the tea leaves at the Times, there was the story of the diminishing returns of a regional newspaper company versus the much greater potential of an ever-expanding information brand.

Nor did it seem like happenstance or mere hospitality that Arthur, with his banker friend, Steve Rattner, was hosting this conclave of moguls.

Not long ago, a former *Times*man I know had occasion to talk with Arthur Sulzberger Sr. and to ask conversationally what he thought of his son's paper. The senior Sulzberger replied, without directly answering the question, that the heyday of the *Times* was in the seventies.

This may not have been as much a reflection on his son's stewardship, or on the quality of the paper itself, as just an acknowledgment of a world where flagship-driven, proprietor-run media companies once happily thrived. The seventies, after all, were the heyday for Time Inc. and the three networks and the *Washington Post* too.

Arthur Jr. is in a different world—which he may or may not successfully navigate. But it's his ship.

It's his company. He's the mogul.

The strategic question that the profane, smart-alecky, impatient publisher always seems to be asking at his favored form of discourse, the corporate retreat, is, How profoundly does the *Times* change? The tactical question is how to keep the extent of the metamorphosis from people in the newsroom. Or, more complicated: how to get the people in the newsroom to facilitate the change without their being aware that that is what they're doing.

You wouldn't want to appear in the third-floor newsroom and try to explain that the *Times* has many good qualities that are worth preserving, but the paper and its publisher also have ambitions in a larger, polymorphous media world. Where the audience is different. Where the values may be different. Where the priorities are different. Where being the newspaper of record is an equivocal value proposition. Where cross-platforms demand a certain . . . plasticity.

Even Arthur wouldn't want to just blurt this out. This requires some finesse.

Anyway, Arthur was making more or less charming remarks at the dinner, including, in a Dean Martin sort of way, going on about the virtues of many martinis.

22
THE FINAL
DINNER

I was seated next to John Sykes, who ran Infinity Communications, the second biggest radio network in the country (after Clear Channel) owned by Viacom.

There were seven or eight tables, each with six men and one woman, with everyone served a very big piece of meat, without vegetarian option.

The deal was that at each table, we were supposed to discuss the future of the business (topics provided) and, once again, try to answer that hoary question: *What's the next big thing?* Then, over dessert, Charlie Rose would lead us in a Socratic inquiry. (I'm not kidding.)

Now, it is hard to imagine that most people here did not find this a little childish, or bush league. On the other hand, because this was the media business, the *mass* media, there is always an effort to re-create or imitate the bush league and the childlike—to be like ordinary folk. Also, I think, famous people like to see other famous people subjected to a measure of control and discipline—just a whiff of humiliation. This was, of course, a room of sadists.

Then, too, everybody here is a performer of some order—and wants to go to the head of the class.

And then there was the Sulzberger *New York Times* thing—*we should be serious.*

Still, I think everybody found the topic to be somewhat embarrassing. First, because it was old-hat. At the very least, two years out-of-date. What's more, there was the pervasive sense that there was no next big thing. Or certainly no big thing in the way the question was meant, no coming wave of enthusiasm, no profound and transforming fork in the road, no *voilà!*

It was not really a question worthy of this kind of firepower.

But a parlor game was a parlor game.

There was a brief exegesis on the room we were sitting in by one of the officials of the National Museum of the American Indian. She hurried through the presentation.

Then Steve Rattner gave a short after-dinner welcome and turned the floor over to Charlie Rose.

I wondered if Charlie was at all put out about having to perform for his supper like this.

But there was something reassuringly itinerant about Charlie. He was willing to ply his trade.

The discussion got off to a lackluster start with Zoe Baird talking at some meandering length. Zoe Baird is most noteworthy for having been the first Clinton nominee for attorney general and then having been dinged from the job and semidisgraced because of having failed to pay taxes for her nanny. But she had risen after that and taken over the Markle Foundation—a sponsor of the conference—which had, in the go-go years, opportunistically rededicated its mission to the Internet, a subject that Baird, like so many other people who got onto this particular bandwagon, knew next to nothing about. What's more, the foundation had been recently excoriated in a long article in the *Times* for wild overspending and expense account abuses and failing to accomplish most of what it said it would accomplish. Baird spoke blandly and earnestly.

Walter Isaacson also spoke blandly and earnestly, but it was his particular ability to make the bland and earnest somehow of moment. He lent it intensity. He lent it at least the expectation of intelligence. When Zoe Baird spoke nobody listened; when Walter spoke everybody listened.

Everybody was very earnest. It was like a book club meeting or a really painful wedding.

Nobody had anything above the level of uninteresting to say.

But the real point was that nobody knew the answer to the question.

And this was not an insignificant point.

Everybody here, in greater and lesser ways, was seriously fucked. And while nobody was going to come out and say that, nobody was going to give a good-times-are-just-around-the-corner speech either. It was, finally, a very awkward choice of topics.

Barry Diller, when Charlie called upon him (Charlie knew that everybody always wanted to hear Barry speak) was the only respondent to move off the bland and earnest. He expressed with equal parts wit, condescension, befuddlement, and even a certain sort of humility that he did not remotely have an answer here to what was the next big thing. (And, in fact, he may have known.)

Mostly I was waiting for this to be over. I found it all awkward and embarrassing. You wanted it to pass. You didn't want to participate. You didn't want to be that sort of hotdog. To participate was just to call for attention—which prolonged everyone else's agony. And yet, a few times my eyes brushed past Charlie's. I wasn't entirely listening here, and every time I did listen I got more annoyed because nothing was being said—and even more annoyed because people were going through the motions of saying it—and, so, expressing my impatience, as well as my deep need to go to the head of the class, I caught and, for a just a second, held Charlie's eye.

He called on me.

I wasn't any less self-serious than anybody else.

But I thought, why not? What was there to lose? And might not there be something to gain?

Nail the thesis to the door.

The next big thing, I said (and took a breath), was that we were going to find out how unhappy everybody is in the media business.

I said I knew this because "the people who work for you" call me up constantly to complain. Even some of the people in this room have called me up to complain about how rotten and unsatisfying and dispiriting and ridiculous the business is.

Hello?

Nobody, I went on, can possibly enjoy or get satisfaction from working inside such colossuses. Everybody's in their particular Soviet Union.

There is a dark and growing rage in the ranks. While we partied, the media business was rebelling from within. (Granted, there was not a lot of evidence of rebellion—still, there was certainly lots of passive aggression.) It would be pulled apart by a bigness-induced psychosis, as well as by the ever-growing pressure and sure futility of the search for the next big thing.

Charlie was looking at me with some concern.

And there was that pin-dropping silence feeling.

I had surely gone too far. I'd brought too much emotion here.

What could anyone say? Yes, we've mismanaged everything. We've screwed it all up. Sucked the big one.

But I was right. And, if the people here didn't think it was true about their own companies, they certainly thought it was true about other people's companies.

I thought I should just charge on. I should force this point. I had the floor. I should hold it. Fifty of the most important people in the media business gathered together—a veritable Mafia retreat—I should make them listen.

Instead, I sat down. Sank. Was ashamed of myself for trying to say this, was ashamed of myself for not insisting further.

Charlie called on Ken Auletta. I interpreted this as a further slap. It was sort of, Let's hear from an adult journalist. A real inside journalist. A voice of experience. I had a sudden, overwhelming, blind hatred for Auletta. For his prissiness and sanctimony and his willingness to stroke these guys and his interest in being on their side.

He said, rising, "I think Michael is right."

And, as though there were a sudden rising background musical score, the entire tone of the room changed.

This was partly, on Ken's part, just kindness and generosity— the same kindness and generosity which made everyone like Ken, and, which, on Ken's say-so, now made them think better of me.

And yet, if Ken was saying this too, or accepting it, what everyone realized, and what I understood too, is that the conventional wisdom was in fact heading in the direction of what I was saying.

And indeed, the question of the next big thing was, in so many words, just another way of locating the conventional wisdom.

There was a gravitational pull here; the forces of negativity were out there and getting stronger every day. Various people in this room were going to have to pay for other people's dissatisfaction and unhappiness.

Ha!

23
BARRY
TRIUMPHANT—
SORT OF

In the morning, Charlie and Barry took to the stage.

This was very exciting. Barry is imbued with all kinds of currents. Violence and humor and playfulness and toughness and sensuality and hard-nosed financial acumen.

You want to get close to hear what the legend has to say, not least of all because you don't know which legend will be talking: the charming or the surly.

It's quite unfiltered too. Reflexive. Depending on his mood. What he had for dinner last night. *Who* he had for dinner last night.

Here's my precious Barry Diller story: On a Saturday morning a long, long time ago, the *New York Times Magazine* sent me to interview Diller, then the chairman of Paramount Pictures. ("He's the new 400-pound Hollywood gorilla," said *Times Magazine* editor and future movie producer Lynda Obst.) I met him at the home of his then-consort, now wife, Diane von Furstenberg—a flocked-wallpaper apartment on Fifth Avenue overlooking the Central Park reservoir. In an open-neck shirt—as bald at 39 as he is now, a sort of cross between Mussolini and Picasso—and no socks, holding a large glass of juice and sitting in a massive upholstered chair, Diller said to me, shortly into our conversation: "You know, you can't say anything about my personal life." Most shocking was that the 400-pound gorilla had a kind of whiny voice.

"Of course," I said, fumbling, "only to the extent that your personal life is relevant to the story." He was not only a megagorilla but, every whisper agreed, a gay one in what was still, in the late seventies, a highly homophobic business.

"No. I don't think you understand," he said in his discordant whine. "I would kill you."

(Note to libel lawyers: While I did not actually believe that he would kill me, I do not think anyone had or has ever spoken to me in exactly the same way before or since.)

After a horrifyingly long pause, he said, suddenly brightening: "Well, I understand Simon & Schuster"—a Gulf+Western–owned company, as was Paramount—"is going to be publishing a book of yours soon. I hear great things about it. We'd like to take a look at it at Paramount."

Imagining my film career, I called the *Times Magazine* that Monday morning and resigned the piece. In due course I found myself on a conference call with Michael Eisner and Jeffrey Katzenberg—then Diller's lieutenants at Paramount—asking me to explain to them what I had told Barry to get him so interested in my book and offering me a first-class ticket out to the Coast. In short order, I was sitting out by Barry's pool in Coldwater Canyon—just Barry and me and houseman—as he talked in the most contemptuous language I had ever heard about the power elite of the movie business. This was dissing of an extraordinary order.

Oh, yes, he never did buy my book.

Still, for years afterward, I could do a parlor trick. I could dial Barry Diller's office number and he would immediately come to the phone.

Nearly twenty-five years later, when he was told that this was a story I circulate about him, he responded, winningly, with the epigraph for this book: "I should have killed him when I had the chance."

The threat, the charm, the joke.

He was Sinatra—as perfectly and as classically and as elegantly and as frighteningly Hollywood as you could ever be. Even Barry's suits equal the perfection of Sinatra's during the Capitol years.

And he was as successful as Sinatra and in similar ways. People were afraid of him. The fear thing was huge. A vast business advantage. People gave you what you wanted; they didn't risk offending you with negotiations; they didn't cheat you at the edges. They gave you wide berth; they gave you more rather than less; they tried to curry favor.

Fear is a great business tool.

Everybody in this audience was looking at Barry and was a little afraid of him. You could feel the way people were on the edge of their seats. If Barry had turned to this audience and smiled and then said "Boo!" everybody would have jumped an inch.

Barry's story was surely the story of the moment and there was the sense that it would all, very shortly, come to its dénouement.

What would he do with Universal?

He was toying with this company. He was the big cat and the company was the little mouse.

You sensed his tactile pleasure—he held the company, torturing it.

They hated him at Universal. No, "hated" is not strong enough.

By all accounts, Ron Meyer, who had been running Universal for the past several years, who had withstood Bronfman and Messier and ill fortune of so many kinds, and Doug Morris, at Universal Music, who was pretty much the only guy in the music business to still be running a viable enterprise, weren't just at odds with Diller, the part-time chairman, but were made physically ill by him.

There was sadism here.

And yet Barry was doing his job. His job was not to protect Universal—not yet, at least—but to protect his odd interest in the company, the money, the various billions due him, and to preserve his options. To buy the company for the lowest possible price, even to lower the value of the company, certainly to probe all of its weaknesses, so that he would know what he was buying, and know more than the people who were selling it to him.

Here's another point: Barry had become unhitched from the corporation, from even the idea of the corporation.

The corporation—that is, these big, dumb, blundering, blind collections of almost invariably badly run and underperforming assets—was there for him to abuse.

There are guys who grow up in the corporation and then, because of ill winds, get set adrift and they never quite get anchored again. But then there are guys, like Barry, cut off from the mother ship who realize that they hold all the secrets, they have seen the blueprints, know the playbooks, possess the exact same DNA. Hence, they can become a kind of evil twin.

Having been inside, and now outside, you know every deal, and you know every deal-maker, and you know where all the money is, and you know too much for people not to want to make a deal with you, which, because you know what you know is going to be a good deal—you're always buying low and selling high—so more and more people want to do deals with you, want to be on your side (although, of course, they never really are on your side), which means you are the man.

The cash flows.

You're a predator.

Yours is a protection racket.

Everybody wants you inside pissing out.

It *is* all about you.

You really are free.

If, as Barry surely does, you see the world as a world of numbskulls and incompetents and servile morons, then it is an ideal place to have arrived at.

It's an interesting order of corporate nihilism.

Yes, seeing Barry as the media nihilist makes sense. The last mogul. The angel-of-death mogul.

What you had to suspect is that he did not like the media business at all. That he saw, and was taking advantage of, not just its flaws, but its fatal flaws.

This is, of course, the perfect place to be: To know that death is coming before everyone else knows. It makes you God. Or the devil.

That's what it had come to. Everybody was kind of thinking that Barry knew what was going to happen.

Because he didn't have to justify one of these sucker companies—was the only practicing titan who didn't—his was the only objective eye.

Hence, the Internet stuff.

His company, USA Networks, was a hodgepodge of things he had been able to acquire. It would be hard to say that there was a method here other than availability and affordability. But Barry had imbued it with enough Barryness that it had to be taken seriously, enabling him to get it to the point where he could credibly do his first killer deal with Edgar Bronfman Jr., and then his second killer deal with Jean-Marie Messier (killer in the sense that it killed both of those men). At which point, after selling off the theoretically good stuff he had bought, he was left with only the theoretically bad stuff (the Internet stuff), which he pronounced to be not just the real good stuff but the gold.

And because he had so ably screwed so many people in so many deals (and saved himself on so many occasions when people were trying to screw him), you couldn't risk not believing him.

Indeed, he might know something.

Here was the Diller proposition: This stuff that he was left with—either because he had a grand strategic vision, or because this was the luck of the draw—was what media would become.

If advertising—old-time, big-budget, high-production value, impressionistic, image-creating, make-the-consumer-feel-good, make-the-advertiser-himself-feel-great advertising—was going away, then it was reasonable to believe that what it was going to be replaced by was some direct transaction thing.

Advertising itself would be disintermediated.

There would be no need for the advertisement.

The idea that you would be entertained and while you were entertained you would be further entertained in a way that would suggest to you that you might buy a product underwriting all this entertainment, which was only available through a whole series of disparate steps which most certainly meant traveling to a remote location, would, shortly, be looked at as some incredible piece of commercial inefficiency.

Entertainment and transaction would be united.

In fact, pursuing the malling-of-America and shop-until-you-drop paradigm, the transaction would become the entertainment.

Diller, he would have you believe, was the transaction guy.

With Match.com for dating, Expedia for travel, and Ticketmaster for access to entertainment itself, he had established this empire of buying stuff. As more and more of the world was reduced to digital lots or digital notions, or available by digital access, Barry would be the person to sell it.

While the media business would continue to struggle to create products based on an increasingly futile model of advertising support and unit sales—struggling painfully with ever-dwindling margins—Barry would be the King of the World, levying his transaction fees as everything digital passed through his hands.

Media was dead. Long live Barry.

Or, conversely, this was just the blah blah.

The point was not the reinvention of media.

The point was maintaining the illusion of Barry.

It was a classic three-card-monte, flimflam thing. You always wanted to keep people distracted. Keep their eye off the target. Keep them from seeing when the switch took place.

Barry didn't want to be seen as just another media business hustler and wannabe.

What would that make him besides another version of Marvin Davis, the oilman who briefly owned Twentieth Century Fox (who Barry had worked for, briefly), who was, all of a sudden, vaingloriously, back in the game trying to buy Universal, or, even, another Edgar Bronfman Jr?

In the entertainment business, you never wanted to be thought to be looking for a second act. That would always cost you. That was a kind of desperation that would reliably jack the price.

Barry had solved that problem, and avoided that scent of neediness, by creating this alternative business life.

He wasn't in the *old* media business anymore. That was just something that was trying to drag him back.

What's more, this sense that he could go back into the real media business, that he could go back, hugely, as a conquerer, as hero, but that he didn't want to, was prepared to forsake all that, for this, *interactivity,* made his interactive business seem so much more valuable.

So, he was not interested in the business in which he was making his big money (reluctant deals, if-you-insist deals, let's-just-settle-up deals), but vastly interested in the business where, in fact, he wasn't making any money at all.

Barry was a big flirt.

He was a true free agent.

He was the operator.

This was war. Somebody would always get rich. Somebody would always get dead.

He was terrifically, and appealingly, flirtatious with Charlie. You could see the tough guy, but it was the appealing side of his toughness. He was open enough. Showy enough. There was great, theatrical animation to his face (nearly Milton Berle–like at moments). He was talking to Charlie and having a perfectly intimate-seeming conversation with him, and, at the same time, having another, parallel, perfectly intimate conversation with the audience.

And enjoying himself, obviously.

Anyway, no, he wasn't going to say what he was going to do about Universal. But this didn't seem like avoidance, or that he was hiding anything, but more that you should not ask a woman of a certain style and status her age.

Nobody here really wanted to hold Barry accountable in any businesslike way.

We understood—and appreciated—that his whole business methodology was to tease.

Brains and charisma and a sense of humor and a killer instinct. That makes for a great stage presence.

No, no, he wouldn't say, didn't have any plans, wasn't looking to do anything, just wanted to protect his company's assets. That's all. Not an issue.

It was still possible of course that he would leave this stage and begin a course that would deliver one of the world's largest movie studios, some of the world's choicest theme parks, the world's largest music company, etc., into his hands; that, as he spoke, this was all in progress, and we were all being played for little fools; and too, that he would go from there to acquire a network and many of the pieces of the devolving companies that he had once coveted and become something like the last action mogul.

But unlikely.

He had achieved a greater thing: to be wholly in the game and yet entirely independent.

He had started the last decade with modest wealth, and now was sitting here one of the richest men in the business.

What's more, he had slipped the bonds of true, mortal responsibility.

He wasn't going to be blamed.

He was free and ready for the next thing.

Everybody sitting in their seats was, at the moment, in love with Barry.

24
WALTER

And then there was the Walter panel, the last panel: "The News Business—Profits and the Public Interest." It was Walter, Karen House, the publisher of the *Wall Street Journal* (who was awkwardly married to the president of Dow Jones, the *Journal*'s parent company), Arthur Sulzberger Jr., and Andy Lack, the president and COO of NBC (and before that, the head of NBC News). The panel was moderated by Michael Elliott from Time—Walter and Andy's neighbor in Bronxville.

But it really was Walter's panel.

Walter is, at heart, a panelist.

I have seen him, reassuringly, on many such panels. So much so that I've occasionally thought of him as a Bennett Cerf figure—a *What's My Line?* type. An educated celebrity. Someone you thought could tell you something—someone who could explain it all.

And, of course, everybody wanted it explained.

Oddly, news was still at the heart of this—news was still the theoretical raison d'être of the media business. It was the thing that had to be rationalized, or at least bowed to.

There yet remained in so many striving media people an earnest, civics-minded boy or girl.

And a fundamental tension in the business, of course, was whether or not the moguls and suits and Hollywood smoothies had that interest—or how far their interests diverged from ours.

Or we still pretended that tension existed.

At least the snobbery still existed.

The process of reconciling our earnestness with a widespread lack of interest in our earnestness was also a part of the tension.

I've sometimes wondered if the AOL deal wasn't born out of some desperate effort to force our earnest values into the great new technology.

Walter as the head of CNN was in some sense the final flowering of all those rationalizations.

I was thinking, at that moment, of Walter on another panel a few years ago—when he was still running *Time* magazine.

The panel was Walter and *Time*'s legendary presidential correspondent Hugh Sidey, with Henry Kissinger. The occasion was the opening of an exhibit of photographs celebrating the American presidency and *Time*'s relationship to it—one of various events that Walter was always staging when he was managing editor to herald the rebirth (under him) of *Time*.

The panel and exhibit were what a marketer might describe as a snapshot of the *Time* franchise: proximity to power, indelible images of great events, the best and the brightest journalists.

It would be hard to find a Watergate- or earlier-generation journalist who didn't think that the pinnacle, even the essence, of the profession was to cover Washington and the presidency. But, in the exhibit, the opposite point was being made too: Looking at these photographs and listening to the indefatigable Kissinger, it was clear that the presidential, sweep-of-history *Time* had been dramatically contracting, and a new *Time,* concerned with issues like genealogy ("How to Search for Your Roots") and blockbuster movies (the *Star Wars* keepsake issue, which we pore over in our house), had taken its place. *Time's* beat, in other words, under Walter, was no longer America-writ-large but the various private preoccupations, emotional and aspirational rather than ideological in nature, of large blocs of Americans who don't much relate to great events or great men—or read a newspaper, or even watch television news.

After all, the headline form itself is a relic—we know what's happening pretty much the moment it happens. Washington's status as the news capital is heading the way of Detroit's status as a center of economic strength; there's no lower-selling type of news than political news. The news business, which was once dominated by a small circle of players, is now a competitive free-for-all. Add to that the demographic revolution: Everybody has his or her own socioeconomic, psychographic, ethnic-gender-generational view of what's news.

And one more thing: The overwhelming sentiment in any news organization is insecurity. Hardly anybody thinks he will be doing the same job he's doing now five years from now.

Practically speaking, none of us is really in the journalism business anymore—not even the most Reston-ish or Lippmann-esque or pompous among us. We're in the magazine business, or newspaper business, or television business, or, even, online business—we're in, of course, the media business—trying to answer the one question many of us imagined we'd never have to answer: What is the unique selling proposition of our product? *News* is not unique.

Under Walter, *Time* managed to come up with a sort of answer—*Time* as a lifestyle magazine, *Time* as a feel-good book, *Time* as the outside-the-Beltway, salt-of-the-earth journal.

Part of Walter's elevation in the media business was that he could wear this humiliation with some verve and confidence.

I'm not sure there is anyone of our around-50 generation who is as self-consciously a journalist as Walter. His sense of his own importance and his almost otherworldly identification with the profession's grandest gentlemen (you can hardly have a conversation with him without his evoking *Time*'s former editors and various Washington-press-corps grandees) are still a cause for wonder among his classmates at Harvard. (Imagine being the most self-important person in your class at Harvard.) Walter was clearly born to be the prime minister of the Fourth Estate and to confer with his peers at State and on the Hill and at the White House and to bring the concerns of the powerful to the people.

He even speaks with that old Luce-ian, American Century, Teddy White *Making of the President* tone; you never quite feel you're saying something important enough when you speak to him.

Still, he was never—not even for a second—defensive about *Time*'s new, more modest interests.

"We used to have great access to great events and report them with Lippmann-esque certitude. Now our goal is to tell stories that connect with the way we live," he once explained to me. "We want to know about the debates happening around the dinner table rather than the Senate committee tables."

Still, while he was willing to throw over the old *Time* augustness, I was never sure he entirely appreciated the social changes he was speaking to.

"Walter, I'm not sure anyone sits around the dinner table anymore," I found myself pointing out.

"Hmmm. The water cooler, then."

It was almost quaint that Walter, as he deconstructed the

polemical and pontifical *Time,* was still thinking about people having debates and about journalism as the basis for social discourse.

Among Walter watchers there are many explanations for his constant adaptability in the face of overwhelming obsolescence. There's the Nixon-in-China analysis about Walter: He was the one person who could lead *Time* out of the death throes of pompous white-man news, because his pompous white-man news credentials are better than anybody else's. And there's Walter-as-a-Clinton-surrogate: Walter, like Clinton, recognized the nineties-style notion to make it personal, that people relate more to the trivial, the local, than they do to the momentous.

And then there's Walter-as-company-man, the ultimate media conglomerate factotum: Walter gave up being a journalist in favor of being a mediaist, even a synergist, and what he did was turn *Time* into an amalgam of the company's other, more consumer-friendly "products." *Time* became a little bit of *People,* a little bit of *Entertainment Weekly,* a little bit of *Money,* a little bit of *Parenting,* and a little bit of *Health,* along with a small remaining bit of *Time.* Walter, in other words, was the packager-in-chief.

Which is how, in one of the great media career leaps, Walter got to be the chairman of CNN.

Now, news guys—like Walter and NBC president Andy Lack—no matter how close they come to power, don't usually get the power themselves. They don't usually run nations or corporations, but watch, warily or admiringly, the people who do.

Of course, that was before the media world changed and news and information "became so vital to our portfolio," as Lack has described NBC's collection of programming and cable channels.

Such a paradox! While nobody wants news anymore (not news, at least, in the old-time sense), a newer sort of news (or let us call it nonfiction programming) is now among the most valuable currencies of the current television age—if only because it's cheaper than sitcoms and hour dramas to produce.

So having news credentials can, counterintuitively, make you something special. A major-hitter media executive.

Of course, neither Andy nor Walter is *just* a news guy. I don't think that just *any* news guys could have gotten the jobs they've gotten. It's not like Edward R. Murrow, were he 50 and living in Bronxville, would have gotten the job. Andy and Walter are *new* news guys. They demonstrated they could match the news to the market.

Under Andy, *Dateline,* with its "storytelling" mix of consumer exposés and real-life crime dramas and survivor sob stories, became the mainstay of the NBC schedule. It's news, but—in the manner of Walter's *Time*—this was news in the largest, broadest, most entertaining sense.

"It's all about unlocking value," Andy once told me, talking nonnews talk.

Of course, it's possible that Andy and Walter were being allowed to run networks because the guys above them didn't think that running a network was as important as it used to be. Network guys at Andy and Walter's level (as opposed to the more abstract strata of men who engineer massive distribution shifts) are just content producers—and content hasn't been king in a while. NBC, in the era after the departure of GE's media-loving Jack Welch, will also, likely, be rationalized in a more corporate way. And CNN, post–Ted Turner and post–Fox News, is just a problem on top of other larger problems in the AOL Time Warner calamity.

In the tons of email I get from disaffected people at dysfunctional media companies, nobody vents more than television people.

The tone of my mail from CNN is rage that Time Warner fucked the company up, and now it's all coming apart. The tone from NBC is more existential: *What will become of us?* (Though one correspondent did point out that a bad day at NBC is still better than a good day at ABC.)

It could even be that some smart management person realized you don't want professional television guys (sales, finance, and affiliate guys) to be running the television business now, because whatever happens is bound to be a disappointment for them—and you don't want depressed executives bringing everybody else down. All numbers in the television business will get smaller—that's the only certainty. The television business is a hardscrabble business. Which is why the content guys were given a shot, because they didn't know that it was all downhill.

I'd even argue that television, with its ever-more-specialized topics, smaller and smaller audiences, more and more complex distribution routes, increasingly meager profits, and ever-expanding dial of choices, is the new print—which, for television people, is possibly the worst news.

So what did Andy and Walter see in it besides the job titles and the dough?

As news president, Andy was faced with the daily (and, for a news guy, thrilling) task of deciding what was important in the world; as head of the network, it was his decision whether to air *Weakest Link* on one night a week or two, and how *Fear Factor* could keep topping itself (there are millions of dollars in profit margin dependent on clever humiliations and gross-outs). As for Walter, I've heard him talk about television before, and judging from his I'm-trying-to-be-with-it tone, I really don't think he watches television much.

Neither guy was necessarily a natural.

I'm tempted to think this was hubris—that Andy and Walter both overreached.

Then too, I can't help thinking that they both made a sort of devil's bargain. They would use their Serious News Guy rep to front for the fact that they were running dumb-it-down businesses. For whatever news talents they might have, they were being employed now for their other talents—as semilowbrow packaging whizzes.

Getting on their bellies with Fox may be, in the end, what they'd both been hired to do (something Tom Johnson, Walter's predecessor at CNN, seemed to have no heart, or talent, for doing).

But I also suspect that I'm not seeing the full breadth of the career moves here. That I'm stuck in an old idea of form and function. After all, so many of the careers that we planned on and are now stuck in have eroded or don't quite exist anymore (which is the real point of these emails from the disaffected that I get all the time). Even Walter, on track to get the job he'd prepared for all his career, the Time Inc. editor-in-chief job, the Henry Grunwald job, understood, I think, that this job doesn't exist any longer—you can't be the editor in chief of 64-plus magazines; you can't even *read* 64 magazines.

Andy and Walter, I think, have realized that they aren't really journalists anymore. They've mutated into mere mediaists.

Being a mediaist has to do with having some finer understanding of the almost-impossible-to-grasp function of a massive media company. In other words, Walter and Andy may get it, while the rest of us mostly don't. It's alliances, it's leverage, it's transactions, it's franchises, it's platforms and what all.

At NBC, for instance, there has been a telling change in vocabulary. The news division, if you're in the know, is called a nonfiction-production unit (sometimes a "multiplatform nonfiction-production unit," feeding content to myriad outlets). The point being distribution and convergence and modularity and interactivity, rather than just news.

So it isn't about journalism. In fact, it may not even really be about television, but rather whole new demanding levels of ambition, canniness, charm, and survival skills.

This seemed to me what they ought to be talking about here—not news, not journalism, but their own careers in the media business.

Because they were both up against it.

Most everyone here knew the background, too. So there was a poignancy.

Walter and Andy were expendable.

They had been put in harm's way because a natural ambition, or hotdogism, propelled them blindly forward.

They caught the mogul thing.

They really thought they could be, just might be able to be, moguls.

That they could ride astride one of those great and ridiculous companies.

Why not try, was their point. They knew that what they did—this journalism job—was over with. At least in any high-cultural, go-to-the-head-of-the-class sense. So they had to segue.

Unbeknownst to them, they became a kind of executive fodder.

In their own efforts to be a part of the mogul class, they led the news business into its transitional phase.

But it was not likely that they would become moguls or transform news—at least not without enduring great setbacks.

That's what they both looked like now. Guys enduring.

Possibly it was Fox that had driven them both to the brink of despair. Andy Lack had, more and more at NBC, two dysfunctional cable stations, MSNBC and CNBC. Fox, the rough beast, had reinvented the cable news genre, and made MSNBC and CNBC pathetic.

As for CNN, its crisis was larger. In some sense, it carried the burden of liberalism itself. What a fate: Walter would be responsible not just for the end of news, but for liberal democracy as well.

But it was not just Fox they were up against.

They were, of course, up against themselves. This desperate need for position and approval and visibility, to be at the center of everything, is what brought us all into the media business—this mogul gene or virus or monkey on the back that we all possessed— sustained the business and would continue to sustain it long after it was ready to collapse. We held it up by our comical weaknesses.

I stood in the back of the room with another Walter watcher. We deconstructed him as you would any serious man of great power and stature: his flagging skin tone, the droop of his shoulders, the oomph or lack of oomph of his voice, the fading quality of light in his eyes, wondering how long he could last.

The room was starting to recede. Walter and company turned out not to be such good closers. As they wound down, the audience, one by one, made its excuses, and began to scuttle from its seats.

Ennui mixed with anticlimax.

The world is as it is was the message, which was actually reassuring to many people.

The media business was a vast, excessively complicated, capital-intensive industry. There would be shifts of power among the existing powers, and there would be the establishment of new fiefdoms—Rattner's fiefdom, possibly—and there would be the decline and fall of older fiefs. But its power and influence would not go away quickly or easily.

That was, anyway, how you would see it if you were in the middle of it.

Otherwise, you had an industry built by singular men all who were in, pretty much, final scenes of last acts. You had a system that, on its face, had little long-term logic to it: amass, buy, aggregate, assemble, consolidate, take over, until somebody makes you stop. And you had a business which was inevitably plagued by what all businesses came to be plagued by: ensuing generations of weaker and weaker leadership.

Still, it was the kind of thing that certainly wouldn't change today, and, if it changed at all, would change only in hindsight, and when that did happen, by regulation or technological innovation or new and unimagined cultural trends, then that was the opportunity that everybody here was charged with divining and getting in on.

The other possibility, of overthrow—of rapid, helpless transformation, of the thing turning against itself, of a time and generation passing and then a sudden deluge, of a stunning, visceral, breakdown in the value proposition—wasn't much, I don't think, on anybody's mind but my own.

Certainly, none of these people, even if they had the jitters, would be sharing them. Their very job was not to have the jitters—or not to let on.

This is why the inevitable always took so long.

I said good-bye to Heilemann and Battelle and Rattner and took the subway home.

EPILOGUE:
WINTER
AND SPRING

An odd thing happened: Lots of people started to get pissed off about the FCC's decision in the spring of 2003 to relax the media-ownership rules.

Even in Congress there was a wholly out-of-character march to undo the undone rules.

This pissed-off-ness was rightly unexpected by both the media conglomerates petitioning the FCC and by the FCC commissioners. After all, it wasn't that easy to explain what the rules were in the first place—and what would be different if they changed. For instance, before the rules were relaxed, no one conglomerate could own television stations that reached more than 35 percent of the U.S. audience; after the change, the conglom could reach up to 45 percent. So what's the big deal? The FCC seemed genuinely perplexed. What's more, if there was to be a hue and cry about consolidation and the commonweal's vested interest in media independence, more logically it should have happened ten years ago—before Time and Warner, before Viacom and Paramount, before Disney and ABC—rather than now, when all but the final gasp of consolidation had already taken place.

But possibly it was the finality of this, the sense not just of victory on the part of the media conglomerates but of obnoxious victory. They had it all anyway, now they wanted more—always more. This was what, after so long, seemed to be galling to so many people. It was a mindless grab. The arrogance of it was, finally, just too irritating.

And then there was the FCC commissioner himself. I don't think the negative effect should be underestimated of a public figure giving people the creeps. Michael Powell was not just puffed up—at once epicene and porcine—and he was not just full of these shiver-inducing black-is-white bromides ("consolidation increases choice"), but he was the son of the secretary of state, for God's sake. How could everybody not feel the fix was in everywhere? That the game was rigged.

And then there was radio: Clear Channel—and its PR geniuses. Radio was everybody's media touchstone. It was comfort media (we weren't couch potatoes as much as front-seat turnips). But in the space of a few years, as Clear Channel's holdings climbed from a handful of stations to more than 1,200, radio was altered and disrupted. Radio—wherever you went in America and on the drive-time dial—was as regulated, as planned, as bureaucratic, as formatted and formulaic, as removed from personal interaction and bedside manner, as an HMO. Clear Channel was Kaiser Permanente.

And then there was Fox. For the first time a television network was not dissembling about its power. It was not talking about the public good and the public airwaves and the public interest. It was not bowing and scraping to the usual FCC shibboleths. Quite the opposite, it was openly ridiculing those things. *We report, you decide.*

And, in doing so, it was courting and amassing, and even creating, dramatic political power. There arose something of a collective "Yikes."

But it was not just Fox. Rather, where Murdoch went, everybody went. This was perhaps never more apparent—and unsettling—than during the Iraq war.

Indeed, let me follow a thread between the search for the weapons of mass destruction and the FCC's move to relax the media-ownership rules.

First, the weapons: The Bush guys had obviously played Saddam for a fool. He wanted to have those weapons. He was a broken man without them. The Bushies, by their wild accusations, conceded to him the very illusion of power that they knew he would happily and fiercely cling to and that they could then set out with appropriate fervor to protect us from and to take away from him.

Saddam had a get-out-of-jail-free card: He just had to reveal to the world that he was bereft of resources, spent as a force, bankrupt as a ruler. But Rummy and Wolfowitz and Perle, and everybody else in the Bush administration who had been obsessing about Saddam for fifteen years, understood that it would be at least as difficult for him to admit to not having such power as to get tarred for having it.

He needed to appear threatening. They needed him to appear threatening.

They needed him to dissemble. He needed to dissemble.

Everybody was party to the creation of an alternate—and, likely, entirely false—reality.

There was even a neat moral justification for letting Saddam hang himself: While the Bush people surely had an extensive understanding of the truly dismal nature of the Iraqi military resources, Saddam's squirreliness allowed them to maintain an iota of less-than-absolute certainty (and then, of course, Wolfowitz and company couldn't help throwing in a little bogus intelligence). Indeed, North Korea, threatening to blow up the world in the middle of this, turned out to be helpful. Here was a down-on-its-luck regime apparently producing serious offensive weapons—so it *could* happen. (But since we weren't running to the barricades on this, it probably meant that the weapons produced by a down-on-its-luck regime were of limited usefulness; or, on the other hand, it meant that if we did really fear that a rogue regime has them, we would tread very carefully.)

Even in the aftermath of the war—when looking for the weapons had become something of a Monty Python routine—the Potemkin-village logic continued:

If we can't find them, they still must be here—or they must have been here—because Saddam could have avoided all this if he had just admitted he didn't have them (and while he did say he didn't have them, he didn't say it as convincingly as he would have said it if he really didn't have them).

The logic of the war was the logic of the Jesuitical arguments popular on right-wing television and radio. It had been war by syllogism.

We settled—and continued to settle—for an abstract deduction over actual proof.

Still, this deduction was not so ironclad, or brilliant, or irrefutable, that it could not be disassembled.

And yet this low-rent logic remained, in the public mind, largely unassailable, because nobody—certainly not with any concerted attention—had assailed it.

Why not? It was a setup. A ruse. A cheat. *Hello?*

How had the Bushies gotten away with this?

Now the FCC:

So every news organization from CNN to Fox to the networks to the big newspaper chains to the *New York Times* (although, heroically, not the *Washington Post*) was eagerly petitioning the Bush FCC for the freedom to substantially alter the economics of the news business. For the newspaper companies, the goal was to get out of the newspaper business and into the television business (under the old rules, it was a no-no to own newspapers and television stations in the same market). For networks with big news operations, the goal was to buy more stations, which is where the real cash flows from. Anyway, the whole point here was to move away from news, to downgrade it, to amortize it, to minimize it. And as the war got under way, everybody knew the FCC decision allowing the media conglomerates to do precisely that would come shortly after the war ended.

You've got all of these media organizations that wanted something for the most basic reason up-against-the-wall companies can want something: because they think this is what will save them (by transforming them). There's almost nothing—really—they won't do for this. Indeed, these congloms had already spent many years and millions of dollars trying to make the FCC change its rules. What's more, all of these companies were in lockstep (save for the *Washington Post*); nobody was breaking ranks.

All right then. The media knew what it wanted, and the media knew what the Bush people wanted.

So is it a conspiracy? Is that what I'm saying? That the media—acting in concert—took a dive on the war for the sake of getting an improved position with regard to the ownership rules? Certainly, every big media company was a cheerleader, as gullible and as empty-headed—or as accommodating—on the subject of WMDs as, well, Saddam himself.

But *conspiracy* wouldn't quite be the right word.

Negotiation, however, would be. An appreciation of the whole environment, the careful balancing of interests, the subtleties of the trade (at this point, the ritual denial: "There was no quid pro quo").

The interesting thing is that in most newsrooms, you would find lots of agreement with this view of how businessmen and politicians get the things they want. A general acceptance of the realities of ass-kissing, if not a higher level of corruption. You'd find nearly everybody saying, *Yes, duh, everybody gets something in return—but not when it comes to the news. Not like that. Not so . . . quid pro quo.*

Now, this is not entirely true. The people at Fox certainly wouldn't swear on the life of their grandmothers that the news wasn't customized for larger business purposes.

And everybody at NBC seems to understand that if Bob Wright, NBC's chairman and GE's man on the scene, doesn't like what he hears, he'll be calling the control room.

And ABC and Disney, *oy.*

And CBS and Viacom and Jessica Lynch! (CBS, in an effort to get Jessica Lynch, the captured POW and most famous foot soldier of the Iraq war, to give her first interview to CBS News, offered the private a book deal through its Simon & Schuster division and the possibility of a talk show at MTV.)

Still, it comes down to the literal point of influence. Who said what to whom? Did anybody in any news organization actually say, "Go easy on the war"?

We tell ourselves it doesn't go that far.

But do we believe it?

Although the BBC meticulously dismantled the Jessica Lynch rescue in the weeks after the war, the U.S. media was not just defending the story but bidding for it.

Even the term *WMD* is a nod to an inside joke—that the existence of the weapons has been established only by constant repetition.

And it was telling to examine the war justifications in context of that particular media moment in time, when the theme was not to give anybody any wiggle room. Anybody in any position of authority—political, business, journalistic—was being held to the strictest interpretations of meaning and context and responsibility. This cannot equal that. Transparency is the grail. Except for the Bushies. They had a media pass.

The war was one of those great, suspicious, excessively justified, what-you-see-is-*not*-what-you-get, dubious-accounting, reality-distorting, even Clintonian (although it seems far vaster in its plasticity than anything the Clintons ever did) endeavors. The Bushies piped it.

And yet as the whole mess unfolded, it remained, in the media mind, a pretty good war, with or without the discovery of the weapons of mass destruction.

And the FCC thing graciously sailed through.

And then there was something else. Not the power of the media, but its weakness. Finally, in the midst of the most dismal year the media industry has ever had, with each company in some not inconsiderable turmoil, with the future as uncertain as it had ever been, with nobody deserving of any sort of confidence, it was starting to seem obvious—to employees and shareholders and even consumers—that consolidation was just some further example of failing upward.

These are the people you wanted to give more authority to, more responsibility, more companies to screw up—the folks who gave us AOL Time Warner?

AOLTW had created a simple but profound disturbance in the equation. If the biggest company was strong, then all other companies had to strive to be big. But if AOL Time Warner was vulnerable, then the entire superstructure was, with a little critical interpretation, potentially ready to blow.

Steve Case went down early in the winter. He went down sulking, aggrieved, hurt—apparently not understanding why he had to be blamed. But somebody had to. Somebody else, somebody more, had to be blamed. The company had steadily fed bodies to the blame monster. Now it was hurriedly trying to reform and cleanse itself, hoping that it would accomplish some transformation before the next body had to be sacrificed.

But the transformation was not going well. The plan was to sell some assets. To mini-disaggregate. The first step was to roll out the cable company in a public offering—but as plans got under way for this IPO in the early months of 2003, the Wall Street signs, the word on the Street, were not propitious, and the move was delayed. A deal was floated about selling or spinning off the AOLTW music company, but this too got bogged down. And the book company was put up for auction, but, without anyone bidding in a meaningful way, was withdrawn at the last minute. A broken auction.

Nobody seemed to want the whole deal—and nobody seemed to want the cast-off pieces either.

More and more the question was not so much how to fix the company or how to turn it around, but, much more existentially, what to do with it. What did AOL Time Warner mean?

There were different answers from different parts of the company. Indeed, there was less and less a sense of any center of the company—of any actual AOL Time Warner entity.

A Wall Street/media business/consulting guy I know was chatting me up one day a few weeks after the Foresquare conference, talking about his various projects and possibilities, as consultants do, when he said he was doing a little work for Warner Bros. studio—giving some advice "related to the possibility of an eventual public life for the studio." What this meant, it occurred to me, was that the various parts of the company were each planning their own exits. Everybody was pulling away.

Including Walter.

The week Case resigned, Walter announced he was giving up the chairmanship of CNN—instead, he would take over the Aspen Institute, a think tank for liberal internationalists.

It was always worth paying attention to the nuances and direction of Walter's career moves.

If he got out of new media and the Internet because it was doomed, and got out of magazines because they were in trouble, and, arguably, got out of journalism itself because it was so over with, he was, likewise, getting out of CNN now because it was hopeless, and, as the ultimate brush-off, out of AOL Time Warner (where he had spent his entire career) because there was just no longer any advantage in being associated with it.

Trust me, if Walter was going, AOL Time Warner was gone.

Indeed, Walter, by taking over the Aspen Institute, was not just getting out of AOL Time Warner, he was *getting out of the media business.*

(A prediction: The well-endowed Aspen Institute, which had been in minor eclipse, will now rise to great new prominence by virtue of Walter's publicity talents. It will provide Walter, in Washington and New York and Aspen, with a platform from which to say reasonable and intelligent things and get great press. He will host innumerable cocktail parties—which are, in many ways, his real medium. He will find a solvable conflict and broker at the Aspen retreat a big peace in the world. And when the Democrats emerge from their wilderness years, there will be, I promise you, one inevitable secretary of state: Walter.)

Walter wasn't the only brilliant careerist making meaningful career moves early in 2003. Walter's good friend and Bronxville neighbor Andy Lack announced he had been lured from the presidency of NBC to run Sony Music—which, on the face of it, made virtually no sense.

There were two areas here of interesting and telling desperation: the network mess, which no one was going to be able to fix, ever, and the music mess, which no one was going to be able to fix ever either. And yet it was possible to argue there was some management art, or something that might pass for art, in substituting a guy who had not been able to fix the mess in television for a guy who had not been able to fix the mess in music. The logic here would be, I think, that a guy who hadn't created a particular mess (although he might have created other messes) had a better chance of fixing the mess than the guy who, in fact, had created it. At Sony Music that would be Tommy Mottola, one of the great talent handlers (indeed, he sometimes married the talent), but who, in this age of angst and uncertainty and profoundly unanswerable questions, was nobody's idea of a philosopher king.

What was going on here, with Andy Lack who knew nothing about music replacing Tommy Mottola who apparently too did not know enough about the music business—or the *new* music business—was this move toward an acknowledgment of a generalized condition in which nobody really knew anything anymore about what they were doing. (In fact, this was not a small bit of the psychology behind putting Walter, a career print guy, in charge of CNN in the first place—Walter might not know about television, but then who did?)

If consolidation didn't work, if technology was providing con-sumers with the wherewithal to steal the stuff that consolidation produced anyway, and if, on top of that, whatever else happened, the one thing that you could count on was that audiences, invari-ably, got smaller and smaller and more distracted—then fuck it.

The only chance you had was to do the wrong and even ass-backwards thing and just hope that it would—capriciously, serendipitously, randomly—turn out to be the exact right thing. It was all more and more a blind experiment.

These were the people who wanted the FCC to let them buy more stuff that they wouldn't know what to do with.

There was, it was true, one person who seemed to have figured out how to make it work. Poor martyred Martha Stewart, possibly the only media genius of the age (she didn't need special dispensa-tions from the FCC), our Newton, was indicted in the spring.

Actually, there was somebody else who had figured out how to make it work, but who, it seemed more and more certainly, had fig-ured out how to make it work through a growing antipathy to the media business.

In March 2003, Barry Diller gave up his role as chairman of Vivendi Universal.

What exactly, everyone asked, did this mean?

What did it mean that we were left here and Barry was now somewhere else?

There was, it seemed, even an implicit contempt here on Barry's part for the media industry—he was giving us the finger.

More and more, it became clear that he had this other, parallel business life, as the head of one of the largest online companies in the world—indeed, with 24,000 employees at companies including Expedia, Match.com, and Ticketmaster.

And that by embracing this life instead of the old mogul life as head of a television and movie and music company, he was walking away from the thing we did.

The fundamental idea that we would entertain and inform and call attention to ourselves and make a buck doing it was what he was walking away from.

Media does not equal content.

Stars were passé; stardom, as the great media accomplishment, was over.

You didn't need an expensive television show to make people want to buy stuff. There were more efficient ways to skim pennies off of a transaction than having to make up stories and hire actors and produce hits.

What's more, in some final slap, Barry seemed to be turning against moguldom itself. Rather, he was an efficient, by-the-numbers, entrepreneurial businessman. No excesses. No grandiosity. No show.

Indeed, it was Edgar Bronfman Jr. who was back trying to get control of Universal. Edgar Bronfman Jr. was the once and future mogul—which surely said something about the status and character of moguldom these days.

Of final note, Barry—in something of a classy good-bye to all that—was the only mogul to oppose the FCC rule change.

And what of Rupert? And Sumner and Mel? And Michael?

Their intransigence and invulnerability and fierceness and mastery of all the elements of keeping and amassing greater and greater amounts of power along with the obvious fact that they couldn't go on forever—that, indeed, a countdown was in progress, secret office pools were forming—had begun to give them all something of a comic book quality.

"Anyone," I happen to have heard the 79-year-old Redstone say to an 80-year-old Don Hewitt as they left the CBS Christmas party that winter, "who thinks age is chronological is an asshole."

After bickering for a year, Sumner and Mel signed a truce in the winter of 2003 which would let them, together, continue to run Viacom. And yet there wasn't anybody who wasn't aware that the two were trying to behave well in public. And that control of this company would soon enough pass to people—Redstone's children, who already held titular posts in the company—who, it is likely, could not maintain control. The waiting was the game—or, rather, the game was to live for the moment. Within these companies—possibly as a reflection of their hard business heart—there is no mechanism by which to consider death. Or natural transition of any sort. It is the dictator thing—a narcissism which can't acknowledge anything after itself. In fact, everybody assumes that in some sense they die too with the Patriarch, or at least, life as they have known it is over with, and something unknowable, something that can't be planned for, begins. So . . . fuck it.

Meanwhile, the idea, which gained at least conversational credibility through the winter—that Mel Karmazin would replace Michael Eisner at Disney—was suddenly off the table.

Eisner was alone again and still standing. Again the conventional wisdom was that he had one more season—of television and movies and theme parks and deals—to save himself. And yet, this one-more-season thing was in many ways his own myth, his own measurement. It was his way to say that he was judged as everyone else was judged, but, in fact, he had been putting this one-more-season thing out for years now. The message was clear: There was no orderly transition possible here. Here, too, everybody just waited. Until something happened nothing would happen. But when something happened it would happen cataclysmically.

And Rupert.

The odd accomplishment of Fox News was that it had created itself as the media insurgent (indeed, in the early days, this stance was aided by Time Warner Cable trying to keep Fox off of its cable systems so it would not compete with CNN). The subtext of its agenda was always that there was a media which was keeping the truth from you—a big, monolithic, liberal media. Fox had succeeded in part by demonizing the rest of the media. *The established media.*

The great and hilarious irony here is that it may well be this take, this opposition, that has helped crystallize the idea that a vast, ungoverned, ungovernable media actually does exist. Indeed, that the media, the idea of media, the system of media, is a negative force. And, if to some of the rabid faithful, Fox is an antidote to this negative force, to a larger silent majority, Fox of course is inevitably part of the antimedia analysis.

The further irony is that it was ultimately Murdoch himself (through Roger Ailes) making an argument against the great media oligarchs. It was logical to wonder, in fact, if the Fox faithful even knew who Murdoch was—and what would they think if they did know that Fox was the product of the greatest media oligarch who ever lived. An Australian at that—with a Chinese wife.

When the forces against consolidation and the FCC rule-change started to wake up from their long sleep, it was quite obviously Murdoch himself whom they would choose to demonize—it was his grim and forbidding face put to effective use in the ad campaign by the anti-FCC-rule-change organizations. Rupert became the poster mogul for the campaign against moguls.

As much as Fox, it may have been the DirecTV deal that woke up everybody.

Again this has to do, I think, with Michael Powell's Orwellian logic. In essence what he said was not just that EchoStar's purchase of DirecTV would be monopolistic, but it would be more monopolistic than letting Rupert Murdoch buy the satellite system. In other words, giving the nation's biggest satellite system to the world's leading media oligarch, who already controlled newspapers and television networks and movie studios and book publishers, who regularly retailed his own politics through his far-reaching media apparatus, was better for the public than giving the satellite business to somebody else who just operated satellites. No matter that giving Murdoch DirecTV is the ultimate anticompetitive, content-distribution-stranglehold media play. That he'll have the power to make a hermetic News Corp. content world. He'll be able to black out, or downgrade, or otherwise screw with NBC and CNBC and MSNBC or, for that matter, CBS-MTV, ABC-ESPN, and any other offshoot of any content producer that doesn't have a distribution system that can threaten massive retaliation. Pay no attention . . .

Enough. This was, on Powell's part, some serious bit of tone deafness.

But let me add a further irony to this: Honestly, I don't think Murdoch is buying. I think Murdoch is selling—or preparing to sell. Or to devolve.

Now, he could be as blind as any parent. He might really think that his sons, Lachlan and James, are thoroughly created in his image and can truly run his creation. But as likely, he is also as clear-sighted as any parent, with a loving understanding of what his children can and can't do. And, reasonably, they can't be their father.

Bear with my speculation.

He now owns two other satellite companies: BSkyB in the Euro market and StarTV in the Asian market. The satellite strategy has been his technology-vision thing, and also allowed News Corp.

to maintain that it is the only truly global media concern. But it's also a business that has failed to achieve predicted levels of market penetration, tied up an enormous amount of cash, and seen other technologies supersede it (like the whole digital revolution). What to do with this business has long been the Murdoch conundrum.

When he first tried to do the DirecTV deal two years ago—before he was ultimately rebuffed by General Motors, DirecTV's main shareholder—he envisioned it in a financial structure that would have included his other satellite properties and that would have taken substantial third-party investment from the likes of Bill Gates and John Malone. Indeed, News Corp. would have been left with something like a 30 percent stake.

While News Corp., with its minority interest, would have been in control of the new entity, control is a complex and variable condition—especially when you're the minnow in an enterprise full of really big-fish investors (i.e., Gates and Malone). As such, it was a company that would have, inevitably, mutated beyond the Murdoch interests.

Nor would this be the first instance of such an independent entity within the great News Corp. conglomeration: Murdoch has already done a "carve out" with the Fox group—the studio, network, and stations—creating a separate public entity.

The view has always been that this is part of the News Corp.'s brilliant or cunning financial engineering. But, as possibly, there's something here that is larger and more poignant and even more far-seeing.

It does make a certain sort of sense, after all, that, just at the penultimate moment of consolidation, Murdoch, who always sees things first, would, of course, begin to deconsolidate.

It's reverse-engineering the corporation. It's breaking the unwieldy nation into city-states. It's a plan for a more or less sensible network of loosely affiliated enterprises, over which Lachlan and James might ceremonially, and less powerfully, preside.

So here it is, my theory: that he really wants to buy DirecTV and to have the FCC further relax its rules so he can give up control before he loses control anyway.

Part entropy and part sensible business.

And then there is the *New York Times*—and its unfortunate spring of 2003.

In some sense there is no more successful moguldom than that of the Sulzberger family. They have amassed great wealth and profound influence and have held it for a hundred years. Indeed, in many ways, they have transcended mere vainglorious, craven, temporal moguldom.

But suddenly, in the middle of scandal—Jayson Blair, a 27-year-old *Times* reporter, is revealed to have made, with the tacit support of the newsroom's managers, a mockery of the *Times'* valued probity—it seemed like Arthur Sulzberger Jr. was not at all a sun god, but merely a mogul manqué.

The *Times* seemed, in fact, to be caught between seeing itself as a special media circumstance—the one true church—and a desire to be a bigger, newer, hipper, cooler, more exciting place.

Glib Jayson Blair was part of an effort to modernize, deritualize, give up the Latin mass.

Though, in the midst of the scandal, the *Times* rushed back to defend the religion. Indeed, those who are in the Church of Our Gray Lady believe they suffer ever so much more than others. They flagellate piously—and assume they deserve special forgiveness because of it. They confess copiously. (One reporter from an Italian newsmagazine called me in the midst of the scandal wondering if I could help him understand "why the *New York Times* would shoot itself in its own balls.")

And yet it was hard not to also see the other impulse—the modern media managerial impulse—all over the place.

The furies descended most heavily on the unpopular executive editor Howell Raines. Now the *Times* has long suffered under newsroom despots and egotists. But Raines seemed to be something different. Not just a son of a bitch but a son of a bitch out to change the world—or, worse, the paper. To make it a different kind of *product*. A stronger *brand*. Howell seemed clearly to be the agent for the transformation of the *Times* from its cautious, culturally insular, frequently obsessive-compulsive identity as World's Greatest Newspaper into a more freewheeling, glamorous, un-*Times*ian World's Greatest Information Brand. While the rap, in the angry-white-man interpretation, was that Jayson Blair, who is black, had been given favorable treatment for reasons of race, the more savvy view was the he was favored because he was un-*Times*ian—not dour, literal, grave, but amusing, charismatic, and eager to please. Not to mention, he could turn a phrase. Jayson was slick.

And, slowly, it started to dawn on people that this was happening—the apparently careless elevation of Jayson Blair—by some larger design and higher authority.

It was hard to have observed this crisis and not have seen Sulzberger as something more than titular. Even though it probably would have benefited him to be more distantly preoccupied on the fabled fourteenth floor, he inserted himself at almost every opportunity into the mess.

He was signing memos along with Raines to the newsroom staff, in a departure from long tradition; it was his mug that the paparazzi shot; he officiated at newsroom meetings; he issued voluble statements to the media ("It sucks," was how, in Arthur-speak, he described the Blair affair); he empowered the multiple committees and investigations.

Sulzberger made it clear that he was in charge—and not reluctantly.

In some sense, this may have been reassuring, or at least it was supposed to be. It's one reason why monarchs exist—to be there when mortals fail.

But in another sense, it was harder and harder for everybody to avoid the conclusion that this was Arthur's show, and had been for a long time, and that, with Raines (and managing editor Gerald Boyd) sacrificed, he was the remaining player in this drama.

There was even a sense among the conspiracy-minded, as well as the more pragmatically business-minded, of the unseen hand of Steve Rattner.

You take a banker and you take a proprietor (an asset holder) and you have the stuff of big-media dreams.

The tip-off was not just the ever-increasing emphasis on brand and franchise and platforms as the *Times* discussed its business. *Maximizing asset value.* All that talking the talk. There was something else. Something much larger. There was, and you couldn't miss hearing it, more and more a suggestion that nobody really believed in the business anymore. At least nobody who really knew anything.

Newspapers, news, information: If you knew anything about anything, you understood them to be not just equivocal businesses but plastic concepts. They were in transition and if you weren't ready to be part of that transformation you and your business would die. This reasoning is how the *Times* found itself in its unlikely role as part of the consortium of media companies petitioning the FCC for permission to be an ever-expanding media conglomerate.

This was all basic media-banker theory. And it wasn't necessarily wrong. After all, the average age of people who regularly read a newspaper increased every year. This was so predictable that you could, on an actuarial table, pretty much locate your last reader. And while Arthur seemed up against it that Jayson Blair spring, there was no reason to believe that anyone in his family saw it differently from the way he saw it: the diminishing returns of a regional newspaper company versus the much greater potential of an ever-expanding international information brand.

Whatever that is.

And that, finally, seemed to be the point. A mogul was an adventurer, a soldier, a conquerer, even a crusader, and, yes, a savior, willing to march off and take territory and subdue populations and embrace the unknown and do whatever was necessary to do to make the future possible—no matter what that future was.

The idea was certainly not to preserve the past.

Index

369

INDEX

INDEX